Selected quotes from
Shakespeare 400 Chicago

On *Measure for Measure* (Cheek by Jowl):

"For some decades now, feminist insights into Shakespearean staging have insisted that Isabella, who is given no lines of reply, can choose to walk away from such a proposal. Her refusal of the Duke's offer has nearly reached the status of *de rigueur*. How remarkable, then, that this Isabella, though surprised at first and indeed decidedly skeptical at an idea that the audience too finds unexpected and amusing, agrees at last to dance with the Duke in a gesture of acceptance. The final stage image is of three dancing couples..."

-David Bevington

On *Tug of War: Civil Strife* (Chicago Shakespeare Theater):

"Magical reality in theater takes us closer to history, not away from it, moving us toward the other history below and beyond politics or economics or warfare. This is the interior history of human suffering. As York says when his enemies have foolishly provided him with soldiers: 'You put sharp weapons in a mad-man's hands.' In opposition to those weapons stand our knowledge of the past, and the power of theater to reproduce it. We pray they are the tools of sanity."

-Clark Hulse

On *Romeo & Juliet* (Joffrey Ballet):

"...the lovers steal away to meet in private for the famous balcony scene—here set in a mirrored elevator that gives us several Juliets in reflection, suggesting that this young lover represents many others. Even during this intimate scene, though, the lovers are not alone. As they dance an ecstatic *pas de deux*, other dancers hover silently at the back of the stage. Much as Romeo and Juliet would like to imagine the possibility, the scene implies, they will never inhabit a world to themselves; they remain very much in the world of their families, a world of violence and social control."

-Rebecca L. Fall

On *King Lear* (Belarus Free Theatre):

"Fittingly for a company on tour in exile, the Belarus Free Theatre evokes maximum effects from minimal sets: a trunk full of dirt becomes the country to be divided; that same trunk filled with empty mugs then becomes Lear's hundred knights. Water shaken vigorously by the cast on a blue tarpaulin becomes the storm that drenches the King in his rage..."

-Alfred Thomas

On *Falstaff* (Chicago Symphony Orchestra):

"…*Falstaff* moves into another realm altogether, giving the best reply I know in all art to perpetual questions about the meaning of life. How deliciously it thumbs its nose at stupid stereotypes of aging that dominate culture, now as then. (Slowing down? Crumbling? Halting? Try: assured mastery, new power of insight, fizzy rapidity, and a newfound ability to laugh at the body, at sex, at vulnerability, even at death.)"

-Martha C. Nussbaum

On *Songs of Lear* (Song of the Goat Theatre):

"They perform as a single choral body engaged in polyphonic song and ensemble movement, aimed at the most concentrated expression of the very human desires, passions, and grief that have defined dramatic tragedy since classical times. In the process, they largely leave behind Shakespeare's language and the play's plot. Certainly a few lines from the play find their way in, both spoken and sung, and Bral himself narrates some of the plot, but in many ways Shakespeare's play, as we know it, is absent. *Songs of Lear* becomes not a staging of *Lear*, but a staging with *Lear*, in relationship to *Lear*, because of what Shakespeare's play makes possible."

-Ira S. Murfin

On *Celebrity One-Man Hamlet* (David Carl):

"And there's the rub. Or rather the rub that first got me thinking: why did Carl choose to bring these two things together, Gary Busey and Hamlet? I mentioned above that on the surface this show is a joke about Gary Busey. But there's more to it than that. Busey and Hamlet are both famously 'mad' characters, but further than this there's a question with both of them of if and where there is method in't."

-Casey Caldwell

On *Richard III* (The Gift Theatre Company, in association with Steppenwolf Theatre Company + The Rehabilitation Institute Of Chicago):

"At the end, the stark image of Mr. Thornton out of his wheelchair and stripped of any other support calling for a horse gives a power to Richard's last line that it could seldom have had in the long history of the play's performance."

-Joseph Alulis

On *The Winter's Tale* (Cheek by Jowl):

"...the pent-up negative energy of the two men is enhanced by the extraordinary choreography of this production where, unlike most stage presentations in which everyone stands still whenever the main characters are speaking, here everyone seems to be in perpetual motion, like electrons around the nucleus of an atom, like matter itself, expressing in the ensemble the inner restlessness of the two central male characters. Moments like that change one's understanding of a great play forever after."

-Wendy Doniger

On *What Are We Worth?* (Michael Sandel with Illinois Humanities + Chicago Shakespeare Theater):

"Sandel has been called 'a rock star moralist' in *Newsweek* and 'the most famous teacher of philosophy in the world' in *The New Republic*. With a handful of interesting debates and moral dilemmas as examples, he guided the evening's packed house through a series of complex questions about the purpose of money and markets, ethics, and the ways Shakespeare's plays help bring these questions into relief."

-Andrew S. Keener

On *The Complete Deaths* (Spymonkey):

"...*The Complete Deaths* illustrates Shakespeare's philosophy of theatrical death at large: a good death is memorable and eloquent, a bad death is quick and obscure, because a good theater death needs to live on in audience memory. What weds the maudlin and absurd in this particular show, at least for me, is its full-hearted embracing of chaos as an existential concept contributing to tragedy and comedy alike insofar as such chaos recalls the uncertainty, inevitability, and apparent unfairness of death."

-Lydia Craig

On *(In) Complete Works: Table Top Shakespeare* (Forced Entertainment):

"...[Household] objects begin to take on personalities and characteristics that prove a testament to the strength of the connection forged between artist and audience. In this day of the now, the new, the viral, these performances remind us how extraordinarily captivating, dynamic, enduring, and nostalgic the practice of simple storytelling can be, even with the tales we have seen countless times before."

-Raashi Rastogi

On *Culinary Complete Works: 38 Plays. 38 Chefs*:

As a theatrical chef, Shakespeare can serve you up some pretty wild dishes. His menu might begin and end with *Richard III*, starting with a vegetarian first course with ingredients of Richard's "green and salad days," and ending with "good strawberries" from the Bishop of Ely's garden. The featured dish in the middle of course will come from *Titus Andronicus*, where Titus prepares a pasty made from Queen Tamora's two evil sons. Tending bar will be the two Sirs, John Falstaff and Toby Belch."

-Clark Hulse

On *Shakespeare a cappella* (Chicago *a cappella* + Chicago Shakespeare Theater):

"The value of a celebration like Shakespeare 400 is that it provides us all opportunities to do for Shakespeare's work what Shakespeare's work does for its audiences: it makes the familiar strange and the strange familiar. Hearing Shakespeare's words sung not only highlights the innate musicality of the language, but plucks that language out of its native environs, allowing the audience to watch it bloom in new surroundings."

-Lise Schlosser

On *Battle of the Bard: High School Shakespeare Slam* (Chicago Shakespeare Theater + Chicago Youth Shakespeare):

"They used Shakespeare to examine their own multilingual and multicultural worlds—to work through very modern concerns in ways that made Shakespeare's historically distant and rhetorically difficult language seem completely familiar and immediately relevant...This is what Shakespeare should be. This is what Shakespeare will be. And this, the students definitively demonstrated, is what Shakespeare *is*."

-Timothy J. Duggan

Shakespeare 400 Chicago

Reflections on a City's Celebration of Shakespeare

Chicago Shakespeare Theater

Barbara Gaines
Artistic Director
Carl and Marilynn Thoma Endowed Chair

Criss Henderson
Executive Director

Doreen Sayegh
Festival Producer,
Shakespeare 400 Chicago

Marilyn J. Halperin
Director of Education and Communications
Ray and Judy McCaskey Endowed Chair
City Desk 400 Curator

Kevin M. Spellman
Keely Haddad-Null
City Desk 400 Producers

ISBN: 1539329844
ISBN-13: 978-1539329848

Chicago Shakespeare Theater
800 E. Grand Ave. on Navy Pier
Chicago, IL 60611 USA
312.595.5600

www.chicagoshakes.com

Acknowledgments

Special thanks and much gratitude to
Chicago Mayor Rahm Emanuel and Ms. Amy Rule
for their support of this unprecedented international event.

Shakespeare 400 Chicago would not have been possible without the
generosity of our Lead Sponsors:

MacArthur Foundation

PRITZKER MILITARY
MUSEUM & LIBRARY

Julius Frankel Foundation

Contents

FOREWORD
Clark Hulse

Imagine a Shakespeare festival in three dimensions. Not the physical dimensions of height, width, depth, but the artistic dimensions of Place, World, Experience.

First, Place: a city festival that draws together the cultural institutions of Chicago, each programming in parallel, spread across the city's many neighborhoods, with Chicago Shakespeare on Navy Pier at its hub. Participants range from high-cultural institutions to public libraries, parks, restaurants and high school ensembles.

Second, World: a global festival that draws to Chicago artistic companies from twelve countries, with 863 events, over twelve months, performing Shakespeare in eleven languages and fourteen art forms. In addition to theater, there is opera, symphonic and rock music, film, comedy, ballet, academic lectures, culinary events, and exhibitions. A global festival is mapped onto a Chicago festival, with performances at venues around the city.

Third, Experience: thirty-two writer-scholars, drawn from nine universities, attend performances and record what they see, hear, think, and feel in blog posts that draw a worldwide audience of over 10,000 readers.

This is the astonishing scope of Shakespeare 400 Chicago, a commemoration of the occasion of the 400th anniversary of Shakespeare's death, but more importantly a celebration of the rich legacy of performance that shapes our diversity of cultures today. All told, it comprised 1,151 artists, and 863 events spread over 231 locations, reaching an audience of 1.1 million participants. Accurately and therefore not immodestly, it can be called one of the world's largest and most comprehensive celebrations of Shakespeare's legacy. The quantity is boggling. The quality was, in my own voracious but still partial experience, remarkable.

Finally, add a fourth dimension: Memory. Performance is gloriously ephemeral. Each iteration is slightly different in the energy among the performers and between performers and audience. Variations in rhythm, phrasing, posture bring out nuances of the Shakespearean text, texture or action. This is true for theater, music, dance, dessert, and even, yes, for lectures.

The essays in this volume capture these moments. Each reflects a single performance, and a singular reflection by a particularly observant spectator. They are as immensely varied as the writers—some are spoken as "we," some as "they," some as "I." Some have the shape of critical reviews, some are brief scholarly articles, some are personal reflections. All are reproduced here as they were written in the moment, memorializing the ephemerality of the particular performance and the immediate response.

Underlying all of the festival's rich diversity, certain questions recur. Why Shakespeare? What about his work holds our interest after 400 years? What happens when his language is turned into another tongue and spoken in foreign rhythms? What makes him so infinitely adaptable to different art forms? When does an interpretation push so far that it is something different, and no longer an adaptation? Above all, what does Shakespeare mean *now*?

The posts are arranged to reflect the rough calendar of events— rough, since there is a kind of counterpoint among the dates: when an event opened, when this or that blogger saw it, and when the entries were posted. This heightens the flow of entries into something like a fugal movement of thoughts and ideas, flowing and ebbing as the performances move from the serious to the sad or joyful or melancholy.

The essays were written over the course of the four seasons of a full year. In the abstract, they form a record of events, but they also suggest various modes of reading. They may be consumed at short intervals, or in a grand sitting, like binge-watching all fourteen parts of the new season of your favorite show in two days—or in one indescribable vigil of sleeplessness. There are other ways to read as well. You can follow the recurring thread of a single author, or measure the clustered and contrasting voices of a single production, or follow a particular play, like *Othello,* through its manifestations in different art forms. So the volume you have here is more than just a memorial or a historical record of Shakespeare 400 Chicago, more than just a monument to a miraculous year. It is a concentration and distillation that intensifies that year into an avalanche of immediacy, laced through with reflection.

Come and show me another city
with lifted head singing so proud
to be alive and coarse and strong
and cunning.
…
Bareheaded,
Shoveling,
Wrecking,
Planning,
Building, breaking,
rebuilding…

      -Carl Sandburg, *Chicago Poems* (1916)

O brave new world
that has such people in't.

      -William Shakespeare, *The Tempest* (ca. 1610)

CHICAGO + SHAKESPEARE

Marilyn J. Halperin, Chicago Shakespeare Theater
December 1, 2015

Shakespeare 400 Chicago. An unlikely pairing, perhaps? Perhaps. But know this: Chicago is no novice when it comes to shape-changing events. Our city's first quadricentennial (delayed a year by Congress) dates back to 1893 and the World's Columbian Exposition. Galvanizing and inspiring a city to become more than it was, the Exposition reshaped a boomtown, known already for risk-taking, determination and, yes, audacity.

Those qualities stuck. And now the city is once more at the threshold of a citywide celebration honoring a legacy that would forever change how we see the world.

As Shakespeare wrote his *Tempest*, England's tentative settlement in Jamestown still struggled for a foothold. Two more generations would pass before the first Europeans (though not the English) set eyes upon this western shore of Lake Michigan, site to Chicago's future. By the time "Chicago" made its presence known on a map, Shakespeare was dead. A king, beheaded. One revolution, lost and won. London, burned and built once more. And while Europe imagined its Renaissance and conceived the Enlightenment, bison roamed the great prairie, hunted and revered by the Native Americans.

What might Shakespeare have written about this New World and its people...

We were unknown to him; he was by no means unknown to us. He was part of the fabric and soul of this place. The colonists staged productions of his plays. Our founding fathers quoted and collected his works. The settlers carried his books and pioneering spirit with them. And our Midwest native son Abraham Lincoln grew up reading Shakespeare by firelight in his family's one-room log cabin.

Chicago grew topsy-turvy, until the Great Chicago Fire in 1871 burned a third of the city to the ground. Like London, it refused to remain in ashes, emerging at the epicenter of a vast continent's routes of trade, transport and culture. We grew up, rough edged, unruly, untamed.

Chicagoans inherit this legacy. We have taken our rightful place among the premier orchestras, operas and dance companies of the world. Hog butcher for the world is today a world-class culinary destination. Our museums of art, science and the humanities are internationally renowned. Ours is a city that fuels the most dynamic theater community in the country. Our great universities are unparalleled in talent and breadth. Our architectural pedigree, rendered by Sullivan, Wright, Olmsted and van der Rohe, is as imposing and original as our city skyline and lakefront.

A longing for exploration and for freedom of expression severed our New World from the old. The most adventurous, independent and nonconforming were lured westward, to the Great Lakes and tallgrass prairie, to what seemed to our ancestors an endless expanse.

This same longing for exploration brings us back to Shakespeare, to a boundless geography he left behind for us, as wide as the infinite spaces of our histories, our emotional lives and our imaginations. We are relentless, audacious searchers for new meaning and expression, inspired by the most exquisite body of words extant.

Chicago is where Shakespeare has chosen to live. And we will never have a better chance to get to know him than here in 2016.

Note: The following essays appear as they did at the time of publication on the "City Desk 400" site. Chicago Shakespeare Theater has not made substantive edits to any essay and views expressed by scholars are not necessarily representative of those of Chicago Shakespeare Theater.

CHEEK BY JOWL + PUSHKIN THEATRE, MOSCOW
MEASURE FOR MEASURE

by William Shakespeare
directed by Declan Donnellan
designed by Nick Ormerod
presented by Chicago Shakespeare Theater

Johan Persson

A Triumphant Production of *Measure for Measure* in Russian
David Bevington

This is a stunning production, certainly the best *Measure for Measure* I've ever seen. It is highly experimental in design in a way that remains brilliantly faithful to Shakespeare's text and theatrical genius.

The staging focuses on several large box-shaped structures, the modern equivalent, perhaps, of the *periaktoi* of ancient Greek theater: that is, devices that can be thrust forward onstage and rotated to reveal changes in scenic intent. At the beginning they are arranged backstage in a row, separated from one another by spacious gaps so that the entire acting company (thirteen in all) can process between them and out onto the stage. The acting company swirls about, disappears, and re-emerges, serving as audience for one scene and then another. Key actors drop out of this swirl to become the figures of a given scene. At key points, three of the large boxes turn and open to reveal characters, one at a time, about whom we have been anxiously waiting to learn their fates. The staging concept is thus one of discovery, and as such is a terrific rendition of the way Shakespeare has structured his play.

The actors are all members of the Pushkin Theatre in Moscow, speaking in Russian. Rapidly moving supertitles provide the theater audience with Shakespeare's text. Unlike the script of Grigori Kozintsev's wonderful film versions of *Hamlet* and *King Lear*, in which Boris Pasternak's Russian translation is re-translated into English with occasionally wide departures from what Shakespeare wrote, this production mostly gives us the original. The text is cut, to be sure, very adroitly so, providing us a brisk and taut two hours, wisely without intermission. Costumes are simple, modern, understated. Few props are needed, as was true of Shakespeare's Globe stage.

Sexuality is, for much of this production, an insistently dismal affair. When Angelo (Andrei Kuzichev) reveals to Isabella (Anna Khalilulina) his intent to possess her sexually as the price of sparing her brother's life, he underscores the point by lifting her white sisterhood gown, spreading her legs as he forces her down on to a table, and kneeling before her as he insults her virginal body. The motif recurs when Claudio (Petr Rykov), told by Isabella that she can save his life by giving herself to Angelo, panics at the thought of dying and begs that she do what Angelo has asked by making his own sexual attempt on her. This ugliness of male importunity is well suited to the production's pointed depiction of prison life; no play of Shakespeare spends so much time inside the prison's walls. The dark prison humor is splendidly augmented by Lucio (Alexander Feklistov) and his partners in the play's wry scenes of humor.

Incarceration and spying are thematic elements that unite the show into a devastating critique of human carnality. The Duke of this production (Alexander Arsentyev) is brilliantly in control, but from behind the scenes. Whatever his reasons for leaving his city under the too-easily-corrupted authority of Angelo, the Duke is aware of what is going on. The final scene shows him at his most enigmatic and forceful. The play is seen as intensely political, and in a way that silently comments on a nation like modern-day Russia. The Duke knows how to arouse the adulation of his subjects. As he gestures with his arms, their roar of approval, heard over the sound system, swells and subsides in orchestrated waves of popular hysteria. Power of this sort is intensely dangerous. Angelo has attempted to abuse such power in the most craven manner possible; the Duke, conversely, is a charismatic figure who, almost miraculously, knows how to use power in the service of forgiveness and reform.

How would this magnificent production, I wondered, handle the business in the final scene of whether Isabella accepts or rejects the Duke's proposal of marriage? For some decades now, feminist insights into Shakespearean staging have insisted that Isabella, who is given no lines of reply, can choose to walk away from such a proposal. Her refusal of the Duke's offer has nearly reached the status of *de rigueur*. How remarkable, then, that this Isabella, though surprised at first and indeed decidedly skeptical at an idea that the audience too finds unexpected and amusing, agrees at last to dance with the Duke in a gesture of acceptance. The final stage image is of three dancing couples: Claudio with his fiancée Juliet (Anastasia Lebedeva) and their newborn child, a disconsolate Angelo with his Mariana (Elmira Mirel), and, center stage, the Duke and Isabella. She has managed to find a comic resolution to this play's insistently dark view of human depravity. Love and marriage offer themselves as a choice one must perilously make if one is to avoid existential despair.

Measures Immeasurable
Clark Hulse

My esteemed colleagues David Bevington and Alfred Thomas praise Declan Donnellan's Russian-language *Measure for Measure* at Chicago Shakespeare Theater almost as if it were two different plays, one "brilliantly faithful" to Shakespeare and the other speaking truth to power with "an important new non-Anglophone perspective." How can they both be right (which I think they are)?

The simple fact is that *Measure* almost always feels like several plays woven together. Donnellan captures this halfway through, when the stage suddenly explodes. Claudio, naked to the waist, stands astride a stringed bass while the cast, hands linked, swirls around him to mad music. The Duke shouts out to the chaste Isabella and lascivious Marianna how they will trick his lieutenant Angelo out of rape and into marriage.

It is a stunning *coup de theatre,* utterly changing the pace and dynamic of the drama. Up until then, Vienna has been a quagmire of vice and hypocrisy, overrun with prostitutes, pimps, and fornicators. The Duke is indecisive, uncomfortable with power, and afraid of his own people. When he goes underground, leaving the "prenzie" Angelo to lead a crackdown in his absence, things get progressively worse. The Duke, disguised as a monk, seems overwhelmed by the social chaos from below and corruption of power from above. Then he hears the corrosive exchange between Claudio and his sister Isabella, in which Claudio begs his sister Isabella for his life after she refuses to submit to rape in order to save him. In a second, the Duke changes, the play changes, and everything in Vienna changes.

The manic dance around Claudio solves the three problems that haunt productions of *Measure.* What is it about—the general corruption of man, the abuse of power, the fear of death, or all of these? How are we to take this Duke, who seems derelict at the beginning and overly manipulative at the end? And what are we to make of an ending that forces the protagonists into marriages in order to put a "comic" cap on a savage satire? Modern productions have looked for a way to make sense of it. Should Marianna refuse to save Angelo, or Isabella refuse to marry the Duke at the end? Should she just kill herself? Or kill him?

What is the play about? All of the above. It careens through throat-choking moral issues without time for breath. Prostitution is no victimless crime here. Rape, murder, bribery are all in the air or before our eyes. As the Duke searches for a way to postpone Claudio's execution—it's really judicial murder—suddenly the Provost, who commands the prison, moves to the foreground. Until that moment, he has been just another Shakespearean extra known only by his title. But confronted with a clearly immoral directive, he must decide. Will he just follow orders? Step by step he rises to moral action, first protesting merely with words, then acquiescing to the Duke's proposed subterfuge, and then finally devising the way to put a stop to Angelo's crime.

The Duke himself puts off the monk's habit in which he has disguised himself, and reemerges as a preening alpha-dog politician. With tightly controlled, Putinesque gestures (this is in Russian, after all), he manipulates his subjects in what feels more and more like a show trial, making each figure realize that his displeasure signals death. None can be sure who will be the victim, until the jaws of his malice close around Angelo.

So justice is dispensed, if justice it be, at the hands of an all-wise authoritarianism. As the couples pair off and begin their marriage dance, Donnellan stages his final *coup de theatre*. When Isabella tries to embrace her brother, Claudio turns from her in disgust, and takes in his arms his partner and their newborn child. Life and human warmth spurn cold moral rectitude. Gazing on their happiness, Isabella relents, takes the hand of the Duke, and submits to the dance.

How does one speak truth to power in the veiled police states of Elizabethan England or Putin's Russia? Shakespeare rarely spoke truth directly into the face of power. He danced and mimed his way around it. This Russian *Measure,* without an actual Shakespearean word, does its own dance around power, toying with our desire for moral absolutes, and showing how power slyly speaks back to us with enchanting falsehoods.

BELARUS FREE THEATRE
KING LEAR

by William Shakespeare
directed by Vladimir Shcherban
adapted by Nicolai Khalezin
presented by Chicago Shakespeare Theater

Simon Annand

"Machinations, hollowness, treachery, and all ruinous disorders:" Belarus Free Theatre's *King Lear*
Alexandra Bennett

"Will it be in English?" my companion asked when I invited him to join me in seeing the Belarus Free Theatre production of *King Lear* at Chicago Shakespeare Theater earlier this month.

It's a reasonable question: *Lear* is now generally hailed as Shakespeare's greatest tragedy, a play in which a man alone on a heath faces the uncaring tempestuous skies as he slowly loses his reason once his identity is stripped from him. "Who is it can tell me who I am?" he asks. Bereft of Shakespeare's rich verse, who does Lear become? Can any rewritten version measure up to the original?

This production proves that the play loses none of its force in translation. I cannot think of a company more suited to reinventing this story: like Kent, Cordelia and Edgar, all of whom risk their lives in the face of tyrannical wrath, the members of the Belarus Free Theatre have all faced persecution in what is now the last remaining European dictatorship. Several company members live in exile. Banned on political grounds and forced underground, the company is committed to principles of social justice, freedom of speech, and artistic expression, and defiantly performs in Belarusian, the forbidden language of their homeland. In their hands, *King Lear* is shockingly immediate, by turns an effervescently funny and savage portrayal of power and its corruption.

The show begins by highlighting the systematic degradation of the young by their elders: in dividing up his kingdom, Lear (Aleh Sidorchyk) pours handfuls of dirt from a battered trunk into the outstretched skirts of his two eldest daughters, making them appear incestuously pregnant with the land itself as they clasp their expanded bellies upon receiving their rewards. After their respective sexual and patriotic musical numbers extolling Lear as the father of the nation to gain his favor, Cordelia's brash irreverence comes as a blast of welcome air for which her father brutally batters her to the ground. Subsequently, we see Edmund (Kiryl Kanstantsinau) forced to wait on his own imperious wheelchair-bound father, who expects his son to catch the chaotic arcs of his urine in a bedpan and then callously uses his head as a towel to clean his lap afterwards. Such monstrous misuses of power by those on top lead us in the audience, perhaps somewhat to our surprise, to sympathize initially with characters frequently demonized as villainous. (Edgar, by contrast, is portrayed as a partying wastrel before his exile and transformation into Poor Tom.) At the same time, we witness the horror of those once traumatized by servility becoming monstrous in their own experiences of power and the rush it brings: Goneril and Regan quickly trade their simple folk dresses for glamorous gowns and fur coats, ultimately snarling and snapping at one another over the country's spoils.

Power and humanity alike are ultimately stripped to their bare essentials here: Lear himself is neither loved nor feared in this production; rather, all but Cordelia (Victoria Biran) and the musical Fool (Elias Faingersh) kiss and bow down to the heavy steel gauntlet he brandishes on his right hand throughout the play. Until, that is, the rebels strip it from him in prison and mockingly use it as a puppet: the symbol of might exposed for the hollow prop it actually is. When a terrified Edgar (Siarhei Kvachonak) decides to disguise himself as a madman, he strips down to stained underwear and smears himself liberally with excrement to become Poor Tom. During the storm, Lear, Kent, and the Fool all strip as well to hide with him under a tarpaulin on a wet and shit-slicked stage (the audience is warned in advance of the liberal use of peanut butter as a prop in the show in the case of allergies, but the scene is no less effective).

Fittingly for a company on tour in exile, the Belarus Free Theatre evokes maximum effects from minimal sets: a trunk full of dirt becomes the country to be divided; that same trunk filled with empty mugs then becomes Lear's hundred knights. Water shaken vigorously by the cast on a blue tarpaulin becomes the storm that drenches the King in his rage; later, a red tarpaulin borne onstage by the cast singing a military anthem becomes the play's violent battlefield and its bloody aftermath.

The production deliberately upends many traditional expectations: Lear is relatively young and vigorous (shedding the unsteady crawl and long white wig under which he initially totters in his first entrance), even strong enough to spin in place while Goneril and Regan cling to his neck. This king's claim to being "more sinned against than sinning" is deeply problematic: rather, Goneril and Regan appear here as having learned how to wield power all too well from their tyrannical parent. Meanwhile, Cordelia is as harsh as her sisters, callous and defiant even in the reconciliation scene, suggesting that some pasts simply cannot be forgiven. Gloucester is a demanding bureaucrat in the style of his master; both he and Kent are presented as disabled while serving at Lear's court, though Kent leaves the wheeled cart in which he's been kneeling when he disguises himself as Caius. Rising from his knees in exile is a stunning literal depiction of revolutionary action requiring standing on one's own two feet.

Almost all of the characters, including Edgar and Kent, end up brutally dead at this production's end: the show closes with a final song to the audience comprised of key lines from the play and the chorus "Good God!" as the final spotlight focuses on the empty gauntlet downstage center. Distilled, energized and relentlessly interrogatory, this *Lear* becomes a formidable experience indeed: we are left to confront our own reactions to power and the dangerous implications of silence.

Shakespeare under Tyranny: A Belarusian *King Lear*
Alfred Thomas

In 1609 a group of English Catholic players named the Simpson Brothers performed an anti-government play in which a Church of England minister is carried off to hell by the Devil. The interlude was performed in Gouthwaite Hall, the home of the prominent recusant nobleman Sir John Yorke of Nidderdale. A local Protestant diehard denounced the production to the government in London. According to the manuscript of the proceedings of the Court of Star Chamber, which documented the trial in 1614, Sir John, his wife and his kinsmen were charged with "permitting a company of players to act a scandalous interlude, designed to exalt Popery and bring the Church of England into derision, and of maintaining secret chambers at Gouthwaite for the entertaining of Jesuits, seminary priests and other disloyal persons." Sir John ended up spending many years in prison for failing to pay the crippling fines imposed upon him for his obdurate recusancy. Among the items confiscated and examined by the government was a list of plays previously performed by the Simpson Brothers; two of these were *Pericles* and *King Lear*.

It is interesting to conjecture why Shakespeare's bleakest tragedy about power and its abuses might have appealed to these religious dissenters so far from London and the direct control of Westminster. Perhaps they saw their own fate as a persecuted minority reflected in the arbitrary punishment and exile of Kent and Cordelia; perhaps they identified with Edgar, the faithful and legitimate son of the Earl of Gloucester, who is betrayed by his illegitimate brother Edmund just as, in their eyes, the true Catholic faith of England had been usurped by the false heresy of Protestantism. For a multitude of reasons *King Lear*, has inspired radical political interpretations across the centuries, as early—it seems—as Shakespeare's own lifetime. From the disaffected Catholics of Jacobean England to the renegade actors of the Belarus Free Theatre— several of whom have been persecuted for joining the group and banned from working in their own country—*King Lear* seems to resonate with the most personal experiences of those who stage and perform it.

Commissioned by the Shakespeare Globe Theatre in London and first performed on May 17, 2012, as part of the international Globe to Globe Festival, this raw and powerful production of *King Lear* has garnered immense praise and admiration in the West. Reflecting the repressive political conditions of life under Europe's so-called "Last Dictatorship" (personified by Alexander Lukashenko, the president of Belarus since 1994), it audaciously interpolates non-Shakespearean words and songs into the original play text. From the powerful choral chanting of folksongs, which burst through the spoken text with explosive force, to the sinister lines added in the scene of Cordelia's hanging—and involving masked executioners cataloging the victims' confiscated goods in the manner of modern totalitarian bureaucracies—the production powerfully echoes not only the recent experience of political oppression in Belarus but the entire tragedy of twentieth-century eastern Europe. This is hardly surprising, since it was in this part of Europe—what Yale historian Timothy Snyder has termed the "blood lands" located between Hitler's Germany and Stalin's Soviet Union—that the worst atrocities of World War II took place. According to Snyder, between 1939 and 1945, about fourteen million non-combatants lost their lives in Poland, Belarus, Russia and the Baltic states, most of them outside the death camps. Belarus lost about a third of its population, and the scars of the past are still evident in its government's inability to shed its oppressive Soviet-era legacy.

This bloody history of eastern Europe in the twentieth century is brilliantly and powerfully evoked in the civil war scenes in which corpses lie scattered beneath a red plastic sheet stretched across the stage. Amidst the carnage we see Edmund and Regan violently copulating, his hand clutching her throat. What struck me most about this production was its unremitting pessimism about human nature even as it energetically asserts the right of human beings to express political freedom. As Lear first enters slowly and painfully pushing his suitcase on a pram, he pulls off a long white wig as if to shed the traditional interpretation of the role as an exhausted patriarch anxious to repudiate power and "crawl towards death." (In Peter Brook's famous film version of *King Lear* the British actor Paul Scofield plays the abdication scene in precisely this way as an old man slumped on his throne and seemingly on the brink of death). By contrast, this Belarusian Lear (played by the youthful and athletic Aleh Sidorchyk) has no intention of relinquishing his power even as he goes through the rhetorical motions of doing so. Armed with a prosthetic metal gauntlet, he bullies and terrorizes his daughters and subjects, giving Cordelia a bloody nose and clasping Goneril's throat in a vice-like grip. After he has divided up his kingdom (symbolized by a suitcase full of dirt which he pours into his daughters' laps), Regan, Goneril and their spouses—suitably wearing Russian fur caps—kneel to kiss the metallic gauntlet like groveling boyars at the court of Ivan the Terrible.

If Lear lacks compassion, it is not surprising that his favorite daughter Cordelia is presented as equally callous and uncaring. Far from the meek daughter of standard interpretations, this Cordelia (played by Victoria Biran) resembles her father and her sisters in her self-destructive anarchism. In her response to the King's foolish demand for absolute love, she not only refuses to play her pre-scripted sycophantic role, she does so in a comic song-and-dance routine that resembles her sisters' similarly lewd performances. This interpretation of Cordelia as a female anarchist is effective, since its extremism helps to motivate Lear's sudden shift from fun-loving fool to furious despot. Later in the play we see Cordelia—now Queen of France and married to a crippled and blind old lecher rather than a chivalrous prince—as a wine-drinking dipsomaniac; and in the scene of reunion and reconciliation with Lear she does not even address the infirm King directly (slumped in a wheelchair and covered with a sheet) but speaks her lines in the opposite direction. And as she is being selected for execution, she tells the henchmen to hang "the old fart."

Through his crude despotism Lear has not only lost the love of his youngest daughter, he never possessed it in the first place. His three daughters may have different responses to his ludicrous demand for unconditional love—two compliant and sycophantic, the third defiant and contemptuous—but they are all equally cynical. Goneril's flattering speech suggests carnal, sexual desire rather than daughterly devotion as she seductively writhes like a striptease artiste. All three daughters replicate their father's violent bombast. This is a family that prefers hatred and cruelty to love and compassion. It is this terrible insight that there is no love to start with that makes the final scene so utterly bleak: even in suffering and death there is no redemption, only self-delusion. The final scene echoes the opening one as Lear slowly wheels in Cordelia's dead body. But this time he is no longer feigning old age and decrepitude but has become its very embodiment. Lear's final soliloquy is all the more powerful and effective for contrasting with the splenetic bombast of his previous speeches: here is a man utterly broken in spirit as well as body.

In a similar pessimistic vein, we are given no moral contrast between the "evil" Edmund and the "virtuous" Edgar. Edmund is a drug addict shooting up early in the play, while his brother Edgar is a dissolute, spoilt playboy who later, as Poor Tom, strips naked and besmirches himself with his own excrement (effectively simulated with crunchy peanut butter). In the subsequent storm scene all the actors on stage strip naked and take shelter under a blue sheet inundated with water while Regan and Goneril—attired in expensive fur coats to symbolize their sudden rise to power and wealth—scour the stage with flashlights as if to track down the enemies of the state. Later, in his scene with blinded Gloucester, demented Lear emerges wearing a mock-crown consisting of a birds' nest and eggs, which he later smashes on the ground as if they were the skulls of his enemies ("And kill, kill, kill, kill!"). Blood, water, excrement and egg yolks become the ingredients of a morally corrupt world, flooding the stage and defiling the actors' bodies as if reducing all and sundry to a common state of depraved inhumanity.

Like Lear's daughters, Edmund and Edgar are the inevitable products of this dehumanized universe. In this sense this harrowing production does not chart a downward spiral of moral corruption and escalating violence but manifests them as the norm from the very outset—a world in which a father punches his recalcitrant daughter in the face while she in turn contemptuously exposes her backside to him; a world in which a wheel-chair-ridden Gloucester beats his son Edmund with a belt only to be punished in turn when Regan and Goneril bite out his eyes. By the time we reach the horrific scene of Gloucester's blinding we have become so desensitized to violence that it seems almost anti-climactic. Although the sustained fortissimo pitch of this violence might seem to detract from the play's power and effectiveness, it actually enhances it. The final scene, in which Lear crouches next to his daughter's crumpled body, is entirely spoken in hushed whispers as if the massive energy that preceded it has fizzled out into a pathetic whimper.

Returning to my opening account of the Simpson Brothers and their anarchic anti-government interlude performed in Yorkshire in 1609: One of the court deposition accounts of the friction between the Church of England minister and his Catholic tenantry describes a scene in which the tenants would assemble near the churchyard on Sunday with a piper: "And there with theire piping and revelling wolde make such a noyse in time of praier, as the mynyster could not well be harde." In the account of the interlude in the play there is also evidence of the same boisterous and disdainful humor toward those in authority. As I watched this raucously entertaining and subversive production of *King Lear*—including the Fool's cacophonous bursts on the trombone and the frequent lapse into Brechtian song and dance—I was reminded of those early modern carnivalesque techniques of using discordant noise and riotous song in order to drown out the language of political intolerance and mock the self-deluding pretensions of those who wield absolute power.

CHICAGO SYMPHONY ORCHESTRA
+ CHICAGO SHAKESPEARE THEATER
A MIDSUMMER NIGHT'S DREAM

conducted by Edwin Outwater
adapted + directed by David H. Bell

Todd Rosenberg

A Dream Reimagined: CST and the CSO Teach
Mendelssohn and Shakespeare
Rebecca L. Fall

Last week, Chicago-area elementary students and families were treated to a rare event: a live production of *A Midsummer Night's Dream* accompanied by Felix Mendelssohn's incidental music for the play, directed and adapted by David H. Bell, performed by the Chicago Symphony Orchestra and actors from Chicago Shakespeare Theater. Both Shakespeare's drama and Mendelssohn's score were heavily edited and highly abbreviated, for this entertaining production at the Symphony Center functioned effectively as a teaching text for younger children. Taking the role of emcee, Maestro Edwin Outwater regularly paused from conducting to offer background about Mendelssohn and his music, introduce the play's characters to the young audience, gloss major plot points, and even act as a meta-theatrical conduit between players and orchestra: "Maestro, can you give us some cool, swag, hip music for our entrance?" asked Bottom as the mechanicals prepared to perform their disastrous *Pyramus and Thisbe*. "I've got just the thing," Outwater replied before launching the symphony into the players' "Prologue."

As Outwater reminded his audience, Mendelssohn (1809-1847) grew up enamored of Shakespeare. He and his sisters amused themselves as children by acting out various scenes from Shakespeare's plays, and Mendelssohn continued to draw inspiration from those texts throughout his life. The Mendelssohn family acquired a German translation (Schlegel) of *Midsummer* in 1826, when Felix was 17, and their young prodigy promptly composed a piano duet based on the comedy to perform at home with his sister Fanny. He went on to orchestrate the piece shortly thereafter, transforming it into a concert overture; its 1827 debut would be his first public performance, and the Overture would go on to become one of his most famous compositions. Later, in 1843, King Frederick William IV of Prussia commissioned him to write incidental music for a stage production of the play, the finished version of which incorporated and expanded upon his earlier Overture.

Throughout his career, Mendelssohn established a strong interest in recuperating and reimagining older texts. He was a devoted fan of J.S. Bach's baroque compositions, which by the early years of the Romantic music period (ca. 1820s) were decidedly unfashionable. In 1829, he conducted a performance of the *St. Matthew Passion* that radically re-arranged Bach's score and refashioned the piece, originally written to accompany a Good Friday church service, into a stand-alone work. This performance established a tradition for performing the *Passion* as a concert piece and reinvigorated popular interest in Bach's vocal works. In 1841, Mendelssohn composed a piano accompaniment to the Chaconne of Bach's Partita in D minor for solo violin. Later Romantic composers—Liszt and Brahms among them—followed suit and rearranged Bach's music for more up-to-date instrumental configurations, re-establishing Bach as a dominant influence on the evolving compositional landscape.

Mendelssohn's musical interpretation of *A Midsummer Night's Dream* is likewise a product of innovative reimagination. Unlike Bach, Shakespeare had continued to enjoy robust popularity throughout the eighteenth century and into the nineteenth, so the composer's interest hardly recuperated any lost public estimation. However, it did sway the course of Romantic music, helping to amplify the growing vogue for thematic compositions that emphasized drama and lyricism. In its initial public iteration as the stand-alone Overture, Mendelssohn's take on *Midsummer* kicked off a fashion for concert overtures—that is, pieces inspired by literature but not intended to accompany a staged production. Concert overtures became an essential form of Romantic music, eventually evolving into the "tone poem," a characteristic form of the later Romantic period. In looking back to Shakespeare's two-hundred-year-old play, Mendelssohn helped initiate an emergent compositional movement.

The second iteration of Mendelssohn's *Midsummer* again reimagined the role of form. As incidental music, the final version was crafted to accompany a staged production of the play. Its movements follow the action of the plot, and also include a number of vocal pieces set to Shakespeare's own verses ("Ye spotted snakes" and "What hempen homespuns," among others). This time, however, Mendelssohn looked back not only to Shakespeare's text for inspiration, but to his own work, incorporating his adolescent Overture and drawing from its musical themes—including the E-minor pitter-patter of dancing fairies and the strings' Bottomesque "hee-haws"—to elaborate characterological motifs and highlight on-stage action.

Such an approach, looking back to move forward artistically, is not out of line with Shakespeare's own patterns of authorship. "The Bard," after all, is not famous for the originality of his plot lines. *Midsummer* itself borrows from classical mythology to tell what is in many ways a distinctly English fairytale. At the end of his career, Shakespeare (like Mendelssohn more than two centuries later) returned to his earlier work in *Midsummer* to reimagine the wedding of Theseus and Hippolyta in yet "another key" in the tragicomic *The Two Noble Kinsmen.*

Last week's performances at the Symphony Center, collaboratively produced between the Chicago Symphony Orchestra and Chicago Shakespeare Theater, effectively presented a new, hybrid text of the two *Midsummers*. Designed with an audience of children in mind, the performance reworked the symphonic and dramatic versions into an accessible spectacle aimed at teaching newcomers about the play and Mendelssohn's interpretation. Shakespeare's text was heavily reduced to highlight the musical accompaniment, and much of the on-stage action was danced and mimed. (The performance, one could say, served to reimagine and recuperate the pre-modern theatrical staple of the "dumb show," putting it to good use for the young audience; the dumb shows throughout the performance allowed the audience to gain a sense of character, place, and musical style without becoming lost in the complexities of Elizabethan English.) The production furthermore underscored the play's potential for fantastical spectacle and physical comedy, showcasing the cast's impressive acrobatic abilities as well as their talents for slapstick. Maestro Outwater provided editorial commentary and historical background, offering an interpretive access point for viewers so that they could grasp not only plot and character details, but listen for the ways that Mendelssohn's score both represents and interprets the play.

This was a production with two clear objectives in mind: to educate, and to inspire appreciation in young people new to the performance hall. Ostensibly it aimed to teach the children in the audience about the plot of Shakespeare's play and the sounds of Mendelssohn's music, but in so self-consciously packaging its reinterpretation as a teaching text, the performance also managed to convey something important about the spirit of Shakespearean authorship and Mendelssohnian composition: what both owe not only to the processes of imagination, but *re-*imagination, too.

THE THEATRE SCHOOL AT DEPAUL
PROSPERO'S STORM

adapted + directed by Damon Kiely
music + lyrics by Mark Elliott
part of Chicago Playworks for Families and Young Audiences Series

Michael Brosilow

Prospero's Storm/Miranda's Story
Richard Gilbert

"I used to be a magician" writes Damon Kiely in his director's notes to *Prospero's Storm*, his adaptation of *The Tempest*. Kiely is talking about the power of a parent to astonish his children with his control over the world—a control which children can only envy until, as they grow up, it becomes less magical; something they can aspire to, and eventually achieve for themselves.

Prospero's Storm may be marketed primarily towards children, but it is not "children's theater," at least not in the pejorative sense that the term often carries. This is smart, sophisticated theater, a thoughtful adaptation which explores *The Tempest* while opening up aspects of the story that inflect our reading of the original—in short, it does exactly what an adaptation should do.

Several of the design elements of *Prospero's Storm* are decidedly Brechtian. The most well-known directive of Brecht's epic theater is that plays should make an effort to remind their audiences that they are at a play, and that theater means something. Like Shakespeare, a lot of people claim to hate Brecht, but like Shakespeare, his legacy lives on in practically everything we do in the theater, especially in twenty-first century Chicago. It lives on in theaters that do explicitly political work, like Oracle and Trapdoor. It lives on in the way that many of his techniques for distancing (or *alienating* as it is often, though problematically, translated) his audience from the world of the play have become so conventional—like directly addressing the audience or using film clips during the play—that they no longer have much of a distancing effect. And it lives on in the worst tradition of children's theater where plays preach to a crowd of young audience members, making sure they understand the moral of the story as if the story couldn't do that itself. Kiely's show is rich with design elements that do the kind of distancing Brecht espoused, without falling into preaching.

Prospero's Storm opens with a voice-over introduction that, amongst the usual admonitions to turn off cell phones and not take pictures, actually tells the audience what the show is about. "The Magical, Musical-Theatrical Tale of the Wretched Wizard Who Sought Revenge on his Enemies with a Terrible Sea-Tempest but through the Power of Love Learned Mercy, Forbearance, and Ultimate Wisdom." For many fans of Shakespeare, this is old news. For others it might be cause for debate. But for the audience of *Prospero's Storm*, it is certainly distancing; a reminder that we are in a theater, and an attempt to tell us how to read the following performance. What makes it fascinating, however, is that it is completely misleading. One can argue about whose story *The Tempest* is, but *Prospero's Storm*, despite its title and despite the prologue, is more Miranda's than her father's. This is not, perhaps, surprising in a play marketed to children; Miranda is a much more relatable character for most young audience members. Much of the intricate plotting of the court—so important to Prospero—is edited out. But then, so is much of the action around the romance between Miranda and Ferdinand. Of course they meet and fall in love, and we get some brief moments of Ferdinand performing the manual labor that Prospero has set for him, but it is not the focus of Miranda's story. In this play, being interested in romance is part of growing up but being a grown-up is about much more than getting married. Again, a message that could be seen as particularly appropriate for a children's show, but which is welcome in any play.

In *The Tempest* we are told that Caliban had attempted to rape Miranda. In *Prospero's Storm* we once again are shown what Shakespeare simply tells, and what we see is Miranda and Caliban, best of childhood friends, tentatively trying out a child's first kiss. Of course Prospero sees it differently, and his reaction is both utterly disproportionate and completely predictable.

Perhaps the most effective new material is Miranda's curiosity about her mother. In *The Tempest*, Miranda wonders what she "is," but we suspect that Prospero's hundred-and-fifty-line exposition of their history is not particularly interesting to her; once begun, her responses are a few questions and several brief assurances that she is listening. *Prospero's Storm* dispenses with the majority of that monologue in favor of a dumb show with placards for a few lines in the style of a silent movie (another Brechtian technique). At the end of it, Miranda impatiently begins to ask, "But who is my..." and is cut off by Prospero putting her to sleep. She manages to ask again later, only once more to be put off. But in the end, during the resolution scene, we finally get to hear the story of Prospero's wife, who is mentioned in *The Tempest* only to make a clichéd joke about fidelity. In *Prospero's Storm* Prospero summons his wife's spirit to sing her story—how when Miranda was born a witch cursed the child to die, and Miranda's mother traded her own life for that of her daughter. All Prospero's magical studies which consumed his attention to the point that he lost his dukedom were to the end of trying to bring her back to life.

Prospero, here, is tyrannical with his powers; he puts Miranda to sleep with upsetting (both to us and to Miranda) regularity. Caliban's monstrousness is cast into doubt, making Prospero's treatment of him more monstrous. Ariel's repeated importunings for her freedom are met with assurances that in this production, even more than in Shakespeare's text, ring insincere. Portraying Prospero with less sympathy strengthens Miranda's role and focuses our attention more on her narrative arc. This pays off beautifully at the end; Prospero refuses to release Ariel and it is Miranda who, usurping lines that Shakespeare gave her father, convinces him to abjure this rough magic, break his staff and bury it certain fathoms in the earth.

Prospero's Storm is a study in how a play can be adapted to tell a different story while still being true to the source. Choices that might seem to lead us in one direction, in the end bring us back to where we thought we had started: by making Prospero less sympathetic, we end up understanding him better. By backgrounding Miranda's marriage plot, we foreground the magic of her growing up. And by distancing the audience from the world of the story, we bring the point more closely into view.

PEMBERLEY PRODUCTIONS + OXFORD PLAYHOUSE
SANCHO: AN ACT OF REMEMBRANCE

written by + starring Paterson Joseph
co-directed by Simon Godwin
presented by Chicago Shakespeare Theater

Robert Day

The Past Is Present: Paterson Joseph Remembers Race
in the Age of Garrick
Gina Di Salvo

What stories get to appear on our great stages and who gets to tell them?

This is a timely question and one that is particularly apt for *Sancho: An Act of Remembrance*. The one-man show about the life of Charles Ignatius Sancho (ca.1729-80) began when Paterson Joseph entered the theater in eighteenth-century dress and identified himself as a black Briton. Born to an African mother on the Middle Passage, Sancho would become a composer, a valet, a businessman and the first black man to vote in England, among other accomplishments.

But when Joseph took the stage and first spoke to us in direct address, he was not yet in character.

Instead, the actor, who also happens to be the playwright and co-director, begins the play as himself and recounts a brief history of other black Britons. There is Sancho from the eighteenth century, there are "too many blackamoors in London," according to Queen Elizabeth I in the late sixteenth century, and there is Septimus Severus, an African who ruled Roman Britain in the early third century. This all serves as a rebuttal to every director or producer who refused to cast Joseph in the plays of Shakespeare or adaptations of classic literature. The problem of casting him was one of authenticity. If there weren't black people in England in 1600, then how can there be, say, a black Hamlet? (Of course, there is never any worry about the audience going along with that bit about the ghost.) Joseph jokes that *Sancho* emerged from his "vanity," and desire "to be in a costume drama." Framed this way, the piece is about excavating a forgotten history, on the one hand, and about the politics of our present theatricality, on the other.

As Joseph ends his induction, he assumes the portly posture and slight lisp of Sancho. It is now 1768 and our subject is also the subject of Thomas Gainsborough, who produced a portrait of Sancho in the same year. Posing before a replica of the painting, Sancho recalls and acts out episodes from the first forty years of his life.

The theatricality of *Sancho* is pronounced. A white cloth that first serves as his gentlemanly cravat becomes his mother's wimple as he narrates her birth pangs aboard the slave ship where she died, and then it transforms again into "the wretched screaming bundle" of the infant baptized as Charles Ignatius in New Granada. Soon after, our protagonist is "deposited ... as a gift" to "three maiden sisters of Greenwich," who costume him as a romance hero for their own entertainment. He is an Arabian Prince, a Pirate, and, finally, Sancho Panza, the clownish companion of Don Quixote. He is educated, secretly, by the Duke of Montagu not only in letters but in culture as well. To demonstrate the sort of music he composed and the dancing of the age, Sancho invites an audience member up to the stage for a quick and charming lesson. In a slight Irish brogue, he quotes a letter from Laurence Sterne, author of *Tristam Shandy,* and he affects his other friend, David Garrick, in his career-making role of Richard III.

All of these overtly theatrical acts highlight the conventions of dramatic performance. On stage, a piece of cloth can be anything. A single man can represent multiple characters, sometimes performing parts of other plays within the play of *Sancho*. It is make-believe and meta-theatre, but of the usual sort that has defined theatre for about the last 2,500 years. It's what we accept when we enter the theatre. It's why twenty-first century audiences don't roll their eyes when the ghost enters in *Hamlet*. And yet, to return to Joseph's opening monologue about black Britons and period dress, our imaginations allow for all sorts of pretending until the question of race comes up and then there is a sudden concern with authenticity and accuracy — in the theater of all places.

Joseph's own quest for a leading role in an English costume drama is part of a larger conversation on the lack of race-conscious casting in classic and historical roles. Last September, *007* author Anthony Horowitz dismissed Idris Elba as "too street" to play the martini-sipping James Bond. In Sunday's *New York Times*, a feature on diversity in Hollywood included an anecdote from Wendell Pierce on being told by a casting director, "I couldn't put you in a Shakespeare movie, because they didn't have black people back then." Hopefully, they've gotten the *Hamilton* memo.

Where else is the Shakespeare in all this? you might be asking. Well, where isn't it?

The improbable and remarkable life of Ignatius Sancho is part of the age of David Garrick and Dr. Johnson, that is, the point in the past 400 years when Shakespeare began to become Shakespeare. Allusions to the works appear throughout the play. Sancho refers to the Greenwich women as "the *Weird Sisters*," he talks about his failed attempt at auditioning for *Othello* (a role only played by white men until 1833), and he twice punctuates his exasperation with racism by quoting Hamlet's "words, words, words." The first utterance occurs just after he describes the trouble he got into as a boy when he was found with a book by one of the sisters. They intended to keep him illiterate, a state suitable to his "rank," not as a servant but as an African. Hamlet's words appear again in the second act of the play, a single day in 1780 in which Sancho participates in parliamentary elections. Between pulling out publications containing arguments for "reducing the number of Blacks," in England and being challenged to prove with his property papers his eligibility to vote, Sancho angrily repeats, "words, words, words." Throughout his life, words, in their written form, have been used in an attempt to keep Sancho in his place. But he has become a man of letters.

At the play's end, Sancho removes the more baroque parts of his eighteenth-century costume and stands before us as he began the play, in his white shirt and breeches. There was a moment there, a pause without the character-defining lisp, in which I didn't know if it was Ignatius

Sancho or Paterson Joseph who stood before me. In my confusion, I think I saw both, and I think I was meant to see both.

Paterson Joseph's *Sancho*: A Life (Re)membered
Cherrie Gottsleben

In his actor's note to the performance of *Sancho: An Act of Remembrance*, Paterson Joseph asks: "Who do you think you are?" Reintroducing this question to the audience previous to his performance, Joseph turns the question to himself, revealing an internal conflict in his response: "I struggle with who people think I am." This response cues the audience to its role as interpreters not only of Ignatius Sancho's life, but of Joseph's own dialogue on that life, a dialogue that participates in a "shared British history," where the narrative boundaries become blurred between Joseph's witty repartee and Sancho's allusions to the "dark" situation of the Black experience in Britain during the 1700s. By linking a sense of his own identity with the character of Sancho, Joseph makes relevant a four-hundred-year-old story to a twenty-first-century audience.

This shared history, Joseph previously thought, began with the Windrush generation (1948), but the British colonization of the Caribbean goes back to the 1600s. In addition in 1555 some Africans arrived in Britain as interpreters for trading purposes. Black musicians played at the courts of James IV of Scotland, Henry the VII and Henry the VIII. We are also well aware that Queen Elizabeth I and James I had African entertainers. The "blackamoor" population so increased in England that Elizabeth I ordered their expulsion in 1596.

Joseph segues from his introduction to the audience into the character of Sancho by visibly getting into costume without cutting his conversational tone. Against the sound of crashing waves, the audience views the opening stage setting, consisting of a tall wooden bench on which hung the actor's costume jackets—or rather Sancho's attire. Three wooden crates also populated the very small stage—one farther back bearing a copy of Thomas Gainsborough's famous portrait of Sancho, one to the left, and another center stage bearing a glass of red wine and resting on a large bright red Persian rug. As Joseph steps into character he transfers Sancho's portrait from the back of the stage to the front in plainer view of the audience; he then strikes a pose as Gainsborough's subject, which seems to (re)member Sancho as the subject of his narrative while he mirrors his portrait. Without breaking his slightly humorous banter he then readdresses the audience with a lisp, as Ignatius Sancho—composer, writer and sometime actor. The aesthetic dissonance carried in the positioning of old wooden crates on a beautiful ornate rug speaks not just to space limitations on stage, but communicates the "oddity" of Sancho's experience, transitioning from his birth on a slave ship in 1729 to becoming a composer, writer and the first Black Briton to vote in 1780.

Throughout the performance the narration punned on "black" and "dark." This punning emerged in reference to the horrendous period of the triangular trade's Middle Passage, and in reference to the always-imminent danger of the "village coven" or oppressive authority. But the vision of the "dark subject" is also introduced in the memory of a "wannabe" actor, stalled outside the theater door with the "indictment" of a speech impediment as reason for his non-entry into the acting profession. As Joseph's Sancho "lisped" his way through the performance it was hard at first to keep from laughing, since the lisp gave the impression of a man thinking too highly of himself as an actor than he ought to think. But the audience, or at least I, sobered up the minute Sancho expressed his disappointment at rejection by widening and bulging his eyes while referring to criticisms about the "booby" actor. Suddenly, the distance between the 1700s and the 1930s and 40s almost disappeared as I remembered the experience of actors of color in early film.

Joseph foregrounds Sancho's self-education, stimulated by John Montagu (2nd Earl of Montagu) who encouraged him to read by lending him books. The degree to which his study of literature became an intimate part of his life is sampled in the actor's numerous Shakespearean quotes, which reveal Sancho's ambivalence toward his relationships with white Britons. For example, the Legge sisters at Blackheath who "owned" him as a boy became in retrospect, the nightmarish "weird sisters" of *Macbeth*, who seemed to smile like *Hamlet*'s "villain."

Sancho's rendering of his musical accomplishments was celebrated with a hearty gulp of wine, and his compositions of songs and dances exemplified his assimilation into a sophisticated and refined British culture. Most of the music played during the performance was Sancho's own compositions, and at one point during his dance, the actor selected a member of the audience, Susan, as his dance partner. Though actors now commonly interact with their audience, what seemed unique to me was that Joseph referred to his dance partner by name a few times while still in character after the audience member had returned to her seat. In doing so he implicated the audience as part of his act, bringing the story nearer to our present reality.

Political double talk on the Black vote pitched "words, words, words" signifying very little for Sancho in his later years. Joseph's Sancho condenses his comparison between the socio-political climate of 1760 and that of 1780 in one fleeting memory of a man who shrugged past him in his younger days. When Sancho asked the man for the time, he replied: "Why it's 1760." When he had the opportunity to vote in 1780, he recalled the incident by asking himself "What is the time?" He answered: "Why it's 1780."

Sancho's interest in the Black vote manifested itself in the socio-political overtone of Joseph's performance, amplified in the reading of an excerpt of Laurence Stern's 1766 letter to Ignatius Sancho. In it Stern asks:

> at which tint of these [from the fairest to the "sootiest"], is it that the ties of blood are to cease? and how many shades must we descend lower still in the scale, 'ere Mercy is to vanish with them?—but 'tis no uncommon thing, my good Sancho, for one half of the world to use the other half of it like brutes, and then endeavour to make 'em so.

During the reading of Stern's letter all stage lights were switched off except for a soft spotlight on Joseph, giving the effect of a gentle urging to meditate. One might ponder not only the situation past, but consider the present status of the Black Briton. Joseph places at the forefront, the modern Black Briton's freedom to vote when Sancho, desperate to participate in elections, finds his permission papers (for voting) in the little cup of his daughter Kitty who died at the age of five. Sancho expresses his joy at the recovery of this document by kissing the cup and shouting his daughter's name. At this point the performance ends and all lights are switched off, leaving the audience with a distilled sense of an ongoing and constantly evolving, unbroken narrative of remembrance.

CHICAGO A CAPPELLA
+ CHICAGO SHAKESPEARE THEATER
SHAKESPEARE A CAPPELLA

adapted + directed by Tom Mula
musical direction by John William Trotter

Jennifer Girard

"Sweet airs that give delight"
Lise Schlosser

The opening number Chicago *a cappella* performed for their *Shakespeare a cappella* concert was Kevin Olson's "Summer Sonnet," a *bossa nova* arrangement of Sonnet 18, which concludes with the lines "So long as men can breathe or eyes can see, / So long lives this, and this gives life to thee." The lines seemed to speak to the spirit behind the concert and the Shakespeare 400 programs of which it is a part. The beauty of Shakespeare's work, the connections we make across the centuries, and the opportunities to see and hear well-known passages anew will continue, it seems, "as long as men can breathe or eyes can see."

Performances by Barbara Robertson and Greg Vinkler, both beloved veteran Chicago actors, punctuated the musical pieces. The choices of text allowed Robertson and Vinkler to display their versatile talents and clear love of the works they were sharing. Like changelings, they were playful, majestic, passionate, cynical, hopeful, and scornful in turn. They embodied the unexpected electricity of Romeo and Juliet's first meeting as convincingly as the well-worn comfort between Doll and Falstaff in *Henry V*. Vinkler played equally persuasively both the monarchical Oberon and the farcical Bottom to Robertson's stately, and then bewitched, Titania. Perhaps my favorite exchange between the two was their turns as Beatrice and Benedick in their initial parley of *Much Ado About Nothing*.

The interstitial spoken pieces reinforced the experience of the musical arrangements; each allowed the audience to hear these often-familiar texts out of their familiar contexts. The recontextualization opened up new interpretations that may be missed when the lines are only a brief portion of a two-hour production. Rather than a few moments that are glossed in an audience member's memory, the attention this production gave each passage allowed the audience to hear the words anew.

The juxtaposition of pieces from different Shakespearean works also provided new contextualizations that created resonances that would have been otherwise impossible to hear. Writer and Director Tom Mula resisted obvious or lazy pairings between spoken and musical pieces, yet each transition proved a harmonic choice. For instance, the singers performed Håkan Parkman's "My love is a fever," an arrangement of Sonnet 147. This sonnet explores the trope of lovesickness and casts "reason" as the physician. The arrangement facilitated the audience's sense of the intensity of the poet's suffering especially with a shift to a minor key at the sonnet's *volta* when the poet reveals that his beloved is "as black as hell, as dark as night." As the applause faded, Vinkler and Robertson began a scene from *As You Like It* where Rosalind (disguised as Ganymede) scolds a lovesick Orlando that, "Men have died from time to / time and worms have eaten them, but not for love" (IV.i.107-108). The lines could just as easily have been directed at the speaker of Sonnet 147.

A similar recontextualization effect occurred for me when the group performed two different arrangements of Sonnet 18. In addition to Olson's "Summer Sonnet" with which the concert opened, the program also included Robert Applebaum's "Shall I compare thee?" Applebaum's darker arrangement provided a stark contrast to Olson's *bossa nova*. Described in the program as "wrenchingly sad, yet exquisitely beautiful," Applebaum's arrangement accents the somber undertones of a poem that is so often associated with the ebullience of a summer's day. The poem, however, does acknowledge that "summer's lease hath all too short a date" and that death will come to the beloved, which is why the poet crafts the sonnet—to give the beloved life for as long as the poem exists. Shakespeare's crafting of exquisite balance in the poem was reflected in the juxtaposition of the two arrangements in performance.

The value of a celebration like Shakespeare 400 is that it provides us all opportunities to do for Shakespeare's work what Shakespeare's work does for its audiences: it makes the familiar strange and the strange familiar. Hearing Shakespeare's words sung not only highlights the innate musicality of the language, but plucks that language out of its native environs, allowing the audience to watch it bloom in new surroundings. Like the opportunities to see the plays performed in other languages, or danced rather than spoken, hearing Chicago *a cappella* perform selections from Shakespeare's works allowed me to hear some of it as if for the first time and to come to a new and deeper appreciation for the art of a man separated from us by four centuries but connected to us by shared human experience.

HAMBURG BALLET
OTHELLO

ballet by John Neumeier
after William Shakespeare
presented by the Harris Theater for Music and Dance

Courtesy of Hamburg Ballet

Shakespeare without Words
Clark Hulse

Measure for Measure in Russian, *King Lear* in Belarusian, *Romeo and Juliet* sung in Italian, *Othello* in—actually, no language. *Othello* the ballet.

A recent post asked if any rewritten version [or re-motioned version] can measure up to the original. But the real question, I would argue, is not *if* it can but *how* it can. And if the result is good, but it's not "Shakespeare"—so what?

The Hamburg Ballet's production of *Othello* uses none of Shakespeare's words (or at least none I could make out). Instead it uses motion to evoke emotion. It defines the core of the play not as the words themselves but as the feelings and thoughts that the words convey—or in Iago's case, with the feelings and thoughts that the words disguise.

In his choreography, Hamburg Ballet Artistic Director John Neumeier creates a vocabulary of motion that ranges from the classically balletic to modern-but-still-dancelike to what can best be called street motions, if ordinary people in the street were wonderful dancers. (This has a striking analogy to Shakespeare's language, ranging from high-poetic to vernacular, always with the condition that it is the vernacular of people who ordinarily talk with the brilliance of Shakespeare.)

Neumeier's (e)motional vocabulary allows him to juxtapose two very different worlds. One is a dream-like Venetian world of hope, love and desire. People are beautiful, their bodies are garbed in white, their movement is a graceful classicism unfolding to passion. Iconographically this world is as much Florentine as Venetian, recalling fifteenth-century Tuscan paintings of classical scenes, with slender figures draped in short tunics. This is the world in which Othello and Desdemona woo each other and wed. But each is attracted as much to a mythical image of the other as to the actual other. For Othello, that other Desdemona is a Botticellian virgin dressed in flowers. For Desdemona, it is a more disturbing figure, an ebony-black body wearing a caricatured mask of red.

So within the white world from the beginning we are allowed to glimpse the jungle fever generated by these mythic figures. It is enacted openly in the world of Cyprus by Othello's soldiers, dressed in camo, and moving with the scarcely controlled violence of the street. In motions so realistic that one can barely still see that it is dance, Iago brutally beats his wife Emilia into meek submission. In alternating scenes, the soldiers molest and gang-rape women in the street, and pummel one of their members who is done up in blackface, as if they were lynching their commander. The sexual and racial violence is hard to watch.

And it is Shakespeare. In the early seventeenth century, at the beginning of the epoch of white-over-black racism, Shakespeare saw this demon that would haunt our own times, saw its entwinement with misogyny, and unleashed their dual fury through his play. Love, desire, trust, loyalty (male/female, male/male), lust, hatred, suspicion, jealousy, murderous wrath, remorse, despair…they all pour out one after another in taut narrative order. What he could not possibly foresee was how deeply those two demons would inhabit our cultures, both high and low. But Neumeier and the Hamburg dancers have the advantage of knowing it, and in each case suit motion to emotion, the balletic equivalent of Hamlet's direction to "suit the action to the word," and draw the picture of civilization entwined with barbarity.

The mythic doubles—Botticelli's virgin and the ebony male nude— reappear at the end for the murder scene. At this point the production flirts with a distasteful cliché, one that an American company might not have dared to put on stage. But in that four-way confrontation, the two mythic figures are cast aside, and Desdemona and Othello are left on stage, alone, to dance out their final steps. It seemed from the beginning that Desdemona knew she would die, even if Othello did not know he would kill her. For a moment it seems like they might reach beyond the situation, and reach each other. But they succumb to their joint destiny, and the performance ends in profound human sadness.

A friend wrote to me afterward, "How could one not be moved to tears? I was stunned by it, on so many levels, stunned. We Shakespeareans always say, 'It's in his language,' and yet here there was none (well, none SPOKEN that was intelligible to us, at least...). And yet filled with language of its own."

The Hamburg Ballet has cast aside Shakespeare's words, cast aside the complex social setting of Venice and Cyprus and the Ottoman wars, cast aside everything except plot, character, the body, its motion and its emotions. Those prove to be more than enough. Preserving the rest, after the silence, would be, perhaps, just taxidermy.

CHICAGO SHAKESPEARE THEATER
OTHELLO

by William Shakespeare
directed by Jonathan Munby

Liz Lauren

Words at Last
Clark Hulse

Shakespeare with words—at last!

I have written here about the Russian *Measure for Measure* and the Hamburg Ballet production of *Othello*—both wonderful. But after these, the Chicago Shakespeare Theater production of *Othello* fell on my ears like a mad torrent.

It is an odd and useful experience to *see* Shakespeare without his words. It brings out how much more there is than just the script. There is setting and costume, expression and gesture, motions of the body, music and laughter, grunts, cackles, and screams of pain and agony.

But restore the words after their absence and they are fresh again. The feeling was particularly strong seeing *Othello* danced by the Hamburg Ballet and acted by Chicago Shakespeare Theater on successive nights.

We are correctly comfortable with the notion that Shakespeare invented a new dramatic language. He inherited the lofty poetic rhetoric of Thomas Sackville and Christopher Marlowe, ideal for denoting the elevated sentiments of noble characters. He then created a second, prosaic language out of the mouths of common people. In between them, he molded a third language in blank verse that is beautiful in the mouth and on the ear, and yet adapted to the rhythms of natural speech. Initially these languages are distributed among the characters according to social class, but in time Shakespeare dares to mix things up, and give gutter language to nobles and poetry to common folk.

From its opening lines, *Othello* rings the changes of Shakespeare's dramatic language:

> **Roderigo** Tush! never tell me; I take it much unkindly
> That thou, Iago, who hast had my purse
> As if the strings were thine, shouldst know of this.
> **Iago** 'Sblood, but you will not hear me:
> If ever I did dream of such a matter,
> Abhor me.

Roderigo's outburst resolves into scannable iambic, only to be disrupted again by Iago's curse, and resolved again—almost—into meter. In the process, their accents, their voices and their characters are established. But quickly we revert to Iago's vulgar prose:

> ...you'll have your daughter covered with a Barbary horse;
> you'll have your nephews neigh to you; you'll have coursers
> for cousins and gennets for germans.

...though even here Shakespeare cannot resist the word play: "coursers" and "cousins," "gennets" and "germans." This wedding of coarse outburst with fantastical figures of speech accelerates as Iago fevers Othello's jealous imagination:

> Would you, the supervisor, grossly gape on—
> Behold her topp'd?
> It is impossible you should see this,
> Were they as prime as goats, as hot as monkeys,
> As salt as wolves in pride, and fools as gross
> As ignorance made drunk.

Many scenes later, as Othello greets Lodovico, the wedding of poetry and gutter speech is consummated:

> You are welcome, sir, to Cyprus.—Goats and monkeys!

Chicago Shakespeare Theater has always distinguished itself with a purity of diction. Shakespeare's language is spoken clearly and crisply, and is joined to gesture and expression. This is quite simply a matter of trusting the language. Any of us who have taught Shakespeare in the classroom have encountered students who believe that they don't understand Shakespeare *because* of the language. The best refutation of this—the best proof to them that they do already understand Shakespeare—lies in the experience of the theater. Carefully spoken, as meaningful human speech, wedded to expression, the language becomes no less intelligible as the life around us.

This might sound like cant or bardolatry. But the demonstrable proof lay in the audience around me at CST's *Othello*. As Roderigo, Iago and Brabantio poured out their swill ("His Moorship...the thicklips...an old black ram...a Barbary horse...the beast with two backs...lascivious Moor...the sooty bosom of such a thing as thou...") I could feel the person next to me—a senior figure in Chicago wealth management—flinch with each racist slur. As Iago worked Othello with each tightening of the screw, the rise of tension in the audience was palpable. People listened even more than they watched, with acute understanding to the words. Such emotionally exact, insanely, rhetorically, over-the-top words as

> It is the cause, it is the cause, my soul,—
> Let me not name it to you, you chaste stars!—
> It is the cause. Yet I'll not shed her blood;
> Nor scar that whiter skin of hers than snow,
> And smooth as monumental alabaster.

Or,

> Set you down this;
> And say besides, that in Aleppo once,
> Where a malignant and a turban'd Turk
> Beat a Venetian and traduced the state,
> I took by the throat the circumcised dog,
> And smote him, thus.

After much silence, speech is a sharpened blade.

Tribalism and Toxic Masculinity in *Othello*
Rebecca L. Fall

Othello is famously a play about difference. Most obviously, it is a play about racial difference. In Chicago Shakespeare Theater's recent production, however, directed by Jonathan Munby and set in a present-day pseudo-American context, "difference" represents a moving target. The lines of difference constantly shift throughout the production to emphasize various models of inclusion and exclusion based on race and ethnicity, to be sure, but also on religion, class, nationality, and—perhaps above all—gender.

The themes of inclusion and exclusion, tribalism and othering, are apparent from the first spoken scene, in which Roderigo and Iago convene outside Senator Brabantio's home, evidently a condo in a building that, in its imposing, stripped-down neoclassicism, strongly resembles those around Capitol Hill in Washington, DC. The men buzz on the intercom to Brabantio's building, initially talking to him through the speaker; a physical wall separates the two malcontents from the Senator. As they deliberately stoke his racial and sexual anxieties, however, Brabantio's alliances shift. He first only deigns to talk through the intercom's speaker, and then opens a window to shout at Iago and Roderigo in person—but still maintains his distance from them behind a wall, remaining physically as well as socially above them.

Soon, though, Iago and Roderigo close that gap by making Brabantio imagine that they all have an enemy in common: the black Othello. Eventually, Brabantio descends and emerges outside, literally joining the same level as Iago and Roderigo. The model of difference in the scene, which was initially drawn according to class—the Senator putting himself above the common soldier and his friend—has now shifted along racial lines. Brabantio sets out with Roderigo—once "the worser" but now "good Roderigo"—to apprehend his daughter and "the Moor."

On a dark city street, Brabantio confronts an impeccably dressed Othello and follows him to meet the Duke. The setting transforms into something that looks suspiciously like the White House's Situation Room, images of which have been widely circulated in the wake of Osama bin Laden's death. The resemblance is disturbingly apt, considering that the Venetian Duke has just been informed of an incoming military threat from an Islamic force, the "Turks," or the Ottoman Empire. This military conflict between the West and the Middle

East, Christianity and Islam, represents one vector of difference at work in the production, and fundamentally informs its approach to the play.

Munby has gone out of his way thus far to establish Othello as a Venetian insider in religious and military terms. Even before Iago and Roderigo take the stage, the performance opens with an extratextual scene of Othello and Desdemona's wedding—a conspicuously Catholic ceremony during which Othello wears his military uniform, marking him not only as a general but also as a member of the Christian Venetian community.

Yet, when Brabantio interrupts the Duke's meeting to complain about his daughter's marriage to Venice's greatest general, he treats Othello as an outsider, tossing around ugly, racially charged language. Othello is Christian, he is a respected member of the military, and he has just been asked to lead a dangerous campaign against a huge empire—but he is still the outsider here. In Venice, it seems he may never fully belong. This will change, however, when the scene shifts to Cyprus.

The DC-like backdrop rises into the ceiling, revealing a military installation closely resembling images of American bases in Iraq and Afghanistan. Sirens sound and lights flash in warning when anyone comes in or out—here, the stakes of inclusion and exclusion are very high indeed. Men wearing desert camouflage fight the elements: high-strung, they are ready for violence and war. But of course, a storm destroys the Turkish fleet and contains the threat of battle. Othello and his men have arrived at Cyprus, ready to kill and be killed, and suddenly have nothing to do.

Also newly arrived is Othello's wife. When Desdemona enters this military zone, she could not look more out of place. In contrast to the soldiers' fatigues, she wears impractically high heels and carries a designer handbag. It is clear that this is not Desdemona's space.

Here, though, Othello is one of the guys. And while the men still sometimes refer to him as "the Moor," Othello's racial difference is downplayed in Munby's Cyprus. In the military, Othello has found a space where he belongs. He wears the same desert camo as the other soldiers. The uniform aligns them all. So, too, does, gender—for Othello is not only a military man on Cyprus, he is a *man*. His wife is now the outsider. And the longer she stays, the more she will stand out.

Take, for instance, the extratextual scene during and just after intermission. On stage, the soldiers entertain themselves with karaoke. Eventually, they will gang up on Desdemona as she enters wearing a fetching, bright blue ensemble: they follow her around the stage singing The Righteous Brothers' classic "You've Lost that Lovin' Feelin'." She giggles and plays along, but her difference from them is never more apparent than it is at this moment. In its blocking and choreography, the scene pits the men, wearing combat fatigues and huge knives at their sides, against a willowy, super-feminine woman. At the back of the stage is a bulletin board with a large sign labeled "Wall of Shame." It's covered in photos of women, presumably the sexual conquests of the men on base. Evidently, the soldiers here treat women as disposable objects. And so however adorable the men's musical bravado may seem, this scene ultimately sees Desdemona standing down a pack of large and frankly intimidating men in a way that grotesquely anticipates the very frightening violence of the play's conclusion.

At that conclusion, as Desdemona dresses for bed, the men who sang to her will return, silently, like ghosts. They will assemble at the front edge of the thrust stage in a line, advancing on the small, lonely woman. She doesn't see them, but they're there, surrounding her. It is a display of an aggressive male gaze on a vulnerable female body. For the life of her, the production tells us, she'll never fit in with them.

Significantly, though, Desdemona is not the only woman on the Cyprus base. Iago's wife Emilia is also present—and in this production, she is a soldier. This treatment of Emilia is particularly interesting. She is a woman working desperately to survive in a man's world. She wears combat fatigues, just like the men, and adopts a masculine posture that contrasts sharply with Desdemona's aristocratic femininity.

Once Desdemona arrives, though, Emilia is treated as nothing more than another woman. Emilia has risen up through the ranks in an environment hostile to her sex, has worked to prove herself, training her body and instincts (as her impressive self-defense skills show late in the play). And just because she is a woman, she has been removed from her duties to carry around the purse of a privileged interloper, Desdemona, who treats her like a servant. As Emilia's face and body language show throughout the first half, she clearly resents it. Eventually, however, in reaction to the frightening masculine aggression of the men around her, Emilia aligns herself with Desdemona. The women slowly begin to unite, creating in the end a community of two. They become more and more physically intimate throughout the second half of the play, finally embracing tenderly in Desdemona's femininely appointed bedroom.

The women will make their own alliance, but it is the hyper-masculinity and endemic misogyny on the base that, in this production, seems to explain something about Othello's quick turn, his willingness to blame Desdemona and do her such violence. He loves her, it seems, but she's not one of them. On the base, she's an outsider, and outsiders are not to be trusted.

Indeed, this toxic, tribalistic masculinity is only exacerbated by the conditions of a war that never comes: these men, Othello included, have been preparing for battle, for violence that has not materialized. It's as if they *need* something to fight, something to exclude and cast out. It should have been the Turkish invaders, but they never arrived. So if the outsider does not show up, the men will find and fight an outsider within.

When Emilia finds Desdemona's body in the last scene, she turns viciously on Othello. Suddenly he is not one of the guys at the base, he is not her commanding officer. He is nothing more than a Moor. Emilia's racially charged language in this scene is often discomfiting for audiences who celebrate her as one of Shakespeare's great feminist characters. But sadly, in this production, which highlights the myriad ways "difference" can be constructed and even weaponized, it fits.

In Venice, Othello was the outsider. Here on the base, the women have taken that role. But in the end, after he has turned on Desdemona for no good reason, Othello must be excluded from the community. Emilia, like the other Venetians, needs to find a way to *make* him different. That's the thrust of the play, really: what can we use to impose difference upon someone we want to exclude for some reason? What can we do or say to make him *not belong*?

As the playtext and this CST production both suggest, the measure of "difference" is unstable and arbitrary. Its goalposts can be moved whenever it is convenient. As such, it is subject to manipulation by the likes of Iago, who in the end goes silent, refusing to explain anything. The play itself, too, refuses to offer any answers. Only this is clear: the real problem is the ideology of difference itself.

An *Othello* for the Twenty-first Century
Andrew S. Keener

Sometime during the mid-seventeenth century, a reader and book collector named Frances Wolfreston recorded her thoughts about William Shakespeare's tragedy *Othello*. Inscribed in a 1655 edition of the play now held at the University of Pennsylvania, her assessment concisely reads, "a sad one." Wolfreston's commentary preceded Thomas Rymer's notorious, but far more famous misreading of *Othello* as "a caution to all Maidens of Quality how, without their Parents' consent, they run away with Blackamoors," and provides a valuable example of literary criticism from a woman during Shakespeare's own century. In their utter simplicity, her words seize on the heart of a tragedy that continues to raise important questions about foreignness and gender.

Chicago Shakespeare Theater's elegantly wrought production of *Othello* delivers on these counts, and is particularly successful in its attempt to present Shakespeare's tragedy to a twenty-first-century audience. Director Jonathan Munby brings us a dynamic rendition, one that seizes upon wartime tensions between foreign and other, us and them. This tension finds expression in the tragedy's central character, the Moorish general of Venice, Othello (played by a venerable and stately James Vincent Meredith) and his relationships with his wife Desdemona (the confident and amiable Bethany Jillard) and the cynical and manipulative ensign Iago (a pacing, charismatic Michael Milligan). Rising above these actors' chemistry, however, is this production's imposing set, a brutalist concrete edifice representing Venice, and a towering medley of chain-link, barbed wire and corrugated metal characterizing the Venetians' stronghold on Cyprus. This scenery produces an inescapable sense of surveillance and enclosure throughout the tragedy. In spite of *Othello*'s insistence upon the foreign and otherworldly (Othello is an "extravagant and wheeling stranger / Of here and everywhere" known for his "travailous history") this production defers and denies that foreignness, only allowing us to glimpse Cyprus briefly through the Venetians' overbearing security checkpoints. The continuity between the two sets offers the impression that Othello and his soldiers do not truly come to know Cyprus, but merely construct a second Venice abroad, an effort that ultimately undoes them all.

Parallels between the Venetians' campaign and the United States' current entanglements in the Middle East are not lost on this production.

Othello, Iago and a convincing and sympathetic Michael Cassio (Luigi Sottile) could be mistaken for modern American troopers with their beige camouflage and cries of "Hooah!" In one of the most intense moments of this production (during the famous "temptation scene" in which Iago plants jealousy in the mind of the Moor of Venice), an enraged Othello plunges Iago's head repeatedly into a water cooler as he cries, "If thou dost slander her and torture me / Never pray more, abandon all remorse!" This breaking point, a disquieting visual echo of waterboarding and other literal torture methods used by Americans against foreigners during the last decade, illustrates brilliantly how Shakespeare's language enables us to confront our personal and political demons. The choice here was bold, and effective.

Another striking decision in this production of *Othello* is a musical number appearing immediately after the intermission, which primes the audience for the heightened sexual and domestic conflicts of the play's final acts. With the set dressed up for a military-style Christmas banquet, a handful of Venetian soldiers dance around the stage as one of their fellows croons the lyrics to Drake's sensational R&B hit "Hotline Bling"—fittingly, a song about a jealous lover unable to get over his ex. This scene of masculine camaraderie is a definite crowd-pleaser, but a poster of photographs paraded around by the soldiers emblazoned with the words "Wall of Shame" testifies to the company's more sinister side. If this only hints at the soldiers' sexual engagements with native Cyprus women, the sudden appearance of the distinctly foreign-accented prostitute Bianca (a tenacious Laura Rook) with Cassio offers a glimpse into the unfortunate human consequences of these entanglements (she ends up in handcuffs). On the one hand, at least in this production, what was meant to be a political conflict between the Venetians and the Turks winds up being a domestic conflict between the Venetians and the inhabitants of Cyprus, whom, with the exception of the Bianca, we never really see. On the other hand, the central conflict truly exists between the Venetians and themselves, though it uses the same terms of sexual corruption. When Othello calls Desdemona a whore, farcically treating Emilia as a bawd and tossing money in a mocking gesture of payment, we witness a man desperately clinging to Iago's poisonous suggestions, desperate to what would keep him sane, what would keep him a Venetian and not a foreigner. At one time or another, all the women characters in *Othello* are called "whore," a word that Shakespeare uses more in this play than any of his other dramatic works.

For these reasons, it was a very smart move to cast the Venetian Duke as a woman and to costume Iago's wife Emilia as a soldier. These decisions offer fresh staging possibilities, but they also amplify the play's crucial questions about gender and power. Though she only appears briefly in the first act, the authoritative Duke of Venice (Melissa Carlson) exists in this production as a dominant and capable woman overseeing the hyper-masculine military world of occupied Cyprus. Meanwhile, clothed literally in a warrior's uniform, this production's beer-drinking Emilia (Jessie Fisher) is an expert in hand-to-hand combat, supporting with her own physical might the claims she makes for women's equality. "Let husbands know / Their wives have sense like them," she says to a seated Desdemona in one of this play's most powerful scenes. For modern audiences, this Emilia makes a case for women's participation in the military, insisting upon the similarities between men and women, and speaking and acting with conviction against her husband's wishes when her testimony is needed most. One might speculate that the women in this successful production of *Othello* would have been of special interest to Wolfreston, whose opinion of this great tragedy—"a sad one"—remains true in 2016.

Military Culture in *Othello*
Verna Foster

Othello is the Shakespearean play *par excellence* that resonates with contemporary concerns over race, class and gender and, more recently, with the complex and often conflicted relations between East and West, Islam and Christianity. Othello, the text suggests, is a black African Muslim prince ("of royal siege") and mercenary soldier who has converted to Christianity (receiving in baptism the "seals and symbols of redeemèd sin"). As a convert to Christianity, he resembles the traveler and geographer Leo Africanus, from whose *Description of Africa* Shakespeare drew in creating his own Moor.

Chicago Shakespeare Theater's production of *Othello*, directed by Jonathan Munby, does not directly address Othello's outsider status as a cultural "other." Nor does Munby make any more of Othello's racial difference than is required by Brabantio's prejudice and Iago's foul mouth. Rather what fuels this fast-moving modern-dress production is its emphasis on military culture and all that it implies about male bonding, machismo, the casual resort to violence — and the consequences of that culture for women and for the native population of an occupied country. The light-colored fatigues of the soldiers, the metallic no-frills barracks, and the relative undress of Bianca (Laura Rook speaking accented English as a Greek Cypriot prostitute) suggest sand, heat, and a masculine perspective. Cyprus easily stands in for somewhere in the Middle East and the Italian soldiers for American troops. In this context Othello's problem is not so much his difference from as his similarity to the other soldiers, black and white.

Munby establishes a setting familiar to the audience through a number of nice touches in the first act in Venice. When Roderigo (Fred Geyer) cannot arouse Brabantio (David Lively), Iago (Michael Milligan) shows his superior intelligence by ringing the doorbell. Roderigo puts money in his purse by accessing his bank account on his smart phone. The female Duke (Melissa Carlson) is super-efficient in a red Hillary Clintonesque power suit. And the Senators use laptops, on one of which Iago finds pornography to illustrate for Roderigo what he thinks of Othello and Desdemona's marriage.

What chiefly motivates this Iago is his pornographic imagination. He wants to destroy Othello out of sexual jealousy. Rather a cold fish for much of the play, Milligan's Iago becomes frenzied when he declares his suspicion that Othello has taken his own place in Emilia's bed. That Othello gave Cassio the lieutenancy he wanted matters to him but not much, and his declared lust for Desdemona seems improbable. Iago is most comfortable hanging out with men, though there is no sense that he is erotically attracted to any of them. Rather he enjoys violent horseplay as long as he can control it. He ensures that a drunken brawl will take place in the barracks by spiking the soldiers' drink. The final scene displays the results of all the mayhem he has caused: Montano with his arm in a sling, Cassio on crutches, and the "tragic loading" of Desdemona's bed. As he exits, Iago pauses to gaze enigmatically at the mingled bodies of Desdemona, Emilia and Othello, the fulfillment perhaps of his ugly sexual fantasy.

Milligan downplays Iago's comic irony; he is too intense for the audience to feel implicated in his schemes. The advantage is that the production maintains an appropriate balance between Iago and Othello. Too often cleverly amusing Iagos upstage their Othellos. In Munby's production James Vincent Meredith's Othello in his demeanor and speech is always the more commanding figure of the two even when he loses his composure. Othello's physical violence towards Desdemona seems to be the product of his military background rather than attributable to his "otherness." When he demands that Iago furnish him with proof of Desdemona's infidelity, he uses a quasi-water boarding technique to make Iago speak. His recourse to brutality is of a piece with the military machismo displayed by the other soldiers in the brawl or when one of them spits in Cassio's washing bowl after he has been cashiered. Cassio (Luigi Sottile) has good reason for the seriousness with which he takes his loss of reputation in this environment.

But it is the women who are most in danger from such machismo. In Cyprus Desdemona (Bethany Jillard) is at first treated like an idol not only by Cassio but by the other soldiers as well. At a Christmas party in the barracks, they switch from a raucous rendition of Drake's misogynistic "Hotline Bling" to serenade Desdemona with "You've Lost that Lovin' Feelin'" (it proves as foreboding as the willow song). But from idol to whore is only a short fall in this play. And Othello soon thinks of Desdemona in the same way that Cassio and the soldiers think of prostitutes such as Bianca. The violence with which Othello knocks Desdemona down is particularly shocking—both times. As a woman and as a member of the native population Bianca is doubly threatened by the military. First sexually used by Cassio, she is finally brutally handcuffed and marched off to prison, a suspect—without any evidence—in the attack on him.

The production's military environment underscores *Othello*'s exploration of gender relations by isolating the women and throwing them onto their own resources. And all three women are remarkably strong characters. Contrary to the usual critical wisdom, Jillard's Desdemona actually becomes a stronger character in Cyprus than she was in Venice, as she learns how to be a wife negotiating with her husband in an environment that is alien to her. She participates gracefully in the social life of the military outpost, though her clothes are packed in suitcases and hanging on walls. At the end she fights hard for her life. Emilia (Jessie Fisher) is a soldier, not just an army wife. Her military position does not quite make sense of her role as Desdemona's maid, but it does emphasize her strength of character from the beginning. Emilia's insights into men and marriage come from her unhappy relationship with Iago. She can recognize Othello's jealousy because she has experienced Iago's. When she offers her lengthy disquisition on women's rights and abusive husbands in her intimate bedroom conversation with Desdemona, she speaks movingly out of her own sad experience, and Desdemona's.

Munby's modernization of *Othello* causes some inevitable problems. We lose wonderful lines like "Keep up your bright swords, for the dew will rust them." But the contemporary focus of the production gives us a new take on Othello. Military greatness is both Othello's glory and his downfall.

TIM ETCHELLS + FORCED ENTERTAINMENT
(IN) COMPLETE WORKS: TABLE TOP SHAKESPEARE

presented by Museum of Contemporary Art
+ Chicago Shakespeare Theater

Hugo Glendinning

Almost Shakespeare
Ira S. Murfin

The work of the experimental British company Forced Entertainment distinguishes itself among much contemporary performance by its unique relationship to the elemental conditions of theater. Forced Entertainment's work proceeds from and responds to the expectations and limitations of theatrical circumstance, emphasizing to extremity (and beyond to Brechtian estrangement) the particularities of theater's most ordinary aspects—narrative, costume, duration, suspension of disbelief, the performer-audience relationship. Their performances tend to either messily exceed the limits of coherent representation or to deliberately underdetermine their own theatricality, always strategically missing the mark. During a rare US residency at the Museum of Contemporary Art these past few weeks, Chicago audiences have experienced an intermissionless 140-minute epic about childhood during wartime read from identical notebooks by two men without acting anything out, and a six-hour-long non-narrative performance in which the company collectively tried to confess to everything.

The third Forced Entertainment project presented in Chicago, *(In) Complete Works: Table Top Shakespeare*, brought twelve of the one-hour versions of Shakespeare's plays created for *Complete Works: Table Top Shakespeare*, which premiered last year in the UK with every play in the canon. Presented here four per night, these performances featured a single member of Forced Entertainment seated at a large wooden table, relating the plot of one of Shakespeare's plays to the audience, using ordinary household objects and products as illustrative props, and summarizing the action rather than quoting the plays directly. The night I attended included *The Merchant of Venice*, *As You Like It*, *Macbeth* and *The Winter's Tale* in a marathon relay between company members Claire Marshall, Robin Arthur, Richard Lowdon and Cathy Naden (remaining company members Terry O'Connor and Artistic Director Tim Etchells were not in Chicago.) Each of these plays deals in part with characters in disguise or substituting for one another, in much the same way that the narrators substituted ordinary objects for Shakespeare's characters, and plot summaries for the texts of the plays.

Organizing everyday objects on the tabletop and synopsizing the stories, the performers engaged the audience with their capacity to approximate the content of the plays using a limited set of tools, which at a different scale could describe the constraints under which all theater operates. After all, Shakespeare also uses summary and approximation where the limits of theatrical representation assert themselves. *As You Like It* has Oliver reporting on his unseen rescue from a lion by Orlando, which Robin Arthur related in much the same way that Oliver presents this pivotal instance of storytelling. And the offstage mauling of Antigonus in *The Winter's Tale* is merely implied by the famous stage direction "Exit pursued by a bear," here satisfyingly cast by Cathy Naden as a half-full bag of trail mix.

Forced Entertainment is able to make use of Shakespeare in this performance about the provisional nature of theater because in the theater Shakespeare is always close at hand, almost to the point of ubiquity. Like the common objects and products sitting in our kitchen cupboards, our bathroom cabinets, our garages and workshops, we may go years without thinking about one of Shakespeare's plays only to find, on encountering one, that it has been there all along, and that it functions much as we remember. Engaging Shakespeare is like riding a bike, or like fixing a bike with an old set of tools you forgot you had and *then* riding. Some assembly is required, but in the end it still works just fine. Given what most audiences for this performance will know, when Robin Arthur, presenting *As You Like It*, says of the bottle he cast as Jaques, "Then he makes a long speech where he compares the world to a theater," it might be argued that it does much the same work as hearing "All the world's a stage..." recited; similarly Richard Lowdon telling us that the old aerosol can playing Macbeth "feels nothing and everything feels pointless" upon hearing of Lady Macbeth's suicide supplies the "Tomorrow and tomorrow and tomorrow..." speech without it being quoted.

An orientation toward approximation and provisionality in dramatic storytelling informs this encounter between the priorities of postdramatic performance and the assumptions of traditional theatre, as it has similarly amongst Forced Entertainment's contemporaries. The Nature Theater of Oklahoma's 2010 *Romeo and Juliet*, for instance, was comprised not of the text of the play, but of transcribed summaries of what of interviewees remembered of the plot. Theatre has become more and more a context to think about theatricality and the dynamics of representation, under which conditions the table has often proved a space simultaneously within and outside of the literal theater where the divides between performance and criticism, actor and audience, the fictional and the actual can be examined and bridged. The non-illusory direct address of John Cage's lectures or Spalding Gray's autobiographical monologues presented at tables much like Forced Entertainment's suggests a theater that is both dramatically coherent and anti-spectacular. But the table is, at the same time, a model for the theatrical dynamic itself, a literal platform behind which sits a controlling intelligence attempting to bring a story to life on that surface. *Table Top Shakespeare* might promise transcendent puppetry, like that of the New York street performer Stuart Sherman who staged his miniature spectacles with ordinary objects on portable tables, but it delivers instead something purposely a bit more static and self-reflexive. By diagramming but never fully realizing the potential relationship between narrator, story and object, *Table Top Shakespeare* tasks the audience with the act of assembly.

Forced Entertainment is insisting on the contingent, provisional, collectively navigated nature of the performance event, and certainly this is not everybody's cup of tea. Indeed, audience attrition appeared to be an anticipated side effect if not a goal of the work. After the single brief intermission in the four-hour program MCA Director of Performance Programs Peter Taub congratulated those of us who had stayed, inviting us to move closer, as if we had passed the test and the evening could finally proceed as intended. One pleasure of durational performance like this is the satisfaction of having *endured*, together with others, and making it to the end (although that could also be said to be a pleasure of seeing any production of Shakespeare.) Among those I shared the theater with, I certainly encountered some who felt that something was missing, some opportunity had been lost, whether the possibilities of representational spectacle or the texture of Shakespeare's language itself. They imagined the clever, acrobatic uses that could have been made of the objects, and lamented the absence of Shakespeare's poetry. But that disappointment, too, might be productive, offering the audience a stage on which to perform versions of the plays they might hope for or imagine or remember. Like much of Forced Entertainment's work, the whole evening felt like both too much and too little—from one angle we had both seen four Shakespeare plays over the course of as many hours, from another we had seen none at all. *Table Top Shakespeare* substituted for something much vaster and more fantastical than any of us saw on stage that night, yet it also insisted that the theater that we had, the theater we were making do with and enduring, was, or should be, good enough.

Masterpiece (Table-Top) Theater: Reanimating Shakespeare's Plays through Condiment Puppetry
Raashi Rastogi

The Bard has taken many avatars over the years; his works have been transformed into films, paintings, ballets, cartoons, video games, action figures, and even a series of feminist fan fiction YouTube videos (featuring the character "Your Sassy Gay Friend"). They have been abridged, adapted, transmuted, invoked, and translated into numerous languages, forums, and contextual spheres. And yet, I'm not sure Shakespeare's famous corpus has ever before taken on the proportions of Forced Entertainment's *(In) Complete Works: Table Top Shakespeare*, hosted at the Museum of Contemporary Art in late February, in which plays are recounted using ordinary kitchen objects and condiments: candlesticks, lotion bottles, aerosol cans, honey pots, bug sprays, vases, and more. *The Merchant of Venice*'s Antonio becomes a towering bottle of limoncello while Portia is a slim vial of rosewater; *Macbeth*'s witches are small balls of twine with a jelly jar for Lady Macbeth; and *As You Like It*'s Touchstone is rendered a can of Heinz beans with the shepherd girl Audrey as a suggestive and comic bottle of Veet.

This series of performance art pieces was conceived by Forced Entertainment, a group based out of Sheffield, England. Comprised of six artists who, together, negotiate and explore "what theater and performance can mean in contemporary life," the company has produced gallery installations, books, photographic collections, videos, a magic show and even a bus tour, and now, their own original take on Shakespeare.

The *(In) Complete Works* (an abridged version of the *Complete Works: Table Top Shakespeare* which debuted in Berlin) presents twelve plays in thirty-five to forty-five minute segments over three nights. Employing only a bare tabletop, each artist intimately and variously presents, recounts, and enacts a different play, manipulating the kitchen objects to trace the movements of the characters. As Artistic Director Tim Etchells explains, the table is "at once the how-to space of so many Internet tutorials and, at the same time, a distant cousin of the 'wooden O' invoked by Shakespeare in *Henry V*" (and indeed, the event is transmitted live over the Internet as it is taking place at the MCA). The effect produces an unusual amalgamation of storytelling with puppets, acting via condiment, and football-esque play sheets that offer a blow-by-blow account of each work.

Forced Entertainment describes the performances as efforts to explore "the dynamic force of narrative and storytelling with the use of language alone." And indeed, in the small, darkened theater, featuring only the bare table and the actor-narrator-storyteller, the familiar plays are transformed into entirely new stories. The famous lines, the characterizations, critical history, theatrical dramatics, sets and actors are all stripped away as the story is mediated by a single artist in a casual, accessible, colloquial, conversational, often comedic and improvisational manner. In one moment, Claire Marshall retelling *The Merchant of Venice*, interacts with the object-characters—exchanging knowing glances with a candlestick Bassanio—and in another moment, she *is* the character—rolling her eyes in place of the friends that scoff at Bassanio's gamble on Portia and Belmont.

The nuances of each play shift and morph in the mouths of their narrators; the tales become less Shakespeare's and more the narrator's own, aligned with her/his own personal identifications, interests, sympathies, and narrative license. Antonio presides over Marshall's *Merchant of Venice*, towering over all of the other objects; he becomes, in this version, a lonely, isolated figure, physically at the center of the play and yet always on the periphery of the action. The retelling begins with him staring longingly and melancholic-ly upon the sea, and ends the same way, concluding with a comment on his sad part in the world, as bittersweet as the limoncello that constitutes him. This narrative is (or evolves into) one more invested in Antonio's—and by extension, all of our own—existential isolation than it is about the poor treatment of Shylock, Portia's proto-feminist heroism, or Bassanio and Antonio's exceptional friendship. Similarly, Robin Arthur's *As You Like It* cast with an olive oil bottle Oliver and a Dove lotion Rosalind transforms the homoerotic and suggestive romance and Rosalind's masterful manipulations into the unctuously hilarious infatuation of giddy teenagers.

Etchells explains of the project that, "What we're doing is like taking the engine out of the car [that is Shakespeare] and putting all the little bits on the ground and then assembling it in order. There's something analytic about it, slightly dispassionate." And yet, at the same time, I'd like to suggest that there's something incredibly compelling about the way these accounts take the tales that are integrally part of our cultural consciousness and refashion these stories into intimate conversations. As bare bones as these stories become when compared to the Shakespearean playtext, they remain unbelievably rich, nuanced, and animated. The "unpromising machinery of the tabletop stirs something deep, through which the stories gain a kind of traction": the objects begin to take on personalities and characteristics that prove a testament to the strength of the connection forged between artist and audience. In this day of the now, the new, the viral, these performances remind us how extraordinarily captivating, dynamic, enduring, and nostalgic the practice of simple storytelling can be, even with the tales we have seen countless times before.

LYRIC OPERA OF CHICAGO
GOUNOD'S ROMEO AND JULIET

by Charles Gounod
conducted by Emmanuel Villaume
directed by Bartlett Sher

Todd Rosenberg

Romeo and Juliet as a French Opera
Martha C. Nussbaum

Shakespeare and opera have an uneasy relationship. Opera offers some resources that promise the lover of Shakespeare further, or at least different, illumination. The presence of orchestra and chorus can supply a heft and depth in crowd scenes that is more difficult to achieve through words spoken on the stage. In the hands of a first-rate composer, music can pierce into the inner life of a character in a way that reveals new, or at least complementary, depths of meaning. Music also offers possibilities of exchange and reciprocity, in tightly scored ensembles, that are more difficulty to achieve in plain words. For all of these reasons, Giuseppe Verdi's three great Shakespeare operas, *Macbeth* (1847), *Otello* (1887), and *Falstaff* (1893) are works that fully equal Shakespeare in power of insight, although they attain slightly different insights and through different routes. (Some would rank *Macbeth* lower, but though its music is certainly more conventional than that of the two great late operas, it is a splendid work in its own light. In some stretches, for example Lady Macbeth's Sleepwalking scene, it markedly enlarges the emotional possibilities of the original.)

On the other hand, opera has some clear drawbacks. Shakespeare's crisp language can become cluttered and overburdened when a second-rate composer adds to it all sorts of musical frills and froth. First-rate singers are usually mature bodies, and thus may be more suited to play some Shakespearean roles than others. Thus, there is no difficulty casting *Falstaff* credibly, but there is great difficulty in the present instance.

Charles Gounod (1818-93) is a close contemporary of Verdi (1813-1901). But he is no Verdi. In general I have doubts about whether Shakespeare ever translates well into French operatic music. Ambroise Thomas's *Hamlet* (1868) is a particularly annoying example, with its chorus about how wine makes sorrows go away, and with its florid tour de force mad scene for Ophelia that makes a good extract for a good coloratura soprano's aria recording, but has little to do with the pathos and tragedy of the original. Gounod is a better composer than Thomas, and his setting of *Roméo et Juliette* (1867) has some lovely lyrical moments, such as Roméo's aria, "Ah lève-toi, soleil." It also uses the chorus to advantage, for the most part, providing a running commentary on the fatal rivalry of the houses. But it is fundamentally an overblown and therefore frivolous work. Shakespeare's tragedy is spare, intimate, pared down to essentials. It does not do well when inflated to enormous proportions, and its haunting fragile story becomes trite when so bloated.

Let it be said that Lyric has staged this work extremely well, thanks to stage director Bartlett Sher, borrowed from Broadway. The action is rapid, clean, and comprehensible. The ever-impressive Lyric chorus, under the direction of Michael Black, enacts a variety of roles with impeccable musicianship and diction, great theatrical skill, and admirably deft staging. Conductor Emmanuel Villaume, a master of French operatic style, leads the orchestra in a nuanced performance. Susanna Phillips, although obviously a strong mature woman, as she must be to sing Juliette's music, which she powerfully does, has been well directed to act girlish, and both Mercutio (Joshua Hopkins) and Tybalt (Jason Slayden), in addition to singing well, act impressively, showing the payoff of good theatrical coaching. Bass-baritone Christian Van Horn, as Friar Laurence, gives perhaps the most fully integrated performance of all, both vocally and theatrically. And the Maltese tenor Joseph Calleja, while making no attempt at all to impersonate a dashing young man, sings Roméo's music with appealing heft and clarity. (His voice overpowers Phillips's at times, creating some musical problems.) The updating from Renaissance Verona to the eighteenth century works well, giving Catherine Zuber the opportunity to create some stunning costumes.

Still, it is ultimately a mediocre work. Juliette's opening aria, the famous Waltz Song, "Je veux vivre," could be taken from virtually any French opera, and it does little to characterize the vulnerable extremely young girl, particularly when, as must be the case, it is sung by a muscular and robust woman in mid-life. And although the opening Chorus, resetting the "Two houses" prologue, as the citizens of the Chorus face the audience solemnly, adds a new dimension of gravity to that part of Shakespeare's work, and although Roméo's aria already mentioned at least provides an element of haunting pathos and lyricism that sits well with the character, there is far too little that shows us anything new or insightful, far too much that seems cluttered and overblown. It is ultimately, therefore, a boring work. Not necessarily a boring performance: but an admirable performance of a boring work.

Don't take all this on trust from me. I happen to dislike much French opera, and I grant that this is the best production of this opera you are likely to see in a long time. So, Shakespeareans, go, but don't expect more than Gounod can deliver. As for me, I wait with eager expectation for my next City Desk 400 opera assignment, Verdi's *Falstaff* at the CSO in April: a magnificent work, performed under the baton of the greatest living Verdi conductor, Riccardo Muti.

Night's "Close Curtain" in the Public Square: Intimacy and Spectacle in *Roméo et Juliette*
Katie Blankenau

Shakespeare's Juliet, that most verbally agile of thirteen-year-old lovers, opens 3.2 with a gorgeous epithalamion anticipating Romeo's arrival. Unaware that her husband has just been banished for killing her cousin, she calls for darkness to hide their "amorous rites": "Spread thy close curtain, love-performing night, / That runaways' eyes may wink, and Romeo / Leap to these arms untalked of and unseen." Juliet dreams that night's curtain will cast a shadow dark enough to free the newlyweds from society's relentless gaze. This desire for private space in the midst of an all-pervasive public sphere is beautifully foregrounded in the Lyric's production of Charles Gounod's *Roméo et Juliette*. Of course a nineteenth-century opera—especially one driven by the spectacles of its ball scenes and duels—is hardly suited for representing private space. Art, and this art form in particular, would rather embrace the happy dagger than go "untalked of and unseen." Director Bartlett Sher plays with this opposition, staging a tragic contest between intimacy and social surveillance that can only end in the privacy of the tomb.

Gounod's opera begins with the chorus's prologue, a variation on the sonnet that opens Shakespeare's play and that sets out the friction between Capulets and Montagues. Sher brings the chorus on while the house lights are still up. They slowly take seats on straight-backed chairs facing the audience, nearly at the level of the main-stage spectators. Their observation is unsettling. The towering wigs and finery of Catherine Zuber's eighteenth-century costumes add to the sense of being stared down by the social elite (a not entirely uncommon feeling when attending the opera). The result is a clever and pointed setup of *Roméo et Juliette*'s claustrophobic community.

The production's set (designer Michael Yeargan) depicts an Italian piazza outside the Capulets' stone mansion, complete with requisite balcony. Filled to capacity for the party scene, the piazza highlights the crowded publicity of its fictional world. Nothing should go "untalked of or unseen" here, where the watchers and the watched trade places constantly (a fact nicely emphasized by the commedia dell'arte characters who first entertain and then observe the partygoers). Throughout the first half, the set feels primarily representational—

realistic stage dressing rather than meaningful space. But Sher and Yeargan undo that assumption after the intermission.

The second half of Act 3 begins exuberantly with Marianne Crebassa in the "breeches" role of Stephano. Her gleeful performance of the charming "Que fais-tu, blanche tourterelle" reenergizes the production just in time for the renewed sense of urgency brought on by Mercutio's duel. His and Tybalt's deaths in the piazza—staged as a public marketplace—figuratively and literally clear the stage for the lovers' melancholy wedding night. The clutter of the market, with its dead bodies and spoiled wares, is replaced by a white sheet thrown over the raised platform center stage. This undulating white square glows in the darkened piazza, surrounded by the now-gloomy grey mansion. It's a theatrically effective and poignant staging decision. What was the dance floor in Act 1 becomes Juliet's chamber and her marriage bed. The sheeted platform is still part of the public arena, open on all sides, even as it demarcates a softer, romantic space apart. The lovers' proximity and the tactile fabric increase the intimacy of their duet ("Nuit d'hyménée"), but the space is still too big for them. The white sheet is a poor replacement for night's "curtain"; visually arresting, it nevertheless leaves the lovers exposed and vulnerable.

Of course, exposure and visibility are inherent components of Gounod's lush, highly populated opera. Sher's staging takes every advantage of this opportunity while simultaneously framing the relentless exposure of the lovers as central to their tragedy. There is no corner in which they can hide from the chorus or our own spectatorship. For me, the most moving moment of the production was when Juliet (Susanna Phillips) wraps herself in a fold of the sheet after Romeo (Joseph Calleja) departs, curling up in the middle of her large, lonely "bed." Later, despairing in the face of her father's pressure to marry Count Paris, she pulls more and more of the sheet around her until it trails behind her like a wedding dress and covers her like a shroud. Here, her earlier declaration that "my grave is like to be my wedding bed" is materialized in a stage metaphor; even the balconied mansion, with its gray arches and columns dimly lit, takes on a sepulchral atmosphere.

Ultimately the grave proves to be the only private place available to the lovers. While in the play Juliet revives only to find Romeo already dead, Gounod and his librettists revise the ending to allow the lovers a final duet. With the platform that was their marriage bed transformed to a crypt, and surrounded by sheeted tombs, the pair sings their finale ("Viens! fuyons au bout du monde!") before succumbing to poison and dagger. Perhaps most surprisingly to an audience familiar with Shakespeare's play, no reconciliation between the families occurs; the opera ends with the lovers' final musical apology to God for their suicide. (Susan Halpern's program notes helpfully put into context the religiosity of the finale.) Although the production's use of the chorus is one of its strongest elements, the chorus isn't missed at the conclusion. Its absence is the relief the lovers have been looking for.

FILTER THEATRE, IN ASSOCIATION WITH THE ROYAL SHAKESPEARE COMPANY
TWELFTH NIGHT

by William Shakespeare
directed by Sean Holmes
music + sound by Tom Haines + Ross Hughes
presented by Chicago Shakespeare Theater

Robert Day

"What Is Love": Sir Toby's Joyful Punk Rock *Twelfth Night*
Aaron Krall

Shakespeare may not have been a punk rocker, but *Twelfth Night* is probably his most punk-rock play. It certainly is in Filter Theatre's version at the Upstairs studio theater at Chicago Shakespeare Theater. The play, a remount of a 2006 production created for the Royal Shakespeare Company's Complete Works Festival and directed by Sean Holmes, revels in the play's chaotic, youthful, and anti-authoritarian plot about a group of ne'er-do-wells partying and plotting the demise of their pretentious overseer. In this play, the carnivalesque context of the Elizabethan Twelfth Night is recast as a rock show, complete with live music, tallboys of lager, and swaggering performances.

The production's concept is visible as the audience enters the performance space, designed to look more like the Empty Bottle, one of

Chicago's venerable PBR-soaked rock venues, than a space for traditional theater. The stage is set with tables loaded with music gear—keyboards, analog synthesizers, MacBooks, and a mixing board—as well as a full drum kit, bass guitar, microphone stands, and assorted props, beer cans, and debris.

The show begins as the performers tune instruments, check microphone levels, and chat with the audience, and the play's opening lines are pitched as brainstorming during band practice. Harry Jardine as Orsino rehearses the first phrase several times, "If music be the food of…," and the audience completes it yelling "love!" This initiates a raucous jam session, with Orsino conducting the other performers as band members. Finally, from the balcony in the audience, he finishes the opening lines: "If music be the food of love, play on, / Give me excess of it." At this point, the relationship between actors and audience is set, Filter takes Orsino's exhortation as a mission statement, and they offer a celebration of excess during their brisk ninety-minute set.

Although this might sound like a jarringly revisionist version of the play, celebrations of Twelfth Night, or the Feast of the Epiphany, in Elizabethan England were notoriously rowdy affairs. By the sixteenth century, the feast day, marking the end of the Christmas season, had evolved into a Feast of Fools, a blasphemous carnival holiday. Anne Barton, in her introduction to the play in *The Riverside Shakespeare*, explains that it was "a period of holiday abandon in which the normal rules and order of life were suspended or else deliberately inverted, in which serious issues and events mingled perplexingly with revelry and apparent madness." The modern rock concert, complete with overwhelmingly loud music, flowing booze, provocative fashion, and occasionally dancing and assorted debauchery, is a fitting contemporary equivalent, a break from the rules of everyday life.

Filter's production emphasizes the punk rock ethos of the play by cutting the script to feature the revelry and hijinks of Sir Toby's gang and Feste's songs. The centerpiece of the production is a rendition of "What is love" as a folk-punk anthem that would make the Mekons proud. It begins with Sir Toby, played by Dan Poole as the center of the party and the only character in ragged Elizabethan ruff, doublet, and hose, waking up in the middle of the night, hung over, and doing physical comedy with a bag of chips, while muttering lines from the song. The scene—and the song—escalates as the audience joins in a game of catch with foam balls and a Velcro hat on Sir Andrew's head. Meanwhile, the crowd is invited to clap and sing along, a dozen audience members are invited on stage to dance, and a pizza guy shows up to pass around boxes of hot slices.

The audience is explicitly complicit in this disorder, and when Fergus O'Donnell's Malvolio shuts it down, he scolds us too. Played as a killjoy heavy metal gear head, he explodes at the late-night musicians, but later—prompted by Maria's deceit—he puts on a show of his own. He struts around the stage and the audience in yellow hot pants, knee socks, and nothing else, dancing and playing air guitar. In this production, our alignment with the revelers, and Malvolio's hypocritical willingness to obnoxiously celebrate himself, makes his eventual downfall more humorous than horrifying.

Through an impressive trick of editing and double casting, the production keeps the small ensemble of performers involved in the party. Jardine plays Sir Andrew as well as Orsino, Sandy Foster plays both Feste and Maria, and Amy Marchant plays Viola and her twin Sebastian—the other minor characters are cut or absorbed. With only minor costume changes—the addition of a clown nose for Feste for instance—the characters move in and out of scenes and songs seamlessly, increasing the velocity of the performance and blurring the lines between the nobles and the servants. Through it all, Foster's Feste punctuates the chaos with her menacing snarl and jittery Ian Curtis-like kicks and punches.

This unruly spirit, and the audience's participation in it, also infects the love stories. When Marchant's shipwrecked Viola arrives in the Illyria rock club, she is wet and staggering through the audience. After marveling at her surroundings, she asks the audience for a disguise, a man's jacket and hat. She tries on a couple of offerings before settling on a leather jacket and a knit hat from the balcony. Placing this costuming choice in the hands of the audience reinforces the collaborative nature of the production and positions the audience as a confidant. Later Viola, in her "Cesario" disguise, is wooed by Olivia with an erotic bass solo, reveling in an excess of love and music much like Orsino at the beginning of the play.

By the time the entire cast performs the closing number, "When that I was and a little tiny boy (With hey, ho, the wind and the rain)," the servants have partied, Malvolio is chastened, true identities are revealed, and pairs of lovers are united. Time has untangled the knots that Viola could not. But order has not been restored—not entirely. The band packs up its gear, and the club turns on the house lights, but there is the sense that things have been transformed. In *Lipstick Traces*, Greil Marcus identifies the punk spirit of the twentieth century in Johnny Rotten growling about anarchy and tearing down walls of British respectability. Filter Theatre is overturning conventions too, but it is also building spaces for exuberance, joy, and love—an excess of it.

Punk Rock *Twelfth Night*...with Pizza
Regina Buccola

London-based Filter Theatre brought Chicago Shakespeare Theater's audience inside the fourth wall for their rollicking adaptation of *Twelfth Night*. Produced in association with the Royal Shakespeare Company, Filter's *Twelfth Night* used clever doubling of roles and direct involvement of the audience to render the isthmus of Navy Pier an Illyrian community that shared in equal measure in the heartbreak of Viola and Olivia, the humiliation of Malvolio, and the romantic surprises of Sebastian and Orsino. A cast of six plus two musicians and the stage manager barreled through the entire play (minus Antonio) in a lightning-fast 110 minutes.

The audience assembled in Chicago Shakespeare Theater's upstairs black box studio with the house lights fully up and musicians Fred Thomas and Alan Pagan in place along with stage manager Christie DuBois. The small stage, a long step up from the floor, looked like the stage in a bar set for a musical act, with mics in stands, black folding chairs, and three tables angled around the rear perimeter of the stage laden with synthesizers, sound boards, and a laptop. Harry Jardine as Orsino took the stage to conduct the musicians for the first few minutes of the performance in raucous music that made liberal use of effects. Establishing the audience as part of the cast and the importance of music for the whole enterprise, he romped up the center aisle to consult with audience members about the quality of the performance he had elicited before returning to the stage to utter the play's famous opening verse line: "If music be the food of ..."

Pretending not to remember his line (as Harry Jardine) or not to know how to complete the sentence (as Orsino), he kept playing this game until the audience accepted their role, and assisted in filling in the blank with "love." The reward for the audience's successful performance was the completion of the speech, affectuoso. Music constituted the main structuring element in the performance—with raucous music the indicator of emotions run riot—and one of the most important links between the cast and the audience, who were incorporated into the production from its earliest moments. In wonderful comedic business, Ronke Adekoluejo's Olivia provocatively bowed an amped bass situated suggestively at crotch level in a desperate play for Cesario's affections; when this move failed to achieve the desired effect in an upright position, Adekoluejo flung herself on the floor, continuing the performance spread-eagled, a screech of feedback signifying the happy ending for her one-woman band.

All members of the cast but one wore *au courant* street clothes; in fact, Amy Marchant, who doubled the twin roles of Viola and Sebastian, affected her cross-dressed transformation into Cesario by borrowing a coat and a hat from men in the audience. The sartorial outlier was Dan Poole, as Sir Toby Belch. A Shakespearean revenant in crushed velvet doublet, puff pants, ruff, and stockings, Toby's concession to the production's modern time signature was to reel across the stage in his period costume quaffing from Budweiser tallboys, toting brown paper bags of McDonald's hamburgers and fries. A hack-of-all-plays, he delivered bombastic snippets of Shakespeareana such as the opening Chorus of *Henry V* ("Oh, for a muse of fire"); Macbeth's hallucinogenic murder speech ("Is this a dagger that I see before me?"); and Hamlet's mournful coda to his pun-laden interlude with the Gravedigger ("Alas, poor Yorick"). He enthusiastically took a seat in the audience periodically to enjoy the onstage action, generously offering his fries to those seated around him.

Throughout the production, none of the performers ever left the performance space, staying to watch the ensuing action either in one of the chairs on the stage, or from the audience. In addition to the doubling of a few of the parts and the elimination of Antonio and Fabian, the onstage technology assisted in the streamlining of the play. The report from Orsino's first messenger to the Lady Olivia, the predecessor of Cesario, came in as a text message read aloud (complete with the dutiful report of crying emoji to accompany her announcement that she would remain in mourning for her deceased brother, and would not, therefore, be entertaining embassies of love). With the exception of appended emoji, the text delivered (and musically performed) throughout the performance was Shakespeare's, though at times it arrived via quirky delivery mechanisms: the responses to Viola's Act 1, scene 2 queries about her whereabouts, and what she should do, now in Illyria, came over a transistor radio, Shakespeare's lines alternating with snippets of the BBC shipping news.

The doubling of roles and the direct involvement of the audience were pointed, and poignant. Demonstrating considerable range, Jardine played both an imperious Orsino and a ridiculous Sir Andrew Aguecheek, an inspired bit of doubling that underscored the sharp contrast between Olivia's two suitors prior to her heels-over-head plunge into love at first sight with Cesario. A clown in the European sense of the word, Sandy Foster doubled the roles of Feste and Maria, simply popping a red clown nose off and on to affect her transformation, and making immediate sense of Maria's ultimate marriage to Sir Toby (a marital union that went unheralded in the production, except via their obvious attraction to one another during a protracted performance of the lyric, "What Is Love?").

Fergus O'Donnell's Malvolio visually paired with Ronke Adekoluejo's Olivia, both of them clad all in black. Filter wittily anticipated Malvolio's gulling at the hands of Maria, Sir Toby and Sir Andrew by having him overhear Olivia's blazon of Cesario/Viola following his/her first visit to her on behalf of Orsino, clearly mistaking its effusions as commentary on him. Already confident of Olivia's attraction to him, Malvolio was insufferable in the late-night carousing connected with a completely debauched performance of "What Is Love," which included getting audience members to toss squishy balls onto a Velcro-stripped fool's cap sported by Jardine's Andrew. He eventually recruited an audience member to similarly attempt to catch balls with his head, and then he and Maria gathered audience members to come on stage to dance along to "What Is Love." Shortly after a pizza delivery to the packed stage, an outraged Malvolio stormed in to throw the party off switch. He upended pizza boxes, slapping slices out of the hands of audience members with such vehemence that some of them flew to the black cinder block walls, their cheese adhering them there.

Malvolio's self-importance and vindictive suppression of fun made it easier to stomach the cruel prank played upon him by Maria, Toby and Andrew. When he found the letter the wily Maria penned, mimicking Lady Olivia's handwriting, and designed to delude him into the belief that his lady longs to make him her lord, Malvolio had to be bludgeoned over the head with the significance of the letters "M, O, A, I" in the riddling letter, the full cast whispering them around the stage perimeter. The longer he struggled, the louder their chant and its musical accompaniment became, the whole audience eventually joining in, shouting the chant until comprehension dawned, and Malvolio stripped down to yellow tube socks and gold lame hot pants, lasciviously running the letter's paper promises over his torso, thrusting his crotch into its folds.

In addition to joining in moments of subplot frivolity, the audience was also conscripted to make one in the main plot. Viola entered for the first time through the center aisle in a cheetah-print poncho, her hair wet. She faced the audience to ask "What country, friend, is this? ... And what should I do, in Illyria?" as she listened to responses from Shakespeare's text on her transistor radio. Olivia entered to Viola/Cesario from the top row of the tiered audience seating to "draw the curtain" and show Cesario "the picture" of her face after Viola repeatedly asked the audience if she was truly the lady of the house. In the play's final scene of recognition and reunion, Amy Marchant faced the audience and delivered all of both Viola's and Sebastian's lines directly to us, rendering us participant-observers of their reunion, both audience and addressee, collectively twinned to her.

How can this black box hold the isle of Illyria? Is this my twin that I see before me, her face toward my face? Alas, poor Malvolio—I knew him, Olivia; a fellow of infinite fuss, of most excellent priggery. When the revels are ended, you will find that you have made one in the comedy in a production in which music truly is the food of love.

THE GIFT THEATRE COMPANY,
IN ASSOCIATION WITH
STEPPENWOLF THEATRE COMPANY
+ THE REHABILITATION INSTITUTE OF CHICAGO
RICHARD III

by William Shakespeare
directed by Jessica Thebus
dramaturgy by Michael Peterson, PhD

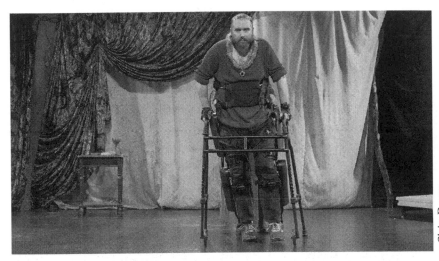

Claire Demos

Confessions of Richard Plantagenet:
The Gift Theatre's *Richard III*
Hilary J. Gross

I had the immense good fortune of seeing The Gift Theatre's *Richard III* on the night of their second preview, and was blown away. The production is thoughtful, beautifully executed, and engaging, particularly in their use of extra-textual theatrical cues to support their reading of Shakespeare's most famous historical "villain." These especially salient technical and theatrical decisions serve to highlight Richard as an outsider in his society, and grant the audience special access to his experience. While Michael Patrick Thornton shares the endearingly emphatic girl-with-the-pearl-earrings with the rest of the cast, he is distinguished visually before we even consider his assistive support (Thornton performs most of the show from his wheelchair). The cast's costuming is united in gray scale, everyone wearing shades of the same black, gray and white, with a distinctive ruff-collar. Richard, of all the characters, lacks the collar, both highlighting his difference and allowing the audience visual access to Richard III's iconic humped shoulder. Richard though is the only character in color, showing red against the shades of gray, giving emphasis to both the interpretive and physical work of the actor's hands in fingerless bright red, and distinctly modern, wheelchair gloves. Richard's dress is not "period," cueing the audience's connection into the world of the play through Richard in contrast to the legibly theatrical dress of the other characters.

That is perhaps what I found most surprising and refreshing about this production. Richard III, often portrayed as iconically theatrical, much like a Falstaff, a Henry V or a Rosalind, here plays down that overly performative connotation. At first I chalked it up to acting style, but as the play progressed I began to realize that, dependably throughout, Richard is not talking like anyone else on stage. The other actors speak with a histrionic, dramatic, recognizably "Shakespearean" declamation, but Richard, even in his most famous soliloquy, "Now is the winter of discontent," breaks with the already established style (since the monologue does not open the show, but is delivered in pieces over the course of Act 1, scene 1). Richard speaks in a realistic, colloquial and thrillingly sardonic mode throughout the play, especially pronounced in his direct addresses to the audience, of which he has many. The comparison between these two modes of performance creates the illusion that Richard is real where everyone else is only performing. When he delights in his ability to manipulate other characters' assumptions about his (dis)ability, so do we, when he flips a situation on its head, taking advantage of the emotional effect of his walker and wheelchair, we cheer. Thornton's style makes us forget he's speaking in iambic pentameter, managing to remain faithful to the beautiful language Shakespeare wrote for Richard, while transforming the cadence and sentence structure to feel completely natural and modern. Richard's language, along with his costuming, casts him as a liminal character, bridging the world of the audience and the historic setting of the Wars of the Roses in late medieval England.

Richard takes full advantage of that liminal status as a *platea* character to manipulate the dramatic action of the play itself. Making literal the stage habit of freezing the play for asides, Richard calls "Stop" to pause diegetic action and "Now" to restart it, moving between the frozen actors to comment on the events of the play and pull us into the role of co-conspirators, in on the machinations of his performance. These moments are visually arresting, granting Richard the only motion on stage, maneuvering around his fellow actor's bodies, now just obstacles, with a sarcastic half-smile. As a conceit, it grants Richard an incredible boost in power. Not only does he have the power to manipulate other characters within the plot, but he has the authority to start and stop the narrative itself on a whim, at times clearly reveling in it, stopping the action just because.

Each of these production choices supports the critical work of this Richard's physical reality. The assistive walking devices that allow Richard to move on stage function as an immensely effective communicative and emphatic mode. Thornton suffered a spinal stroke in 2003, working through The Rehabilitation Institute of Chicago (a partner in this production) to regain the mobility he has today. The Gift Theatre shows Richard in a wheelchair, wheeling himself, or being pushed, depending on the moment, with a walker, with arm crutches, and finally suited in a robotic exoskeleton to mark his coronation as King Richard III. The moment in Act 1 scene 2, when Richard encounters Lady Anne, sticks in my mind as one of the most powerful of the production. When he rises from his chair without help to stand with the walker and approach Anne, punctuating his assertion that "Here" is he "that loves thee better than [Edward] could" (1.2. 148,141), I began to understand the theatrical potential of the supports. As he offers Anne his death, and subsequently persuades her to forgive him, she becomes entangled between Richard and his walker, trapped by him physically just as she will be in their marriage. Though the extent of Richard's (dis)ability in the text is not made explicit beyond his own descriptions of being "curtailed of fair proportion...deformed, unfinished...scarce half made up" (1.1.18-21), we find the critical power behind a modern adaptation of (dis)ability and how an understanding of existing in an ableist world, a world that was not built for disability, particularly here for the realities and limits of assistive walking technology, colors a strikingly presentist characterization of Richard III. My only major criticism is in the framing of the project. The program announces the production's intent to "re-define... what (dis)ability and Shakespeare's great villain look like by *utilizing* both a disabled actor in the title role as well as assistive devices past and present as articulations of Richard's protean identity" (Playbill, 3) [emphasis mine]. While I agree that casting an actor who understands living with a disability physically is essential to The Gift Theatre's reading of *Richard III*, bringing out innovative dynamics from the shadows of the text to the forefront and giving Richard a life beyond his identity as a villain, grammatically posing Thornton himself, a talented actor, as a physical prop to the project feels negligent to me. As an audience member, the overwhelming feeling is not that the production utilizes Thornton in his identity as a disabled actor, but that Thornton, along with director Jessica Thebus, utilizes a 400+-year-old play to make a statement about ableism in our world, exposing the harmful assumptions society makes about (dis)ability on a daily basis while infusing a dynamism into Shakespeare's text, and a sardonic vitality into his lead character, to cast Richard's very villainy as a rebellion against the prejudice of his world, as well as ours.

"An island/ Entire of itself":
Shakespeare's Portrait of the Tyrant
Joseph Alulis

"I am myself alone." These haunting words of the title character convey Gift Theatre's take on *Richard III*. Director Jessica Thebus presents the action as unfolding within the theater of Richard's mind; when he dies, the stage goes dark. In this imaginative vision of the play, by slaying Richard, Richmond destroys the stage upon which his triumph would be celebrated. The rest is silence.

The famous opening lines of the play, "Now is the winter of our discontent/ Made glorious summer by this son of York," are not the first we hear. Rather we see Richard (a masterful Michael Patrick Thornton) brooding by his tent on the eve of battle at Bosworth Field. His first speech, a command, "Give me some ink and paper" (5.3.49), pairs with his last, an entreaty, "A horse! A horse! my kingdom for a horse" (5.4.13), to bracket the action of Gift's production. Within this frame, his last day on earth, Richard communes with the deeds that constitute his life, first the memory of their doing and then the confrontation with their consequences, the dreadful accusations of the ghosts of his victims and the fatal blow of their avenger.

Richard III is the last of a set of four plays. The first three, the three parts of *Henry VI*, tell the story of the loss of England's empire in France, the division of the House of Lancaster, and the Wars of the Roses. The triumph of the House of York bridges *Henry VI, Part Three* and *Richard III*, the former depicting its victory on the battlefield at Tewkesbury and the latter its installation in power with the coronation of Edward IV. (Actually, this is his second coronation but that's another story which Chicago Shakespeare Theater will tell in the fall with Barbara Gaines's distillation of *Henry VI, Parts Two and Three* and *Richard III* as a single theatrical event, *Civil Strife.*) *Richard III* then goes on to repeat the cycle, depicting the division and fall of the House of York. For the first audiences of these plays, the fact that the cycle had not been repeated with the House of Tudor was a public good that outweighed any complaints they might have had against this dynasty.

The decision to include material from *Henry VI, Part Three* in this production of *Richard III* is audience friendly. It makes intelligible the madness and hatred of Margaret (an imperious Shanesia Davis) and explains the appearance of two of the ghosts who accuse Richard, Henry

VI (Martel Manning) and his son, Prince Edward (Jay Worthington). The line "I am myself alone" is also from *Henry VI, Part Three* (5.7.84) as are the lines in which Richard declares his plan to reach the throne: "Henry and his son are gone; thou, Clarence, art next; / And by one and one I will dispatch the rest" (5.7.90-91).

No less than murder, marriage has a part in Richard's schemes and Thebus gives full attention to Richard's two wooing scenes, first with Anne (Olivia Cygan) and then with Elizabeth (Jenny Avery), for the hand of her daughter Elizabeth (who we see walk silently across the stage). Ms. Cygan's Anne shows both the fire and softness of youth, first angry than yielding. The role of a woman of her rank was to be given in marriage for political alliance and to bear children to advance the family fortunes, especially sons to carry on her husband's name, possibly to claim the throne. Anne's father had given her to a Lancastrian pretender, why should she not give herself to a Yorkist one? Richard gloats at his victory, "Was ever woman in this humor wooed? / Was ever woman in his humor won?" (1.2.227-28). But there is calculation on both sides and to Anne the credit of goodwill in playing the role of peacemaker to her father, Warwick's king-maker hence war-maker.

In the case of Elizabeth, the gloating—"Relenting fool and shallow, changing woman!" 4.4.431)—is out of place; Elizabeth has clearly won the engagement. Like the accomplished political person the historical Elizabeth Woodville was, Ms. Avery effectively counters each of Richard's arguments. She does, of course, have the stronger case ('You want to marry your niece?'); she deserves credit for her refusal to be intimidated by Richard and the way she challenges him at every turn. I wish Ms. Avery had shown some of the courage and control of this encounter in her portrayal of Elizabeth's growing alarm and grief as Richard destroys her family.

Before he can assail Elizabeth, Richard must face his mother, the Duchess (Caroline Dodge Latta), the last of the four strong woman of this play, who speaks her final word to her son: "take with thee my most grievous curse/ Which in the day of battle tire thee more/ Than all the complete armor that thou wearest" (4.4.188-90). Ms. Latta, who also plays the Bishop of Ely, one of Sir Thomas More's eyewitness sources for his *History of King Richard III*, delivers these lines with unexpected energy.

As the action is presented as the usurping tyrant's recollection, all of it occurs before the steady gaze of Mr. Thornton's usually wheelchair-bound Richard. Though Richard's deformity is noted, his mental acuity as the wily Machiavel is foremost in our mind and, as in Hamlet's dumb show, we expect to see it bodied forth in physical stealth, nimble villainy. Its absence in Mr. Thornton's case, however, does not detract from his Richard but adds menace; his massive form makes palpable the motive Shakespeare gives Richard: he is "determined to prove a villain" because "cheated of feature by dissembling Nature" (1.1.30, 19). In speech, gesture, and movement Mr. Thornton enables us to see into Richard's soul, desirous of command, sternly controlling, and full of malice. He makes us see Richard's pangs of conscience after the visit of the ghosts. When, speaking for both prosecution—and defense—"I am a villain. Yet I lie: I am not. / Fool, of thyself speak well. Fool, do not flatter" (5.3.192-93)—Mr. Thornton's Richard slaps himself, we feel his torment as if we had ourselves been struck. His portrayal of Richard's internal division was the tragic counterpart of Peter Seller's comic Dr. Strangelove. At the end, the stark image of Mr. Thornton out of his wheelchair and stripped of any other support calling for a horse gives a power to Richard's last line that it could seldom have had in the long history of the play's performance.

Thomas J. Cox as Clarence showed him to be the clever reasoner that Richard warned the murders they would find and he made us feel Clarence's terror in recounting his nightmare. (But I regret that this production cut the line, "Clarence is come: false, fleeting, perjured Clarence" (1.4.55), which I had just heard Dan Waller deliver at Court Theatre as the sometime-Shakespearean actor James Tyrone, Jr. in *Long Day's Journey into night*.) Keith Neagle captured both the aristocrat and the player in his portrayal of Buckingham as Richard's enthusiastic accomplice till even he must draw a line. Adrian Danzig gives us the sense of life at court playing both patron and client, King Edward lamenting that none stayed him from signing Clarence's death warrant and Tyrell coolly informing Richard of the murder of his nephews. Their murder as well as that of Anne is shown on stage bathed in eerie blue light in JR Lederle's lighting design, which at every point, not least the dramatic ending, strengthens the vision of this production. This is an excellent production of one of Shakespeare's most popular plays; a fitting tribute to Shakespeare's artistry in this anniversary year.

CHICAGO SHAKESPEARE THEATER
SHORT SHAKESPEARE! TWELFTH NIGHT

by William Shakespeare
adapted + directed by Kirsten Kelly

Chuck Osgood

Welcome to Illyria, All
Timothy J. Duggan

How do we experience love, and how do we handle its intensity? The wish to love and be loved flavors human experience, but as Shakespeare reminds us in *Twelfth Night*, we should be careful what we wish for. Last Saturday, I attended a performance of *Short Shakespeare! Twelfth Night* in Chicago Shakespeare's Courtyard Theater on Navy Pier. I was delighted by the 75-minute production and the conscientious educational scaffolding surrounding it. Even with some thirty percent of the text cut for performance, the cast conveyed the story, spirit, physicality and musicality that make the play a perennial favorite among Shakespeare fans.

Twelfth Night is a flexible text that may be played anywhere between farce and tragicomedy, depending upon which lines and plot points the director chooses to emphasize. Kirsten Kelly's direction opens the text to its target audience: elementary, middle, and high school students. In the service of accessibility and, to some extent, propriety, this production de-emphasizes the implications of gender switching and drunkenness, instead providing an examination of love's giddiness. Each of the main characters experiences the disequilibrium of sudden and consuming love, and each reminds us that losing ourselves in love may make us vulnerable to embarrassment, or even humiliation.

The opening scene features Neal Moeller's likeable Duke Orsino, calling for more music to feed his unrequited love for the Countess Olivia. His request fuels a somewhat discordant ditty banged out on a broken-down piano, eliciting the first laughs that on Saturday would gain and sustain momentum throughout the show. Just as the scene ends, Viola (Rebecca Hurd), who has washed up on shore following a shipwreck that separated her from her twin brother, Sebastian, emerges on top of the piano inquiring of the Sea Captain (Lynn Robert Berg) "What country is this?"

This melding of scenes is made possible by Scott Davis's clever stage design, mixing elements of an aristocratic but disordered residence with mast-like pillars, leaning askew, wrapped in torn curtains/sails the color of the sea. A minimum of furniture provides domesticity for scenes set in both Orsino's court and Olivia's estate, tied together with a large patterned rug. (As this production will travel to schools and parks following its run on Navy Pier, the design must be portable.) Rachel Healy's costumes accentuate an early twentieth Century seaside boardwalk vibe. Viola's decision to disguise herself as a boy, "Cesario," in order to serve in Orsino's court, launches the plot, and when we next see her, she looks like a paper carrier with vest, cap, tie and bicycle.

Viola very quickly falls in love with Orsino, complicating her role as his male emissary in the wooing of Olivia, elegantly played by Krystel Lucas. Of course, Olivia just as quickly falls for Viola/Cesario, believing her to be a young man. Hurd's exuberant Viola, believable in her disguise, confides directly to the audience, "O time, thou must untangle this, not I. / It is too hard a knot for me t'untie." Like a protagonist from an engaging young adult novel, she carries us with her into increasingly absurd situations.

La Shawn Banks, as Olivia's imperious steward, Malvolio, develops an opposing, yet equally compelling relationship with the audience. When Olivia sends him to deliver a ring to Cesario/Viola, he must chase her down on her bicycle, cleverly lit and placed on blocks to give the appearance of fast-paced pedaling, while Banks runs in place at breakneck speed to catch her. In Saturday's performance, the kids and adults in the audience erupted into spontaneous applause as he finally caught her attention. While his "self-love," as Olivia calls it, makes him intolerable to the other members of her household, his almost child-like response to what he mistakenly thinks is Olivia's love note and his hissing impatience with Olivia's gentlewoman, Maria (Lydia Berger Gray), garnered some of the show's biggest laughs.

Cutting the play demands that actors use gesture effectively to convey meaning. Kelly's cuts emphasize plot movement. She features the gulling of Malvolio, engineered by the zany members of Olivia's household: Maria and Sir Toby Belch (Ronald Conner), with Feste (Will Mobley), Fabian (Donovan Diaz), and the doltish Sir Andrew Aguecheek, who is, literally, "as tall as any man in Illyria," thanks to Dominic Conti's stature. Conner's Sir Toby, in the words of the actor himself, is "a guy you love to see show up, and a guy you love to see leave." Mobley, as Feste, ably performs the play's iconic tunes on a miniature guitar and interjects his witticisms as much to the audience as to the other characters. The prankish fight between Cesario and Sir Andrew features boxing gloves rather than swords, emblematic of Kelly's softening of the play's rough edges. Perhaps in the desire to help the audience comprehend the play, a few of the actors occasionally exaggerated their expressions, but not to the point of distraction. The fast-paced movement and dissolution of the fourth wall kept Saturday's young audience members engaged throughout the show.

After Malvolio falls for the bait of Maria's feigned epistle of love from Olivia and shuffles off his usual decorum for smiling, cross-gartering and yellow stockings, Olivia places him into the care of his household enemies. Malvolio's ill treatment—he is bound, blindfolded, and kept in the dark—soon wears thin even with Sir Toby, whose line, "I would we were well rid of this knavery," hangs in the air for a second or two, acknowledging the corrosiveness of bullying. Malvolio is excluded from the happy realignment of relationships occasioned by the appearance of Viola's supposedly drowned brother, Sebastian. In the final scene, however, after swearing to be "revenged on the whole pack" of them and storming away, Malvolio is coaxed back on stage to join the other characters to dance and sing with Feste, "And the rain it raineth every day." This production thus strikes a note of forgiveness that a darker interpretation would omit. Perhaps Kelly is inviting the audience to find our common humanity through our lovesick foibles.

Chicago Shakespeare Theater takes its role as ambassador of Shakespeare's work seriously, and the Short Shakespeare productions feature supports to the performance both before and after the show. For *Twelfth Night*, a folded, 8.5 x 11 quarto program includes a plot summary of the first three acts, several full-color photos from different scenes, and cast responses to the question, "Have you ever been a fool in love?" Just prior to opening curtain on Saturday, Nate Santana, who plays Sebastian, appeared on stage and, in addition to making the typical request to turn off cell phones, provided a short lesson on how to watch and listen to Shakespeare's work, reminding the audience that it is okay to not understand every word, and that paying close attention to gestures, facial expression, tone of voice, and language can help them to follow the story. Immediately following the show, all cast members remained on stage for a Q & A session, deftly and generously hosted by Marilyn Halperin, CST's Director of Education and Communications. Halperin made a point of taking questions from the youngest audience members and distributing the opportunities to respond amongst several cast members. One of the first questions came from a boy of about twelve who asked, "Do you think the other characters were too mean to Malvolio?" Clearly the boy had closely observed gesture, expression, tone and language.

Thinking about how students often experience Shakespeare in school, marching through the text and answering comprehension questions without considering Shakespeare's words as a set of possibilities for actors, I wonder whether theater experiences such as this one would make for far better curriculum than that provided by the current testing regime. On Saturday, the school-aged audience members swarmed the actors for autographs and photos in the lobby following the show, reminding me of John Dewey's assertion that the best kind of educational experience is that which leads the learner to desire another, similar experience.

"Journeys end"? Only Change Is Constant in *Short Shakespeare! Twelfth Night*

Stephanie Kucsera

"Is there no respect of place, persons nor time in you?" (2.3.91-92). If there is one question that Kirsten Kelly's Short Shakespeare adaptation of *Twelfth Night* takes most seriously, it is perhaps this one. *Twelfth Night*, like Shakespeare's other festive comedies, including *As You Like It* and *Much Ado About Nothing*, is a carnival-like pursuit of love and mirth in which the powers of disruption and change, for a time, reign supreme over the conventional forces of order and restraint. In Kelly's production, in particular, the underscoring of changeability—of locale, affections, convictions and identities—seems to be the only constant. Content and form neatly reflect and reflect upon each other in this adaptation that so cunningly makes use of its production elements in order to tell Shakespeare's story in a way that is clear and engaging for student audiences.

Even before the play begins, the ideas that will govern this world are foreshadowed by the production design. The stage is washed in the cool blues and sandy golds of Greg Hofmann's lighting design—a color palette brimming with sea and shore hues—while Scott Davis's cleverly teetering, off-kilter set only adds to the feeling of windswept possibility. The audience is given the distinct feeling that at any moment what appear to be curtains will become sails, pillars will become masts, and what looks like a balcony can then only be a ship's rail. This quickly proves to be the case. Scenes shift fluidly between interior and exterior spaces, and among the residences of Orsino, Olivia, and the seacoast of Illyria. Transitions are aided by furniture that is quickly moved and repurposed and by Ethan Deppe's original music and sound design. Music, the "food of love" in Illyria, is itself a changeable thing here, respecting neither place nor time as hits like Sinatra's "All of Me" and Monroe's "I Wanna Be Loved by You" mingle in a fictional land with an early twentieth-century ambiance lent by costumes designed by Rachel Healy (1.1.1). Scenes are frequently played on top of other scenes as the action in one sphere is suspended in order to shift the audience's focus elsewhere.

Into this world teeming with the power of transformation enters the young heroine, Viola (Rebecca Hurd). After surviving the requisite storm and shipwreck which land her on the Illyrian shore—themselves conventional signs and agents of change—Viola disguises herself as a boy, Cesario, and serves as a page to her new beloved, the Duke Orsino (Neal Moeller). But while Viola embodies the festive potential of a purer, more sincere love given room for expression in the freeing interplay of disguise and mistaken identity, Orsino is the embodiment of the conventional wooer trapped in rigid courtly artifice. The object of Orsino's desires, the Countess Olivia (Krystel Lucas), is herself obsessed with unchanging ritual. She is a vision of chaste, aloof womanhood, withdrawn from the world in mourning for her brother, but her practice of mourning—her own performance of love—is just as life-denying as Orsino's. Both delight in their own unchanging suffering. Oliva's household is fittingly run, then, by the puritanical steward, Malvolio (La Shawn Banks), who enforces a stifling regime of absolute order, sobriety and misguided self-denial.

Yet Olivia also maintains a household fool, Feste (Will Mobley), who is the opposite of Malvolio in every way. Just as Viola (as Cesario) upsets the order of Orsino's and Oliva's lives—Orsino and Olivia, attracted by the paradoxical sincerity of the dissembling Viola, both come to accept the risks of romantic love and of living fully—it is, of course, the fool who challenges the wisdom of the steward's extreme devotion to propriety. Conventional notions of wisdom and folly change places with astounding frequency in this play until the drama is brought to its almost-orderly conclusion. Intemperance is squashed, balance is restored, romantic couples are appropriately paired, brother and sister are reunited. Nearly everyone assumes a place in Shakespeare's transformed Illyria.

But in Kelly's production, the endless changes that began the moment Viola lands in Illyria seem to cease by the close of Act 5. Deprived of its ambiguous ending through the happy inclusion of Malvolio in its ensemble performance of Feste's (usually solo) final song, the resolution of Kelly's *Twelfth Night* could very well be described as too neat and overly reassuring, perhaps even a bit condescending to its student audience. Shakespeare's text, after all, refuses to tell us what happens to Malvolio after his avowal of vengeance on his merry-making tormentors (5.1.378). His potential for future change—for good or ill—remains open. But maybe there is another way to think about Kelly's choice here. By including Malvolio in the play's comic conclusion, perhaps Kelly is not merely refusing to acknowledge that the steward's conversion is still a complex work-in-progress. Perhaps she is including him in the most radical ongoing transformation of all—that of a community's reconciliation through the transformative power of forgiveness.

PROFESSOR MICHAEL SANDEL
WITH ILLINOIS HUMANITIES
+ CHICAGO SHAKESPEARE THEATER
WHAT ARE WE WORTH?

Courtesy of Chicago Shakespeare Theater

Public Humanities Thrive in Michael Sandel's Lecture on "Shakespeare, Money, and Morals"
Andrew S. Keener

"Gold? Yellow, glittering, precious gold?" utters Timon of Athens in the fourth act of Shakespeare's play. "Thus much of this will make / Black white, foul fair, wrong right, / Base noble, old young, coward valiant." Though they don't necessarily shed any light on the playwright's own beliefs, Timon's words demonstrate that Shakespeare clearly had a mind for money. Through a variety of voices in his plays and poems, he contemplated its value, its meanings and its dangers in an era of nascent capitalism. Indeed, in *The Poetics of Primitive Accumulation*, the literary critic Richard Halpern recognizes the pivotal economic moment Shakespeare's England, a moment which witnessed the beginning of a radical transition from political sovereignty toward the surplus value of the market. Following Halpern's lead, researchers have taken great pains over the past two decades to understand the peculiar, distinctly non-modern characteristics of economics in Shakespeare's time and the way

Renaissance-era market values are reflected in his works.

And yet, although the world of emerging capitalism familiar to Shakespeare is in many ways strikingly different from our own, the playwright's works still speak to us. This perhaps was the greatest take-away from "What Are We Worth: Shakespeare, Money, and Morals," a single-night Illinois Humanities event at Chicago Shakespeare Theater featuring dramatic readings from Shakespeare and an engaging conversation led by Harvard Professor of Political Philosophy Michael Sandel. Sandel has been called "a rock-star moralist" in *Newsweek* and "the most famous teacher of philosophy in the world" in *The New Republic*. With a handful of interesting debates and moral dilemmas as examples, he guided the evening's packed house through a series of complex questions about the purpose of money and markets, ethics, and the ways Shakespeare's plays help bring these questions into relief.

Preceding this conversation was a sequence of staged readings by seven Chicago Shakespeare Theater actors: all Shakespeare, all on the subject of money. Dressed not in costume, but in street clothes that brought the playwright's words into a visually modern context, the performers delivered a mix of monologues, exchanges, and an extended scene—the choice of caskets from *The Merchant of Venice*. In this play, the actors reminded us, the distinctions between money, affection and power can be difficult to disentangle. Offering a counterpoint to Portia's extravagant Belmont, however, was a desperate exchange from *Romeo and Juliet*. Here, Romeo buys illegal "mortal drugs" off the Apothecary, only to declare that gold is "worse poison to men's souls" than poison itself for the harms it causes in the world.

Shakespeare's lines, spoken aloud in the theater, set the stage for the conversation to follow. With his engaging, yet colloquial style, Sandel (listed not as "speaker" in the program, but rather "moderator") gave the Chicago Shakespeare Theater the intimate feel of a seminar room. Adding to this effect was Jeremy McCarter, a former student of Sandel's, who elegantly ushered the evening's program from the staged readings to the interactive lecture. McCarter wasn't the only former Sandel disciple in the room, however. "You haven't called on me since 1983!" exclaimed one audience member called upon during the program.

At the program's opening, Sandel proposed we have witnessed a quiet revolution: we have changed from a market economy to a market society, in which almost every aspect of life—familial, medical, educational, legal, civic—is for sale. Withholding direct judgment on these developments, at least at the outset, he guided the audience through a series of situations, asking his auditors to slow down and reflect for themselves. Should there be a free market for human organ donations? Would it be a good idea to offer cash incentives to students for good grades—$50 for an A, and $30 for a B, for instance? With these questions, Sandel urged his listeners to interrogate their own assumptions about the ways money influences our human lives and relationships. (While most in the crowd responded "no" to a free kidney market, cash-incentive schooling resulted in a split.)

It was in the end, after these thought-experiments, that Sandel's argument emerged in full force. Parting ways with economists, he claimed that in the domain of human behaviors and social norms, the practice of buying and selling may change the meaning and value of norms. Referring to the "skybox" effect, in which sports arenas become increasingly luxurious and segment local populations of spectators into a hierarchy, Sandel's conclusion seemed nostalgic, and idealistically so— nostalgic for a democratic past that has often escaped us, but remains worth pursuing. In keeping with Illinois Humanities' excellent public programming, the evening's event offered a challenging and provocative series of questions, truly furnishing for the audience a "theater of learning."

THE TALLIS SCHOLARS

written by + starring Peter Phillips
presented by Chicago Symphony Orchestra

Shakespeare, the Lyricist
David Bevington

Music was extremely important to Shakespeare. Some of his comedies are virtually what one might call musicals, they rely so much on song. The lovely lyric at the end of *Love's Labor's Lost*, comparing the "daisies pied and violets blue" of spring to "icicles that hang by the wall" in winter, was so popular and thematic that it was imported into other Shakespeare comedies in revival in the seventeenth and eighteenth centuries. The song at the end of *Twelfth Night,* "When that I was and a tiny little boy," sung by the fool Feste, hauntingly tells a story of human life as it progresses from being "a little tiny boy" to "man's estate" to marriage and "the rain raineth every day." "A great while the world began, / With hey, ho, the wind and the rain." Earlier in the play Feste has sung the superb "O mistress mine, where are you roaming?" with its thematic echoing of the play as a whole: "What is love? 'Tis not hereafter. / Present mirth hath present laughter. / What's to come is still unsure. / In delay there lies no plenty. / Then come and kiss me, sweet and twenty; / Youth's a stuff will not endure."

Shakespeare is, among his other amazing accomplishments, a superb lyricist. His songs were often sung by professional clowns and by the boy actors who played women in his plays, many of whom had been trained as choirboys. The level of performance appears to have been high, both in the singing and in the instrumental accompaniment. Shakespeare often mentions popular melodies such as "Walsingham" and "Rowland." Part singing was second nature to professional actors, as when Sir Toby, Sir Andrew and Feste sing a "catch" in their drinking scene called "Thou knave" in *Twelfth Night.* Music is the occasion of much mirth, as when Sir Toby replies to Malvolio's complaint that the revelers "squeak out" their "catches without mitigation or remorse of voice," showing "no respect of place, persons, nor time" by insisting that "We did keep time, sir, in our catches. Sneck up!" (2.3). Thomas Morley wrote the music for *As You Like It*'s superb "It was a lover and his lass," which is to say that Shakespeare wrote the lyrics for Thomas Morley. Some songs like this one may have existed before the play in which it appears. Some songs are set to popular tunes.

What was Shakespeare's relationship to the sacred music that forms such a substantial part of the Tallis Scholars' fine program on April 5? Such music came with its own Latin texts and does not gain much prominence in Shakespeare's plays, other than, for example, the singing of "Non nobis domine" at the conclusion of the great Battle of Agincourt in *Henry V*. The phrase "Non nobis domine," "Not to us, Lord, not to us but to thy name give the glory," from Psalm 113 in the Vulgate text or 115 in the King James version, had been the motto of the Knights Templars and was widely popular. Holinshed's Chronicles tell us that King Henry did in fact order his prelates and chaplains to sing "Non nobis" after the victory at Agincourt, while the soldiers knelt at each verse. William Byrd composed a popular canon on this text that one hears sung in Kenneth Branagh's 1989 film.

Even if the high art of contrapuntal church music was not part of Shakespeare's dramatic vocabulary, we can see much of his theatrical interest in music as a sort of counterpoint to the music of William Byrd, John Taverner, Alfonso Ferrabosco, Thomas Tallis and Richard Davy. Such music was at the center of the conflict in the sixteenth century between Catholicism and the new Protestant faith to which England was uncertainly committed under Queen Elizabeth I. Elizabeth's predecessor, her older half-sister Mary Tudor, had been raised a devout Catholic by her Spanish mother Katharine of Aragon, and had done her best to return England to the Catholic fold during her reign from 1553 to 1558. She had married Philip II of Spain in 1554, who thus became in his own eyes at least the King of England co-reigning with Mary, even though he could not read English. Elizabeth's succession to the English throne in 1558 was by no means unchallenged, since in Catholic eyes she was the bastard child of Henry VIII's liaison with Anne Boleyn. A northern rebellion in 1569, the rising in the north, challenged Elizabeth militarily by the northern earls who were in no way reconciled to Protestant rule. Philip of Spain raised a huge armed force to invade England; throughout the 1580s, leading up to the failed Great Armada of 1588, conspiracies in secret support of Mary Stuart, Queen of Scotland, Elizabeth's first cousin once removed, living in house arrest in England until she was executed in February, 1587, incessantly reminded the English that they were in imminent danger of invasion and brought the loyalty of English

Catholics into serious question: would they come over to Philip's side once the invasion had begun?

Throughout all these perilous times, Elizabeth kept England out of war and appealed to her people to profess loyalty to her as head of the English church in its defiance of Rome. Elizabeth's own tastes in religion appear to have been what we would call High Church. She liked to hear the service sung in Latin. She greatly admired the church music of William Byrd, and protected him with the proviso that he was not to flaunt his Catholicism in public. She protected Thomas Tallis by granting him a twenty-one-year monopoly on polyphonic music; he and Byrd were the only composers allowed to use the paper that was used in printing music. With her courtiers, too, she was prepared to tolerate discreet Catholic worship so long as they acknowledged her as supreme head of the church rather than the Pope. Her father, Henry VIII, seems to have imported Jewish musicians from Italy to adorn this court, similarly countenancing their choice of faith so long as they practiced privately.

Where was Shakespeare in all this? His father, John Shakespeare, had been born before the beginning the Protestant Reformation in England. A group of scholars argue that he remained a Catholic, at least in secret, during his lifetime, and chose to die a child of the Roman church. I find this doubtful, since John Shakespeare rose to civic prominence in his town of Stratford, becoming for a time its chief administrative official. Shakespeare himself lies buried under the altar in the town's church that had become Protestant, along with his wife and other members of his family. It is true, nonetheless, that Stratford was part Protestant and part Catholic during these years of the late sixteenth century, like many a town at a distant and northerly direction from London. Some of the schoolmasters in the school where Shakespeare appears to have been educated were Catholic.

In his plays, Catholic prelates are often treated with tolerant respect and even admiration in ways that are not so visible in the plays of Shakespeare's contemporaries. In the late *Henry VIII*, Queen Katharine of Aragon, Henry's longsuffering wife, is a sympathetic figure during the grossly unfair trial that she is forced to endure. She sees a vision of angels as she is about to be gathered to her eternal reward. Friar Laurence in *Romeo and Juliet* is a warm-hearted, caring friend and counselor of young Romeo. Friar Francis in *Much Ado About Nothing* is a champion of the falsely accused Hero. Corrupt priests abound in Shakespeare's early history plays, presumably Catholic since the history is that of the fifteenth century, but they are no more venal than the worldly aristocrats with whom they conspire and struggle for power. The Bishop of Carlisle, in *Richard II*, speaks boldly in defense of the soon-to-be-deposed Richard not for self-interested reasons but out of principle. Shakespeare almost never enunciates matters of dogma, of Christ's resurrection and of salvation through His sacrifice; he is interested more in the human drama of guilt, penance and spiritual recovery. One can imagine, then, that Shakespeare was attuned to the music of William Byrd and Thomas Tallis, his great contemporaries, and others featured in the Tallis Scholars' superb concert under the direction of Peter Phillips, while at the same time living in a more secular world where his dramas of human conflict could thrive.

Songs, Sacred and Profane, in the Age of Shakespeare
Joseph Alulis

For just one night in April the Chicago Symphony Orchestra made it possible to return to Shakespeare's time by the medium of sixteenth-century sacred music. As part of a Symphony Center Presents program at the Fourth Presbyterian Church, the English choral group The Tallis Scholars, under the direction of its founder, Peter Philips, performed seven works written in Tudor England. Two of these works are by composers whose careers ended before Shakespeare was born, Richard Davy (1465-1538) and John Taverner (1490-1545). All allow us to hear the music of worship in a society whose order was almost universally perceived to be divinely ordained.

There were ten singers in all though for the longest work, which dominated the first part of the program, the *Western Wind Mass* by John Taverner, two of the singers left the group though not before one had sung solo the secular song on which the mass is based, "Westron wynde when wyll thow blow?" A scholarly account of English music for voice of the fifteenth century describes what The Tallis Scholars offered us: "in long and elaborate compositions such as settings of the Mass, the words may be set in a very florid and free manner (sometimes the singers will vocalize on one syllable for minutes on end."[1] Taverner's setting of major parts of the Latin mass reminds us that Shakespeare's world was still religiously unsettled following Henry VIII's break with Rome. The April 5 program began and ended with motets by William Byrd (1540-1623), who managed to enjoy great success in the Court of Queen Elizabeth and also to remain Catholic. There is a tradition that Shakespeare was Catholic as well, based in part upon a seventeenth-century report that the poet "died a papist."[2]

In all of the works The Tallis Scholars performed, voices alone, without instrumental accompaniment, supplied the music. Multiple lines, long and melodious, combined and diverged seamlessly drawing the listener's attention now one way, now another and sometimes to both parts together. The two sopranos, Emily Atkinson, an American singer, and Amy Haworth, both of whom have appeared with various early music and baroque ensembles, were especially pleasing for the

---

[1] John Stevens, *Music and Poetry in the Early Tudor Court* (London: Methuen, 1961), 37.
[2] Samuel Schoenbaum, *Shakespeare's Lives*, New Edition (Oxford: Clarendon Press, 1991), 79.

purity of their voices. Dr. John Milsom, a professor of music at Liverpool Hope University describes the developing sound of English choral music after the mid-fifteenth century in this way: "Melodic lines became longer, more ornate than before, and increasingly virtuosic. They developed into flights of extravagant fantasy in which even a single word might blossom into flourishes and roulades of astonishing length."[3] This aptly describes the ravishing sound the audience heard in the imposing neo-Gothic setting of Fourth Presbyterian two weeks ago.

In the second part of the program, Peter Phillips chose to twice pair settings by different composers of the same text: settings of *Salve Regina* by Davy and Byrd and settings of parts of the first chapter Jeremiah's *Lamentations,* Alpha and Beth by Thomas Tallis (1506-1585) and Daleth and Lamed by Alfonso Ferrabosco the Elder (1543-1588), an Italian active in Elizabeth's court. One wonders if the first audience of *Henry IV, Part Two* (ca. 1598) might have thought of such music when the king tells his attendants, "Let there be no noise made, my gentle friends/ Unless some dull and favorable hand/ Will whisper music to my weary spirit" (4.5.1-3). At the scene's end we learn that the room in which the king rests is called Jerusalem; the sound of The Tallis Scholars singing that name is a pleasing memory to associate with this line.

Scholars concur that "singing was an integral part of English life" in Shakespeare's time.[4] In particular, the kind of contrapuntal or part-song music The Tallis Scholars sang was familiar to those who attended his plays. Part song books were published so that "several persons could sing or play from one book"; "to sing your part sure, and at the first sight," wrote Henry Peacham in *The Compleat Gentleman,* published in 1622 was the mark of an educated person.[5]

As David Bevington noted in his review of The Tallis Scholars, Shakespeare's plays, especially the comedies, are full of vocal music, songs we love so well, as those from *Twelfth Night* and *As You Like It.* Peter Seng gives seventy songs drawn from twenty-one plays including Ophelia's songs in *Hamlet* when she has gone mad and Desdemona's "The poore Soule sat singing, by a Sicamour Tree. / Sing all a green

---

[3] John Milsom, "Commentary" accompanying *A Tudor Collection: The Tallis Scholars,* a four CD recording by Gimell Records Limited, 1995.
[4] Dorothy E. Mason, *Music in Elizabethan England* (Charlottesville, VA: Published for the Folger Shakespeare Library by University Press of Virginia, 1969), 2.
[5] Ibid., 8, 4.

Willough" in *Othello*.[6] Music appears in other ways besides the songs. Walter De La Mare writes, "[Shakespeare] lived in the supreme heyday of English music, a music so much beloved by him and so frequently in his remembrance that there are upwards of four hundred references to it in his plays."[7]

For one evening we were reminded of that "heyday of English music" in which Shakespeare wrote. Though not so familiar as Shakespeare's plays, this music is not forgotten. Within the same week I heard The Tallis Scholars, I heard a performance at North Park University of the Vettern College Choir of Jönköping, Sweden, under the direction of Ove Gotting, which included on its program the motet "Let thy merciful ears, O Lord" by the English composer Thomas Weelkes (1576-1623).

The Tallis Scholars performance was so well received, the group returned to do an encore, William Byrd's musical elegy to his teacher, "Ye Sacred Muses." This work concludes with the line "Tallis is dead, and Music dies." Thanks to The Tallis Scholars, we can appreciate the depth of Byrd's sentiment by hearing superbly performed the music that gave rise to it.

---

[6] Peter Seng, *The Vocal Songs in the Plays of Shakespeare* (Cambridge, MA: Harvard University Press, 1967).
[7] Walter De La Mare, "Introduction," *The Shakespeare Songs*, ed. Tucker Brooke (New York: W. Morrow, 1929), xxiv.

THE Q BROTHERS
OTHELLO: THE REMIX

written, directed + composed by GQ + JQ
developed with Rick Boynton
presented by Chicago Shakespeare Theater + Richard Jordan Productions

Michael Brosilow

Shakespeare's Boutique
Casey Caldwell

It has been a good year to live in Chicago if you are a fan of
Shakespeare's *Othello*. With productions by the Hamburg Ballet at the
Harris Theater, on Chicago Shakespeare Theater's main stage and now
Othello: The Remix in Chicago Shakespeare Theater Upstairs, it has also
been a good year if you, like me, regret that *Othello* has become the
standard bearer for the issue of race in Shakespeare. While the Hamburg
Ballet foregrounded race in bold ways, Chicago Shakespeare Theater's
production directed by Jonathan Munby and its production of *Othello:
The Remix* have eschewed issues of race each in their own ways. While I
am discussing *Othello: The Remix* in what follows, I'll point you to
reviews by my City Desk colleagues Rebecca Fall and Clark Hulse if you
would like to learn more about and compare these other productions.

    I want to be clear, however: something like what we mean today by
race is at play or in the process of emerging for the first time in

Shakespeare's tragedy. But what the play really does, for me, is coordinate issues of race, gender, eroticism, ambition, friendship and love around a searing, arc-welding skepticism about the possibility of truly knowing another person. And the catalyst that sets all these issues swirling in this epistemological nightmare is the clash of three great personalities: Iago, Othello and Desdemona. Desdemona has a form of dedication that most audiences today would find grotesque, if not supra-human. Othello is a Moor in a white man's world, with a brutal past and a decisive mind. Iago is a ferocious, improvisatory and patient enemy of the possibility of certainty. Race is but one key weapon that Iago has at hand in a war he wages ultimately even on himself (he makes no real attempt worthy of his intelligence to "get away with it" at the end).

The Q Brothers' *Othello: The Remix* is a kind of *Paul's Boutique* of the dynamic I have just described (the analogy is deliberate: GQ, the Brother Q playing Iago, has a line that nods at their Beastie Boys-esque style). They have sampled, remixed, alluded to, filled out, and resituated *Othello* into something it seems inadequate to call an "adaptation." Playing in the Chicago Shakespeare Theater Upstairs, the stage is relatively bare, with a raised scaffolding area in back, mostly to house the DJ and his mixing table. The all-male cast of four (plus the DJ) plays multiple parts, including female roles, often changing costumes on stage rapidly between distinctly fleshed out—even when cartoonish—characterizations. The two female characters we see acted on stage are Jackson Doran's Emilia and JQ's Bianca. Especially JQ's Bianca is played mostly for comic relief. Postell Pringle, who plays Othello, is the least doubled with another character (a standout exception being a brief turn as a backup singer for Emilia). The show as a whole is a kind of hip hop musical, nearly all of it in rhyming lines that transition from more dialog-like moments to actual set-piece musical and dance numbers.

The Q Brothers have resituated the play's plot within America's hip hop industry. Othello is a leading hip hop star, and as they prepare to set out on tour, Cassio is chosen to be the opener for Othello. This leaves Iago to be the "opener for the opener." In the most striking decision in relation to the female characters in this production, Desdemona is not personated on stage but rather is merely represented as a singing voice drifting in from the theater's speakers. In their first scene "together," Othello is mixing a song with Desdemona, visibly transfixed, his gaze aloft over the audience's heads as her voice drifts in both melodious and inarticulate. Desdemona is never given any actual words to speak. We see Othello offer her a gold chain, taking the place of Shakespeare's malevolent handkerchief, and of course this comes back in the end to act as the device by which he strangles (an invisible) Desdemona.

At first blush, a show in which women are either caricatured in a comic mode or pushed offstage into a distilled singing voice will and has struck some as problematic, to say the least. What I saw was a production that foregrounded the danger of Othello's reductive apotheosis of Desdemona—he's visibly controlling if also wonderstruck in their mixing session, for example. And the show ends with a song about how only love will save us. The laughable incongruousness here seemed to me deliberate: Iago's surgical strike against certainty has functioned precisely to defeat love. And because our view of "love" is so weighted towards Othello's perspective here, the asymmetry of what "love" is for him stands out that much more (c.f. in Shakespeare: "She loved me for the dangers I had passed, / and I loved her that she did pity them). So we're left to wonder if we can be certain we ever really saw love on stage in the first place.

Finally, by setting their version in the hip hop industry, the Q Brothers have not eschewed so much as inverted the role of race in their production. Cassio and Iago are white men in an entertainment industry "coded" as black in popular culture. Othello becomes the spectacle of an insider in this sense. This makes GQ's Iago's hatred for the Moor that much more defined by alienation and self-loathing, in a way that other productions are rarely able to achieve. But it also drains some of the overt stakes and tension from Othello's being encoded in Shakespeare's version as an "other." The military in Shakespeare's Venice represents a unique route a Moor can follow to attain high social status. In Shakespeare's representation of the army's personnel (which includes Cassio and Iago), Othello *stands out* as being black in an institution encoded as white. This is not the same dynamic in *Othello: The Remix*. That in itself is not a problem, but it does point up how one kind of obvious tension surrounding Othello in the original is missing here. Given how smart the Q Brother's production is, then, maybe this should leave audiences with the question of whether that tension was merely lost in the mix or transposed somewhere else in this *Paul's Boutique* of Shakespeare adaptations. I would suggest that one of *Othello: The Remix's* main aims is to ask rather than answer the question of where this tension goes in America's music industry.

Remixing Shakespeare
Kyle Haden

I went to see the Chicago Shakespeare Theater's production of *Othello: The Remix* on May 5. The Q Brothers are known for their hip-hop interpretations of Shakespeare's work—their best-known piece is probably *The Bomb-itty of Errors*. They managed to create an effective and entertaining adaptation of *Othello*, hitting most of the major plot points in seventy-five minutes. As a fan of both hip-hop and Shakespeare, I left impressed.

Hip hop has a lot of parallels to Shakespeare: rhythm, word play. If Shakespeare were alive and creating work in our day and age, he may very well have been a hip hop artist. It therefore feels entirely appropriate that the entire play is rapped by four actors, who play various parts. The Q Brothers clearly have a deep understand and love of Shakespeare's work; many of the characters' rhymes pulled out lines from the original text, as well as other plays in the canon. (These references are also very true to the spirit of hip-hop, where rappers name-check everything from sports teams to designer labels to politicians.) The lyrics vividly paint the picture Shakespeare created, and cover almost every major plot point—in half the time!

The plot, in a nutshell: Othello is the biggest star in the music game, and Desdemona is the hook singer from the suburbs who falls in love with him. Iago, an underground rapper, has been waiting for his man to give him his shot in the spotlight. Instead, Othello selects Cassio, who is much more of a "mainstream" choice. Iago, therefore, plots his revenge. We see all of the familiar characters: Roderigo is an IT nerd; Emilia, the unsatisfied but loyal wife of Iago; Bianca, the groupie in love with Cassio; and Lodovico, the head of the studio.

The performances were high-energy and compelling. GQ's portrayal of Iago, complete with Eminem-like rapping skills, was particularly memorable. The actors constantly interacted with the crowd, and while it sometimes had the feel of a rock concert, they never lost control of the room. Colored spotlights sweeping across the room led to the club feel, as did the equipment trunk that was wheeled around the room to help create different settings.

The glaring hole in the play is the absence of women; the cast is comprised of four men, and the female characters we do see are played in broad, comic strokes. This can lead to some funny moments, but the power of Emilia's character, particularly her powerful monologue to Desdemona towards the end of the play, is lost. Her death is an oddly humorous footnote to the conclusion of the play. We don't even see Desdemona—she exists only as a voice singing a couple of hooks from the booth, forcing the actor playing Othello to face the front of the stage and gaze dreamily at the back of the house. Her absence is particularly problematic when it comes to her death at the end of the play. The trunk stands in for her, and it is an interesting workaround—but how much more interesting would it be to see two people battling back and forth in song and rhyme—a lyrical battle to the death? It's a missed opportunity, and I think the production would be much richer in adding a woman or two to the cast.

As currently constructed, however, the play truly is Othello's story. It becomes a cautionary tale told through the rhymes of the man who was on top of the world and lost it all; only his death contains any emotional resonance for us. Postell Pringle plays the title character with a deft hand; he's full of bombast and swagger when necessary, but he can also find the vulnerability necessary at key moments. The play would be a wonderful companion piece to any full production of Shakespeare's play (indeed, I thought it was a lost opportunity for CST not to have run this in concurrence with their modern-day setting of *Othello*, which closed in April), but it manages to stand on its own as a fully realized, thoroughly entertaining story.

NORTHWESTERN UNIVERSITY
ALICE KAPLAN INSTITUTE FOR THE HUMANITIES
+ MARY AND LEIGH BLOCK MUSEUM OF ART
CATCH MY SOUL

directed by Patrick McGoohan, 1974

The Resurrection of the Desert *Othello*
Gina Di Salvo

A devil character delivers a bluesy recitative, a man blesses his followers on the banks of a desert river and then a tour bus cuts across the dusty terrain. It is the early 1970s, but this is not *Jesus Christ Superstar*. The film is *Catch My Soul* (directed by Patrick McGoohan), a rock opera adaptation of *Othello* set in a Santa Fe counter culture community. Seen by few until recently, the film closed within a week of its premiere in 1974 and then spent the last forty years in archival purgatory.

The premise of this adaptation, which screened at Northwestern University's Mary and Leigh Block Museum of Art last month, sounds strange and, even, ridiculous. *Catch My Soul* is a relic of its time, but no more so than *West Side Story* (1957) or Naham Tate's Restoration-era *History of King Lear* (1681)—you know, the one where Cordelia lives. The setting is transported from sixteenth-century Venetian Cyprus to the American Southwest during the time of *HAIR*. Absent from the film are the accusations of unnatural seduction, epithets related to "the Moor," and militarism. Still, the film remains true to the original play. It's a tragedy of manipulation within an isolated community and the inevitable violence of a culture—even a counter culture—steeped in misogynist paranoia. The plot (spoiler alert) features an allegedly unfaithful new bride and some brief business with that wretched prop, a handkerchief forever embroidered with berries.

But *Catch My Soul* also presents a religious story as much as a Shakespearean one. The tragic hero (Richie Havens) serves as pastor of a desert Christian church and Iago (Lance LeGault) plots against him as Santa Fe Satan (the film's alternative title). And if Desdemona (Season Hubley) has seemed martyr-like before, then this version actively portrays her passive canonization. She often appears on screen as one of the saints in Ade Bethune's Catholic Worker woodcuts, patiently sewing and toiling as she contemplates God. Our final image of her is as a sacrificial icon.

In the introduction to the screening at the Block Museum, Dwayne Mann (a doctoral candidate in the Interdisciplinary PhD in Theatre and Drama program at Northwestern University) pronounced the film "the missing piece." *Catch My Soul* shares a similar history with other rock musicals of the era, emerging first on stage in 1969, circulating as a cast album in 1971, and then, finally, premiering in its cinematic form in 1974, a year after *Jesus Christ Superstar* and *Godspell* appeared on screen. As a film, *Catch My Soul* picks up on and enlarges the tropes of these other works. *Godspell* begins with baptisms in New York City and *Jesus Christ Superstar* opens and concludes with a tour bus in the Israeli desert. A tour bus in *Catch My Soul* remains on screen throughout the film. It's painted completely black, but is full of stark, blinding white light inside and serves, in part, as a demonic retreat. At one point, Iago rolls around in Satanic fits with bloodshot eyes as he moves closer to orchestrating Desdemona's death. Costumed in jeans and a suede vest, Iago croons his curses in a gravelly voice, but beneath the rock star is the medieval stock character who visits Eve in serpent form in the Old Testament and tempts Christ in the Gospels of Matthew and Luke.

Beyond the context of rock musical history, *Catch My Soul* reconfigures Shakespearean filmography from the sixties to the present. The film picks up where Franco Zeffirelli's *Romeo and Juliet* (1968) left off. Zeffirelli's interpretation linked the tragedy to contemporary youth culture and gave religious undertones to the struggle of the star-crossed lovers. Baz Luhrmann extended Zeffirelli's conceptual framework by saturating *William Shakespeare's Romeo + Juliet* (1996) with beach party machismo and Roman Catholic iconography. But the saints and crucifixes that form the sacred kaleidoscope of Luhrmann's late-twentieth century production first appeared in *Catch My Soul* in simpler form. Compared to the montages of Luhrmann's mega-church rock show, this desert *Othello* strums a low-fi Folk Mass. Indeed, Othello's sudden demand of, "Have you prayed tonight?" in Act 5, scene 2 has never made more sense. It finally has a context beyond the everyday Christianity of Shakespeare's stage. Called "pastor" by his followers, Othello wears a tunic and a large cross—a particular moment of him walking through the desert hill recalls Francis of Assisi in Zeffirelli's *Brother Sun and Sister Moon* (1972)—as he builds a new church, sets up altars, and paints saintly scenes. When he enters his church with the resolve to punitively murder his wife, his faith in redemption continues to operate. Desdemona's death not only occurs on the altar of the church, as Juliet's would in Luhrmann's nineties film, but also Othello surrenders her lifeless body to the outstretched arms of Christ on the cross. This is tragedy set apart from the rest of society, something other auteurs would explore in films such as Polanski's *Macbeth* (1971) and Kristian Levring's *The King Is Alive* (2000). But this one stands out in its earnest religiosity.

Beyond all this, the recent resurrection of *Catch My Soul* is a story in its own right. Panned by critics in 1974, the movie quickly disappeared from public view. Our access to the film, which is now available as a DVD/Blu-Ray combo pack, is owed largely to Samuel B. Prime. Less than a decade ago, Prime was an undergraduate student at Northwestern University. He became passionate about *Catch My Soul* during a project for a class on Shakespeare and Music. In an interview with Prime, he recalled that "the idea of a folksy, bluesy version of *Othello*" delighted him. Without the actual footage, he researched the film through its archival remains, including the soundtrack, the script and photographs. He wrote an honors thesis on *Catch My Soul* and then moved to Los Angeles to pursue graduate study in film preservation. Unlike the film's original critics, Prime found that the film "was actually quite special." He explained that "during its initial release, the film was too close to *Jesus Christ Superstar* to consider thoughtfully." An avid cinephile, Prime dreamed of producing a home-release version and admitted that it "was in my mind from the moment I moved to LA." It was just "a matter of figuring out the right partners to make it happen." In 2014, he met the right person, Joe Rubin, co-founder of Vinegar Syndrome, a company dedicated to restoring cult exploitation films. Together, they pitched the project to 20th Century Fox and *Catch My Soul* was re-released through Etiquette Pictures in November 2015. Prime's long-term dedication and collaborative spirit recalls the mission of past archivists and bibliographers, such as the Shakespeareans who formed the Malone Society in the early twentieth century. Thanks to this labor, we can all experience an important and nearly forgotten iteration of Shakespeare's *Othello*.

CHICAGO SYMPHONY ORCHESTRA
BERLIOZ'S ROMEO AND JULIET

conducted by Riccardo Muti
featuring Ekaterina Gubanova, Paul Groves + Dmitry Belosselskiy

Todd Rosenberg

Romeo and Juliet: **The Power of First Love**
Joseph Alulis

Snow in April in Chicago, something more than flurries, is not unheard of; but it's not that common either. The same could be said of complete performances of Berlioz's *Romeo and Juliet* by the Chicago Symphony Orchestra (CSO). But both occurred on April 8 of this year; the swirling snow on Michigan Avenue after the concert felt like the natural complement to the excitement generated inside Orchestra Hall. The audience repeatedly called Maestro Riccardo Muti and the soloists back to the stage with their applause. Famed Berlioz scholar Jacques Barzun writes that a successful performance of Berlioz requires "ice and fire," that is, "great precision" and "forward drive."[8] That this performance had both was evident in the response of all who heard it.

---

[8] "Fourteen Points about Berlioz and the Public," in *Berlioz: Past, Present, Future*, ed. Peter Bloom (Rochester: University of Rochester Press, 2003), 198.

Berlioz's *Symphonie dramatique* is scored for both full and small orchestra, three soloists, and full and semi-chorus. It is divided into three parts in which the mezzo-soprano and tenor appear only in the first and the bass and full chorus only in the third. The semi-chorus sings on stage in the first part and off-stage in the second; the second is almost exclusively orchestral. Berlioz divided each part into sections or movements for which he supplied descriptions of actions from the play. The CSO program numbered these one through seven across all three parts. The second, orchestral part consists of movements two through four, the second scored for full orchestra and the third and fourth for small orchestra. These three movements are often played separately from the rest.[9]

In his *Memoirs* Berlioz writes of his *Romeo and Juliet* symphony, "As regards execution, it presents immense difficulties of all sorts inherent in its form and style and only to be overcome by long, patient, and *well-directed* study" (italics in the original).[10] The phrase "*well-directed* study" reflects Berlioz's experience as a conductor and implies high praise for Maestro Muti's role in the evening's performance. For on April 8 all parts of this massive ensemble performed their roles with the greatest skill and energy.

After an orchestral "Introduction" depicting the fighting of Montagues and Capulets (a rapid fugue) and the Prince's intervention (stately trombones), Berlioz gives us a "Prologue" in which mezzo-soprano Ekaterina Gubanova and the semi-chorus, together and separately, tell the story of the lovers highlighting the moment when Juliet "confides her love to the night" and Romeo professes his love for her. A recitative follows which Ms. Gubanova sang superbly. Following this, tenor Paul Groves sang Berlioz's rendition of Mercutio's Queen Mab speech (1.4.53-95) with half the lines echoed by the semi-chorus. This was light, airy, rapid, very pleasing and all over in a moment. The semi-chorus concludes the first part, treated as a single movement, by narrating the rest of the story: the death of the lovers and how it causes the families to "renounce the hatred" that divided them. Apart from the Queen Mab it is the equivalent of Shakespeare's "Prologue."

---

[9] For some of the detail of this description I depend on the excellent piece by Roger Fiske, "Shakespeare in the Concert Hall," in *Shakespeare in Music*, ed. Phyllis Hartnoll (London: Macmillan, 1964).

[10] Hector Berlioz, *Memoirs*, trans. Rachel (Scott Russell) Holmes and Eleanor Holmes, rev. Ernest Newman (New York: Dover, 1966), 231.

The second part contains Berlioz's musical description of the balcony scene, already mentioned as part of the first part's narrative. Romeo hears Juliet, unaware of his presence, profess her love for him and he responds in kind. Just before, as a foil to this moment of intimacy, Berlioz has the semi-chorus off stage play the role, in his description, of "young Capulets leaving the feast" in what Roger Fiske calls "the most nearly operatic effect in the whole work."[11] But the lovers' encounter Berlioz depicts without human voice because, as he writes in the "Preface" to the score, "he preferred to give a wider latitude to his imagination than would have been possible with words."[12] The love theme he composed is beautiful and the CSO's performance of it that night was exquisite. With strings, wind, and horn it rivaled in music Shakespeare's poetry: "My bounty is as boundless as the sea, / My love as deep; the more I give to thee/ The more I have, for both are infinite" (2.2.133-35). When Juliet calls to her beloved softly in the dark, Romeo responds in a way that acknowledges the expressive power of music: "It is my soul that calls upon my name./ How silver-sweet sound lovers' tongues by night,/ Like softest music to attending ears!" (2.2.164-66). Berlioz makes palpable for the theatergoer or reader the meaning of these words. More extravagantly, Berlioz attributes to Shakespeare's poetry a power possessed by no other. In the recitative for solo mezzo-soprano of the first part he compares "first love" to "that very poetry/ Of which Shakespeare alone knew the secret."

After the Intermission the space above the stage filled with the 140 members of the full chorus. The third part consists of three movements of which the second is the purely instrumental depiction of the deaths of Romeo and Juliet. In the first and third movements, the full chorus sings, first mourning the supposed death of Juliet and then, divided into Montagues and Capulets, brawling over the bodies of the two lovers. At a moment in this brawl, comparable to the arrival of the prince in the "Introduction," bass Dmitry Belosselskiy stood and, as Friar Laurence, began the recitative "I will unravel the mysteries." In this and the three arias that followed, Mr. Belosselskiy dominated the hall with the authority of his physical presence and the power and beauty of his voice. After his last aria, the full chorus joined him for a grand conclusion to the symphony which brought the whole audience to its feet in applause.

---

[11] Fiske, 191.

[12] Jacques Barzun, *Berlioz and the Romantic Century*, 3rd edition, two volumes (New York: Columbia University Press, 1969), 1:322.

Berlioz's symphony does not so much set the story of Shakespeare's *Romeo and Juliet* to music as use that story to give a lesson in the power of love. It begins with the two families fighting; it ends with their reconciliation. In between we see the son and daughter of Montague and Capulet respectively fall in love and die because of their fathers' feud. Romeo and Juliet's love for each other bridges the gulf of hatred that divides their families. The families renounce their hatred because it has killed those they respectively love. In this way, it seems faithful to Shakespeare's intent expressed in the "Prologue": to enact the story of two star-crossed lovers whose deaths "bury their parents' strife."

Berlioz emphasizes the fact that the love of Romeo and Juliet is "first love." Never mind Shakespeare's Rosaline; the David Garrick adaptation of the play with which Berlioz was working had excised her. In any case, that was not reciprocal love. Also, Berlioz gives us the Queen Mab speech twice. In the first movement the tenor soloist, though he is not named by Berlioz as Mercutio the way the bass is named Friar Lawrence, sings Berlioz's version of Mercutio's speech; the fourth movement, the conclusion of the second part, sets the speech instrumentally. Queen Mab, a depiction of dreaming, brackets the love scene. Is "first love" a kind of dreaming? If so, how firm a foundation is that for the reconciliation depicted in the finale? Berlioz makes a representative of the Church the agent of reconciliation, not the state in the person of the prince, as Shakespeare does. Moreover, he has Friar Lawrence call upon the feuding Capulets and Montagues to "swear all of you by the holy cross." But the most powerful kind of love for Berlioz seems to be "first love." Less than a decade after his *Romeo and Juliet* symphony, Berlioz wrote in his *Memoirs* of his own first love, at the age of twelve, for Estelle Duboeuf, six years older than him and he ends his *Memoirs* with a selection of correspondence with the old Estelle, now the widow Madame Fournier.[13] The last words of the *Memoir* are "Stella! Stella! I can now die without anger or bitterness."[14] Following this, as a kind of epilogue, he adds Shakespeare's lines from *Macbeth*:

> Life's but a walking shadow; a poor player,
> That struts and frets his hour upon the stage,
> And then is heard no more: it is a tale

---

[13] Berlioz, 8-9, 519-30.
[14] Ibid., 531.

> Told by an idiot, full of sound and fury,
> Signifying nothing.

Julie Sanders cites Jonathan Bate on "the deep influence of Romantic readings of Shakespeare."[15] Surely anyone who was fortunate enough to hear the Chicago Symphony Orchestra's performance in April of Berlioz's *Romeo and Juliet* with its beautiful love theme would conclude that this work has contributed greatly to that influence.

---

[15] Julie Sanders, *Shakespeare and Music* (Cambridge, UK: Polity, 2007), 50.

CHICAGO SYMPHONY ORCHESTRA
FALSTAFF

music by Giuseppe Verdi
libretto by Arriggo Boito
after Shakespeare's *The Merry Wives of Windsor* + parts of *Henry IV*
conducted by Riccardo Muti
featuring Ambrogio Maestri

Todd Rosenberg

Verdi's *Falstaff*: A Final Masterpiece
Martha C. Nussbaum

Giuseppe Verdi's *Falstaff* made its triumphant debut in February 1893, when the composer, born in October 1813, was nearly eighty, and eight years before his death. "What a joy!" wrote the composer to his librettist, Arrigo Boito (1842-1918). "To be able to say to the Audience: 'WE ARE HERE AGAIN! COME AND SEE US!!'" (Capital letters and exclamation marks are Verdi's own.) Nor has there ever been a more powerful musical expression of joy. And music, I believe, can express the joy of life more completely and transcendentally than non-musical theater. *Falstaff's* cascading sequence of intricate rhythms, soaring lyrical melodies, and what can only be described as sheer musical laughter does, at any rate, soar well beyond what Shakespeare achieved with the exploits of his fat knight.

Verdi's two other great Shakespeare operas, *Macbeth* (1847) and *Otello* (1887), equal their Shakespearean originals in power of insight, although they attain slightly different insights and through different routes. But *Falstaff* moves into another realm altogether, giving the best reply I know in all art to perpetual questions about the meaning of life. How deliciously it thumbs its nose at stupid stereotypes of aging that dominate culture, now as then. (Slowing down? Crumbling? Halting? Try: assured mastery, new power of insight, fizzy rapidity, and a newfound ability to laugh at the body, at sex, at vulnerability, even at death.)

How lucky our city was this April to have three performances of this work, one on the actual 400th anniversary of Shakespeare's death, conducted in a superb concert version by Riccardo Muti (himself age 74), far and away today's greatest interpreter of Verdi's music.

Sir John Falstaff is a much-beloved Shakespearean character. In his *Shakespeare: The Invention of the Human*, critic Harold Bloom even argued that with this character Shakespeare enlarged our sense of our own human possibilities. I have always been a skeptic. The Falstaff of *Henry IV, Parts I and II* is just not very endearing in his grossness. His unbridled self-indulgence does not strike me as very joyous, and his more serious meditations (about honor, for example) make him dark and cynical rather than deep. If someone wants a friendship with a fictional human being who embraces bodily humanity while not ceasing to be articulate and even profound, she would do better to spend her time with Joyce's Leopold Bloom, a distinctly superior and funnier life companion, who has capacities for tenderness and a sense of justice that appear nowhere in the somewhat hollow Falstaff. (There were no Jews in Shakespeare's England.) If we next consider the Falstaff of *The Merry Wives of Windsor*—the play supposedly penned as Shakespeare's reply to Queen Elizabeth's request to see "the fat knight in love"—we find a very superficial slapstick farce, with none of the delicacy or poetic insight of Shakespeare's greatest comedies.

Arrigo Boito has distinctly improved upon Shakespeare. For a start, he has melded the two Falstaffs very cleverly, following the basic outlines of the comic plot of *Merry Wives*, but inserting monologues and asides drawn from the history plays, thus making the character not simply ridiculous. One notable example is the final scene, in which Falstaff seems about to become a mere target of slapstick humor, as the fairies pinch and prod him—but then he shows the capacity for self-awareness and detachment that is his hallmark in the histories, saying, "Son io che vi fa scaltri. L'arguzia mia crea l'arguzia degli altri." "I am not only witty in myself but the cause that wit is in other men," a direct quote from *Henry IV Part 2*, Act 1, scene 2. Boito's Falstaff has a charm, a lightness, that the histories' Falstaff lacks, and at the same time a depth that is surely absent from the buffo fat knight of *Merry Wives*.

But Boito's improvement goes well beyond his reworking of Sir John. For he has simply displaced Sir John from the center of the play, turning it over to the four zestful women who make the plot move. Slenderly characterized in Shakespeare, Alice Ford, Meg Page, Mistress Quickly, and Nannetta (Anne) are given highly distinctive, and endearing, musical characterizations, while at the same time the wives' ensemble plotting is a very model of friendship and reciprocity. (Here the opera bears comparison with Mozart's *The Marriage of Figaro*, with its portrayal of friendship and scheming in the women's world.) And in a pleasing contrast to the constantly plotting mature women, Nannetta, and her lover Fenton, lend the work a gossamer lyricism that Verdi compared to sugar dusted over the top of a cake.

As this description already shows, it is impossible to go far in characterizing the Verdi/Boito achievement without talking about the music. (Verdi could not read Shakespeare's English words, so his connection to Shakespeare was always mediated by the lyricism of his own beloved language, and, above all, by his musical imagination.) Verdi wrote only one other comic opera, the disastrous early *Un Giorno di Regno* (1840). And comic interludes in several of the serious operas (for example the page Oscar in *Un Ballo in Maschera*) are not especially successful. What a surprise, then, to find that he is fully the equal of Mozart as a composer of operatic comedy. Rapid and unpredictable, the score fizzes with all kinds of interrelated energies of love, friendship, humor and playfulness. As Roger Parker writes in the *New Grove Dictionary of Opera*, "The listener is bombarded by a stunning diversity of rhythms, orchestral textures, melodic motifs and harmonic devices." From the dash of the opening (with no overture) to the concluding fugue, "All the world is a jest," "Tutto il mondo è burla," the work moves forward with astonishing energy and variety. Indeed, its polyphonic complexity defeats most conductors, and even the best of conductors can virtually never make it work fully in the theater, a reason why Muti has long favored concert versions of opera generally, and a reason why we should agree with him for this work at least. In Chicago this spring, Muti brought to the work a clarity, a rhythmic precision, and a sheer energy that are rare indeed in performances of Verdi, which can easily slip into the obvious and the self-indulgent. Hearing Muti's Verdi is like looking at a beautiful building that has recently been cleaned of grime and soot. The ensembles of Act 1, which can be heard fully realized in recording but which almost always come apart slightly in staged performances, were rendered here with beautiful crispness, and the concluding fugue was all that it ought to be. In the uniformly excellent cast one can single out the witty and humane Falstaff of Ambrogio Maestri, the zestful Alice of Eleonora Buratto, and the gently lyrical Nannetta of Rosa Feola.

Because *Falstaff* lacks obviousness—no big tear-jerking arias, not even big comic or lyrical arias like those of Mozart, but only the bustle of life in all its earthy delight—its fortunes in the opera house have always been uneven. Championed by great conductors from Toscanini to Muti, it has not been a huge favorite with the opera-buying public. But has more to tell us that any number of tearjerkers.

Shortly after Verdi died, Boito wrote that "this octogenarian" was "the most powerful expression of life that it is possible to imagine." And Verdi did indeed achieve—in life and in his work—a vital and joyful immersion in ongoing living that never yielded to depression or hopelessness. Of all Verdi's expressions of life, Falstaff may be the deepest and most vital, a protest against mortality not through mawkish self-pity but through sheer delighted aliveness and creative power.

I am grateful to Saul Levmore and Jennifer Nou for very helpful comments on an earlier draft of this review.

Riccardo Muti's *Falstaff*:
A Highlight of Shakespeare 400 Chicago
David Bevington

Giuseppe Verdi's *Falstaff*, a lyric comedy in three acts, superbly conducted by Riccardo Muti, with Ambrogio Maestri as Falstaff, Luca Salsi as Ford, Eleonora Buratto as Mrs. Alice Ford, and Daniela Barcellona as Mrs. Quickly, along with other excellent soloists and with the Chicago Symphony Chorus and Orchestra, has been an utterly delightful way to celebrate April 23, the date we conventionally associate with the birth and death of William Shakespeare, some 400 years after he died.

(Actually, Shakespeare was baptized on April 26, 1564, and was buried on April 25, 1616. Trinity Church in Stratford-upon-Avon has preserved these records in an age that regarded baptism and burial as holy occasions of far greater importance than mere birth and death. April 23 is the conventional date for Shakespeare's birth and death because it is St. George's Day, the traditional date for commemorating the death of England's patron saint in 303 AD. A charming myth, don't you think, to suppose that Shakespeare managed to die on his own birthday, and in spiritual company with the saint who is credited with having rescued a king's beautiful daughter from the devil in the shape of a fearsome fifty-foot-long dragon.)

This *Falstaff* has unquestionably been a highlight of Chicago's Shakespeare 400 celebration. *Falstaff* is my favorite among all of Verdi's operas, with *Otello* (splendidly performed in Orchestra Hall in April of 2011 by Muti and company) as a close second. These two late operas show Verdi at his best, fortunately having been brought out of an intended retirement by his librettist, Arrigo Boito. Together, they conceived the brilliant idea of combining the Falstaffian highlights of Shakespeare's *The Merry Wives of Windsor* with immortal moments from his *Henry IV* plays, especially Falstaff's soliloquy on honor from the battle scene of *1 Henry IV* and Falstaff's praise of wine from *2 Henry IV*. These moments show Falstaff as a superb ironist, talking about honor as a quality sought after by brave warriors but of little use to them once they are dead ("Who hath it? He that died o' Wednesday"), and extolling sherry wine for its ability to make the brain "full of nimble, fiery, and delectable shapes." These insights fit neatly into the richly composite portrait of fat Falstaff, who is in many ways a coward, a buffoon, a thief, a ludicrous boaster, and a dissolute alcoholic while also somehow managing to be the irrepressible embodiment of joie de vivre, the apostle of living life to its fullest.

Rumor has it that Queen Elizabeth I was so taken with Falstaff in the *Henry IV* plays that she commissioned a command performance of Falstaff in love. The result, supposedly, was *The Merry Wives*, Shakespeare's truest comedy in the sense of being perfectly funny and romantic without a countervailing tragic or nearly tragic complication. It is also the most perfect example in Shakespeare of city comedy, able to mock gently urban mores with a satiric plot of catching socially pretentious creatures in the web of their own absurdities. Nowhere else does Shakespeare set his comedy in a bourgeois English village which happens to be also the home of a royal residence, Windsor Castle.

A huge benefit of seeing Verdi and Boito's operatized version of the Falstaff story in a concert performance rather than in the opera house is that it enables us to concentrate on the music: on the superb voices of the soloists, on Muti's deft conducting, and perhaps most of all on the orchestra. Here, in Orchestra Hall, we are treated to hear and watch an ensemble that is perhaps three times the number of players that could be accommodated in most opera pits: four trombone players, for example, one of them playing a bass trombone at least eight feet long, four trumpets, five French hornists, two harpists, six clarinetists of various persuasions, seventeen first violinists and an equal number of second violins, thirteen violists, eleven cellists, nine double bassists, and so on. Size is not everything, of course, but to hear and see the violinists executing Verdi's rapidly ascending scales in perfect union is to experience breathtaking perfection. More substantially, we appreciate what the orchestra is asked to do in its witty underscoring of the sung lyrics. No Verdi score matches *Falstaff* in its pyrotechnic versatility and cleverness in providing musical interpretation, as in the repeated joking on the time for Falstaff's intended assignation with Alice Ford, "Dalle due alle tre" ("Between two and three,") or Mistress Quickly's mocking salutation of the fat knight, "Reverenza!" ("My respects!"), or the command of silence, "Zitto!" ("Hush!"). Verdi and Boito should have done more comedy. This is music and voice and theatrical art brought together with sublime success.

Because Verdi's *Falstaff* is an avowed adaptation of Shakespeare's *The Merry Wives of Windsor* (with moments of the history plays thrown in), comparisons of the two are legion. Many are the opera fans who regard

Falstaff as an improvement over its Shakespearean original. My own preference is to cherish both as inimitably wonderful, but I do of course see the point of those who prefer the opera. The Shakespearean plot is simplified and thereby easier to follow. Many characters in the original disappear in the operatic version: the Welsh parson Sir Hugh Evans, the Justice of the Peace Robert Shallow, his dimwitted nephew Abraham Slender, Slender's foolish servant John Rugby, the Host of the Garter Inn (mentioned, but never appearing on stage), Meg's husband George Page, and still more. In Shakespeare's comedy, these are "humors" types, that is, burlesque caricatures who display various features of absurd behavior like jealousy, fatuous self-confidence and French foreign-ness. Many of their quirks of behavior and speech are, in Falstaff, folded over into the "humors" of those who remain: Doctor Caius, for example, is a composite of the jealous Frenchman (Caius) and the testy Justice of the Peace (Shallow), along with his nephew, Slender. Falstaff himself is endowed with "humors" qualities found in other Shakespearean caricatures. The compression provides clarity of plot along with the compression needed in reducing a stage comedy to operatic proportions.

At the same time, that compression and eliding leaves out a lot of rich satirical representation of human folly. The practical joke that the Merry Wives play on Falstaff with Mistress Quickly's help, of inducing him to accept the invitation to an affair so that we can laugh at the lengths to which Falstaff is driven to extricate himself from an embarrassing exposure, is wonderfully funny in *Falstaff* as it is *The Merry Wives*. But Shakespeare's play, by providing one more such escape plot than remains in the operatic adaptation, increases the comic pleasure that we and the wives enjoy in wondering whether this fat old man, having repeatedly been caught at his lecherous attempt, can possibly be tricked into submitting himself to the same danger yet another time. He does submit thus, in the Shakespeare, to the comic credit of his inventive tormenters.

More than anything else, the brilliance of Boito's and Verdi's *Falstaff*, so splendidly performed for us in Orchestra Hall, is a tribute to the greatness of Shakespeare's comic creation. Falstaff has become for us a composite of all the ways he has been characterized, in plays about English history, in a city comedy, and in the opera that bears his name. We are blessed to have him in all these guises and in all these genres.

CHICAGO SYMPHONY ORCHESTRA
TCHAIKOVSKY'S
THE TEMPEST, OP. 18 + ROMEO AND JULIET,
MAHLER'S
SYMPHONY NO. 4 IN G MAJOR

conducted by Riccardo Muti
featuring Rosa Feola

Todd Rosenberg

Maestro Muti's Shakespeare
Cherrie Gottsleben

On a slightly chilly, but beautiful April 24 afternoon, the Chicago Symphony Orchestra, with Concertmaster Robert Chen, and conducted by Maestro Riccardo Muti, gave one of its quintessential performances of Tchaikovsky's Symphonic fantasia *The Tempest,* his Fantasy-Overture *Romeo and Juliet,* along with Mahler's Symphony No. 4 in G major with Italian soprano Rosa Feola. Scott Hostetler played the English horn, Jennifer Gunn, on piccolo, Miles Maner on contrabassoon, John Bruce Yeh on E-Flat clarinet, J. Lawrie Bloom on bass clarinet and Charles Vernon on bass trombone. Principals included: Baird Dodge (violin); Charles Pikler (viola); John Sharp (cello); Alexander Hanna (bass); Sarah Bullen (harp); Richard Graef (Assistant Principal, flute); Michael Henoch

(Assistant Principal, oboe); Stephen Williamson (clarinet); Keith Buncke (bassoon); Daniel Gingrich (horn); Christopher Martin (trumpet); Jay Friedman (trombone); Gene Pokorny (tuba); David Herbert (timpani) and Cynthia Yeh (percussion).

As the audience streamed in, the intermittent chatter was increasingly overwhelmed by a solemnity that expressed an eager anticipation of the performance, but more so (it seemed) in expectation of Muti's entrance. In his autobiography, Muti alludes to the importance of the *forma mentis* on the interpretation of the music score, the interconnectivity of music and words, and to his formative years when he began to discover—even in the simplest compositions—the almost sacred marriage between accuracy and playing with "absolute moral devotion." The audience certainly experienced this devotion in the dramatic texture of Sunday's performance, in its emulation of a natural sensuousness in the context of musical image-making—where (in Sidney's words) "all virtues, vices, and passions so in their own natural seats" enthralled our ears that we seemed clearly to envision them in a "rich tapestry" of feeling.

The performance began with *The Tempest*'s calm sea. In the soft titillating sensations of the wind instruments, the epic echoes of the brass and the rich undulating movements of the strings, one envisioned a natural harmony of both air and sea, but with a faint and eerie prescience that subconsciously restrained us from fully embracing Nature's peace. Texturally, it was reminiscent of the beauty of those "sounds and sweet airs, that give delight and hurt not," of "the thousand twangling instruments" which gently "hum about [our] ears," but also of a secret haunting that blazons in a savage, chaotic storm evident in the strings' sudden cyclonic power, the horns' trepidations, the loud crashing cymbals and the timpani's rumbling crescendo. Between woodwinds and strings, winds repeatedly answered waves diminishing into a sudden halt as the divine nature of the storm is emphasized. The halting silence gave way to lyrical music that introduced Miranda and Ferdinand's love, conveying a romance that proved bold enough to face strenuous opposition. It is a romance that blossoms, holds and outlasts the "storm" of life as we eventually return to the musical theme of the calm sea and the journey home.

Romeo and Juliet, Tchaikovsky's masterpiece was mesmerizing! Its inspiration for many composers speaks to the musical content of the play-text itself, for even Berlioz exclaimed, "Mon dieu, what a subject!

Everything in it seems designed for music." This is not surprising considering the puns (in the play-text) on "consort," "note," "case" and "crochet," the play on musical names of minstrels like "Simon Catling" and "Hugh Rebec," along with the singing of mournful songs and the performance of instrumental music. Though based on Shakespeare's play, the idea of a "fantasy" speaks to Tchaikovsky's own musical innovations on the play-text that move us to feel without words. The symphonic poem opened with a chorale-like introduction to the good friar Laurence with a presentiment of doom hovering in the lower strings. Nerves sat ceremoniously, already knowing what to expect, and alert to "the gray-eyed morn" that "smiles on the frowning night, / Check'ring the eastern clouds with streaks of light." For all its foreboding one could still feel a sense of beauty in pain and "many virtues excellent" with the fluttering sounds of the harp amid the mellifluous tones of the orchestra. However, with an agitative minor chord alternating between strings and woodwinds, we were suddenly carried off into the streets—in media res—to face the fighting Capulets and Montagues whose thrashing swords eventually confronted us in the quick tempo of crashing cymbals. The audience could feel Maestro Muti's emotional investment in his regulated but forceful body motions, his tempered forward lunges, his vibrato-like fists, and his swaying arms. Following an impressive climax, the violence fades into the love theme, incorporating the smooth legato lines of the English horn and violas, and emulating "a bounty as boundless as the sea," and a "love as deep."

We thus moved from deep love to the heavenly pastoral in Mahler's Symphony 4 in G major. In an interview, Maestro Muti says of Mahler's music: "Mahler always brings a kind of deep pain even in the moments where his music seems to be full of serenity or joy." Though Mahler's symphony is unrelated to Shakespeare, it is, I believe, in this sense of "painful joy" that we find its link to the emotions expressed in the first two musical renditions. This is the kind of poignant joy that was sensed in Rosa Feola's magnificent performance of *Das Himmlische Leben* (Heavenly Life). Feola's smooth bell-like voice fused beautifully with the orchestra, bodying-forth the peace of an angelic and bountiful world that leaves behind a life of weeping.

I feel very fortunate to have experienced a sample of Maestro Muti's devotion.

CHICAGO SHAKESPEARE THEATER
TUG OF WAR: FOREIGN FIRE

adapted + directed by Barbara Gaines

Liz Lauren

Making History with the Histories
Regina Buccola

In this year marked by all manner of celebrations of the 400-year history of Shakespeare's legacy, Chicago Shakespeare Theater has prepared an entry for the history books of its own with *Tug of War*. With the inclusion of the apocryphal *Edward III* as the opening salvo in this pair of mini-marathons through Shakespeare' history plays, Director Barbara Gaines has made history with these histories, as the play is rarely staged, and certainly has not been included in other recent marathon or redux versions of the two tetralogies, such as *Rose Rage* (Edward Hall 2004), *The Glorious Moment* (Michael Boyd 2008), and *Breath of Kings* (Mitchell Cushman and Weyni Mengesha 2016).

The first half of a two-part journey through the histories, *Tug of War: Foreign Fire* juxtaposes *Edward III* with *Henry V*, a play with which *Edward III* has sufficient affinities to serve as one of the bases for the claim that Shakespeare had a hand in writing it. Long regarded as apocrypha, related to the canon but not definitively part of it, *Edward III* has increasingly come to be considered a play that includes

Shakespeare's hand. Descriptions of it are now routinely included in collected works (such as the Oxford and the Norton), but productions of the play are still quite rare. Seeing it in performance is a treat in and of itself; seeing it set off against its near contemporary both in composition and content is revelatory.

Both *Edward III* and *Henry V* feature romance elements superfluous to their respective plots' narratives of English military success in France. In *Edward III*, the movement is from the king's romantic distraction with a subject—the wife of one of his loyal soldiers, the Countess of Salisbury—to a focus on foreign conquest, aided and abetted by his (pregnant) queen. In *Henry V*, the movement is from England to foreign wars in France, which conclude with thoughts of romance with the French princess, Katherine.

At the first day of rehearsal for *Tug of War*, Stuart Sherman, the scholar in residence on this production, talked about the echo chamber that reverberates through these plays. To some extent that is created by the Sisyphean struggles, over and over, to conquer the same territory, which is then lost, and conquered once more by a subsequent, successor king. The echo chamber is rendered literal on the linguistic plane, however, as successor kings verbally echo their predecessors. Barbara Gaines adds a visual element to these verbal echoes, by placing the predecessor kings back onstage as ghostly participants in the scenes in which they are invoked. So, for example, in the end of part 1 of *Henry VI*, when Exeter fumes over Winchester's promotion to Cardinal, invoking Henry V's prophecy about the false prelate and his power mongering, John Tufts, who portrays Henry V, returns to the stage to recite the prophecy along with Exeter: "'If once he come to be a cardinal, / He'll make his cap co-equal with the crown" (5.1.33-34).

In addition to underscoring such verbal echoes between the plays by placing the predecessor king onstage for events traceable to their reigns, Barbara Gaines also uses double casting to draw highlight connections across generations. In the first half of *Tug of War: Foreign Fire*, Karen Aldridge plays both the Countess of Salisbury and Margaret of Anjou (among several other roles). As the Countess, she teaches Edward III a powerful lesson about loyalty when he attempts to seduce her, and she rebuffs him, offering to die rather than betray her marriage vows. As Margaret, she inverts this dynamic, marrying King Henry VI in order to gain a level of political power to which her birth alone would never have promoted her, and as cover for her illicit relationship with a married lover among the English nobility, Suffolk. Her refusal to accept the terms of peace that Henry makes with the Duke of York, promising the crown to him, rather than to Henry and Margaret's son, Edward, keeps the civil broils raging between the Houses of Lancaster and York, straight through all three parts of *Henry VI*, and into *Richard III*.

In *Foreign Fire,* the cast is costumed in simple tunics accented with red and blue to demarcate the English and the French, and to identify the various monarchs. The monarchs wear capes emblazoned with their own faces and names, like living, breathing trading cards. These identifying marks are helpful for audiences trying to keep the various monarchs fighting with one another straight, but they also visually signify the extreme self-absorption and narcissism of these kings. I couldn't help but notice, however, that Henry V, who aligns himself with his troops as all "but warriors for the working day" (4.3.110), is seldom depicted wearing his royal robe, but is most often seen in the modest military garb of all of the members of his army. He does not simply give lip service to the idea of being one of them, he is visually identified as one of them by virtue of his attire.

With the exception of the color-coded capes and paper crowns worn by the monarchs, the palette for the production consists of somber hues of gray, and olive drab. The set is stark and plain, gray mud oozing up from the theater floor to meet the wooden slats of the stage, spaced far enough apart to allow for a variety of smoke and lighting effects. Two tires rest one atop the other downstage, and the entire upstage space is bare scaffolding, with two platform levels. Frequently throughout the production, monarchs are depicted watching battle scenes from this elevated position, remote from the main action on the stage, visually suggesting that monarchs create messes with which they do not sully themselves.

A pile of tires is mounded under the left side of the platform as you are facing the stage. A single, gilded tire is suspended from the fly space over the thrust, glowing eerily as the audience assembles, and lowered in to serve as a throne for various monarchs over the course of the production, while other tires drop in during *Henry V* to serve as chivalric steeds. As the visual signifier of what these many kings are fighting for, the gilded tire lacks even the appeal of a gilded lily; it's more like a gilded turd, and the struggle to attain it clearly emerges as a pointless waste of the many lives sacrificed.

One of the most noteworthy aspects of Barbara Gaines's staging of these history plays so full of combat is the utter absence of weapons or stage blood. A simple bit of stage choreography and physical marking is used to indicate the death of a character. As I mentioned earlier, most of the monarchs remain quite detached from the combat that kills so many of their soldiers during the performance. The "death gesture" in performance highlights the fact that Edward III, his son the Black Prince, and Henry V all die of natural causes.

Unlike most performances that have been staged in the Courtyard Theater, this production uses small microphones on all of the actors, so that one can clearly hear their lines through the many explosions that signify battle scenes, and through the music that underscores or accompanies much of the show, which is performed onstage, by a live band. Their full kit is placed under the scaffolding upstage left. Some of this music already has associations with specific wars, such as "When Johnny Comes Marching Home," which dates to the American Civil War. Some of the lyrics come from contemporary popular music, turned to haunting, elegiac effect here, such as Pink Floyd's "Us and Them...":

> Us, and them
> And after all we're only ordinary men
> Me, and you
> God only knows it's not what we would choose to do.
> Forward he cried from the rear
> and the front rank died.
> And the general sat, as the lines on the map
> moved from side to side.
> Black and blue
> And who knows which is which and who is who.
> Up and down
> But in the end it's only round and round and round.

The Dark Side of the Moon, 1973

I have seen several "marathon" or redux productions of Shakespeare's history plays at this point, and the effect generated by moving through history in this way is to produce the dizzying sense that the cycle of violence and bloodshed is a perpetual one: "in the end it's only round and round and round."

Despite the fatalism in the Pink Floyd lyrics, one of the saving graces in *Tug of War* is the music. Much war music (like "When Johnny Comes

Marching Home") is actually quite jaunty, and the cast and onstage band give spirited renditions of it. Another element of Gaines's production that makes the experience rather more enjoyable than it might seem to watch six hours of warfare (and the unpleasant lead-up and aftermath of it) is her focus on ordinary people. Scenes of French women fleeing the onslaught of the English in *Edward III*, for example, are retained here, when such moments that do not actually advance the aristocratic plot are often sacrificed in even stand-alone productions of the histories, to produce suitable running times.

In the end, it's more than round and round and round. It's an emotional roller coaster that, even after six hours, left at least this theatergoer eager for Part 2, *Civil Strife*.

Historical-Tragical-Comical-Epical
Clark Hulse

If there is one word everyone uses to describe *Tug of War,* it is "epical." Six hours, over sixty characters (plus "Soldiers," "Band," and "Chorus"), covering a century of events—and that's just Part 1: *Foreign Fire.*

Few directors can manage anything this massive. Chicago Shakespeare Theater's *Rose Rage* more than a decade ago was memorable, monumental and still only half as long as *Tug of War* will be by the time it wraps up this autumn with Part 2: *Civil Strife.* In the wrong hands, the result would be chaos. But the right directorial decisions instead can make it deeply tragic, leavened with pathos and comedy, so that the lessons of history come home. And that, in the end is what makes it epic.

Barbara Gaines has made critical and daring decisions in assembling *Tug of War* out of Shakespeare's history plays. The top-level decision was to separate out the wars between England and France from those among the English themselves, giving us the two-part structure. The second was to open with the play *Edward III,* now generally recognized as a collaboration between Shakespeare and Thomas Kyd, treating it as a prequel to the very familiar *Henry V* and the less-known *Henry VI Part 1.*

As we would expect from Gaines and Chicago Shakespeare Theater, the production is deeply respectful of the Shakespearean texts. There is no presumptuous re-writing and no awkward attempts to interweave the three plays. Allowing for merciful cuts, they are strung together like beads on a rosary of national prayer.

This in turn creates challenges. The three plays are written at different times and stylistically very different. *Edward III* features the highly rhetorical blank verse that Kyd learned from Christopher Marlowe, interspersed with fits of early-Shakespearean rhyming. It is followed by the mature language of *Henry V,* one moment royal oratory, the next moment the plain speech of common soldiers or the comically rendered accents of various ethnic groups. Then with *Henry VI Part 1,* it's back to an early rhetorical style, with occasional glimpses of Shakespearean magic.

The second challenge is the sheer number of characters. Sixty named characters in five hours running time means introducing a new character every five minutes, if they were strung out evenly. Which they are not.

If the shifty language and multiple characters create two challenges, then scene construction creates a third. Sometimes the action rattles along in nearly indistinguishable short scenes of French and English shouting at each other, followed by incoherent battles. Alternately, there are long, almost slow-motion scenes, as when King Edward III tries to seduce—and then to rape—the Countess of Salisbury, or the famous scene of "Harry in the night" before the Battle of Agincourt. The Shakespeare-Kyd script is like a series of short stories interspersed with the odd novella.

There are a lot of ways to mess this up, but one big way to make it work: Trust the material. I've seen too many contemporary productions that turn to farce, or rewriting, or forced messages, to cover up their lack of faith in the plays. Too bad, especially when Shakespeare shows them the solutions.

First, let the language be. Skilled actors adjust their delivery to the varied contours and pacing of the language, and the audience adjusts too, and quickly. It's when actors are fighting the language that audiences get restless.

Second, double up the characters and give the trusted actors a long leash. The doubling of parts was an economic necessity of the Elizabethan theater, and Shakespeare has constructed his plays to allow for the doubling. When it's done right, it becomes part of the fun. Where will Kevin Gudahl or Larry Yando or Karen Aldridge show up next? Which lead actor is under the hat of the Blue Cap Soldier? And Gaines has indeed given Gudahl and Yando and Aldridge and others their long leashes to be histrionic or solemn or clownish or whatever it takes to move things along.

Finally, let the short scenes be short and the long scenes be long. Abrupt transitions among the short scenes are covered with music or foolery or stylized stage movement. As for the long scenes—they are at the heart of Shakespeare's earliest theatrical innovations. They have a specific contour to them, which he uses with increasing mastery throughout his career. Two characters confront each other. One is in a very fixed position emotionally, but gradually, as the confrontation unfolds, the fixed character begins to give away, and ends up in the diametrically opposite emotional position from where he or she began. Think of the "willow cabin" scene in *Twelfth Night*, when Viola/Cesario comes to woo Olivia, who begins in absolute refusal and ends head-over heels infatuated. Or *Much Ado*, where Benedick goes from resolved bachelor to "horribly in love." In the tragedies, the "closet scene" is a perfect example, where Gertrude begins accusing Hamlet of having "much offended your father" (meaning Claudius) and ends with her heart cleft in twain. Or King Lear beginning as a regal bully confronting Regan and Cornwall, and ending shut out of doors, mad, and weeping.

The *Henry V* scene of "Harry in the night," walking among his soldiers, meditating on his own responsibility for the deaths that will follow, and begging the God of Battles to "think not upon my father's fault" shows the art of the long scene in its mature form. The scene in which Edward III attempts to seduce and then rape the Countess of Salisbury—the very scene that leads to the attribution of the play to Shakespeare—has to be one of his earliest experiments with the technique. It is, as has often been observed, a first draft for his narrative poem *The Rape of Lucrece.* But here Lucrece lives, persuading and shaming the king into conquering his lust.

As the scene (okay—technically two consecutive scenes that play as one) unfolds from its beginning to its long middle, I found myself wondering at first why it was there—what was it doing in the midst of a play-cycle about war? But as the scene evolved, its point became clear, and it was the first iteration of the underlying point of the whole epic. How do we overcome those savage emotional impulses that drive humans—not just *them*, but *us*—to do physical harm to others?

Once upon a time we were told in school that the Shakespearean history plays represented some sort of moral tale about the value of stable, conservative, divinely sanctioned government, but it's hard to give that much credit after the complete savagery of the twentieth century. Instead, Gaines gently de-historicizes the action, partly through the costuming, which I would call grunge-chic, and partly through the stage design. She pulls the action first toward all wars, and then toward *our* wars.

The program is laced with quotes from participants in America's wars, from 1776 to 1918. None is more central to *Tug of War* than Lincoln's First Inaugural:

> The mystic chords of memory, stretching from every battlefield and patriot grave, to every living heart and hearthstone, all over this broad land, will yet swell the chorus of the Union, when again touched as surely they will be, by the better angels of our nature.

The evolution of the long scene in *Edward III* drives us to this stark truth—that the better angels can prevail, though too often, too late. Edward's shame overcomes his lust. At Calais, he again remembers to "master our affections," and pardons the burghers who have offered their lives to ransom the city. At the gates of Harfleur, Henry V restrains the "dogs of war" that would wreak murder and rapine upon the hapless city. Each time, though, the restraint is temporary, and more violence breaks out, just as a long and horrible war ensued before America's better angels restored Lincoln's union.

Gaines has made it her project to show the wars through the eyes of the common soldier. Who better to supply her the material than the wise and eloquent child of a glove-maker, armed with a high-school education, who, legend tells us, poached deer before running off to join the theater? What more to learn from our own long scenes of bitterness than how the better angels of our nature might touch our own heartstrings in this time of violent passions?

ARTISTS BREAKING LIMITS + EXPECTATIONS
TWELFTH NIGHT

by William Shakespeare
adapted + directed by Katie Yohe
music direction by Peter Van Kempen
choreography by Kendra Van Kempen
presented by Chicago Shakespeare Theater

Michael Brosilow

Achieving Greatness
Timothy J. Duggan

Several months ago I was invited to attend the May 28 performance of *Twelfth Night* by Artists Breaking Limits and Expectations (A.B.L.E.) in the Courtyard at Chicago Shakespeare Theater and to write about it for City Desk 400. The A.B.L.E. ensemble is comprised of twenty actors, ages 14-21, each with Down syndrome or other developmental challenges. I accepted the invitation with a combination of anticipation and anxiety. As the parent of a child with significant special needs, I welcome the opportunity to examine extracurricular programs that allow access to cultural and literary enrichment for students who are often denied those experiences in school. As a Shakespeare teacher and performer, I have worked with students for years and know something of the emotional intensity Shakespeare's language provides. At the same time, I am perhaps overly cautious about enrichment programming that places students with special needs in situations that may be overwhelming or developmentally inappropriate for them.

Arriving at the crowded theater and taking my seat, I perused the program and saw that virtually all of the actors are veterans of the company, many of them performing in their seventh, eighth, even tenth production. So there must be something that keeps them coming back. My anxiety was further relieved when Katie Yohe, co-founder of A.B.L.E., came to the stage to introduce the show and explain a bit about the process through which it came to be. She described the A.B.L.E. philosophy that the actors should be able to "have fun" and concentrate on their relationship with their scene partners, rather than worry about memorization. Volunteer teaching artists and facilitators, holding scripts, would physically shadow the actors on stage, speaking the lines in two or three-word bursts, echoed by the actors.

The method worked. Somehow, standing behind the actors, the facilitators in black A.B.L.E. logo t-shirts were able to articulate the lines, project their reading for the audience, cue the actors, and yet *not* steal focus from the actors themselves. For their part, the actors infused their recitation of lines with flourish and intensity original to themselves, drawing the audience into a circle of understanding. Even ensemble members with less developed verbal abilities demonstrated passion for the intentions of their characters through vocal tone and gesture. Simple yet elegant costumes and accessories helped to identify the characters, as each was performed by different actors in different scenes, with each actor playing more than one character during the course of the performance. Occasional physical and verbal ad-libs on the part of the actors added to the levity in the production. Peter Van Kempen, one of the teaching artists, served as narrator to link together scenes. Van Kempen also provided music, along with his brother Paul and Kaylie Honkala.

This show was the third production of *Twelfth Night* I've seen as part of the Shakespeare 400 Chicago celebration, and each production has illuminated a different side of the work. In the rock and roll production by Britain's Filter Theatre, the audience was treated as collaborators and the focus was on the zaniness of the characters and situations. In Chicago Shakespeare Theater's *Short Shakespeare! Twelfth Night* production, a streamlined text and clear direction invited young audience members into the story. In the A.B.L.E. show, the essential experience for me was in witnessing the process whereby Shakespeare's language emboldens and invigorates young people who too often are denied the chance to do serious artistic and creative work in school. I wondered whether I would find Shakespeare in the show, or whether the pleasure would be in seeing the ensemble members perform. The answer was yes and yes. The level of challenge for the actors was both appropriate and rigorous, while the language of Shakespeare—the actual words and exchanges of dialogue, even in a script that was cut liberally—carried the day.

While we might expect that all students are routinely exposed to Shakespeare in school, that exposure is not always authentic. Working in schools throughout the Chicago area, I have seen a growing trend of replacing Shakespeare's language, especially for students with special needs, in favor of more simplified versions called "No Fear Shakespeare" or other "adapted from Shakespeare" resources. As the Lexile scores (a simplistic mathematical formula for determining text difficulty) in the "No Fear" version appear to match what is considered appropriate for struggling students' levels of comprehension (based on equally inappropriate tests), many teachers choose to march students through these lifeless scripts to avoid the difficulty, the confusion, and the ultimate illumination that is Shakespeare's own language. If A.B.L.E.'s *Twelfth Night* demonstrated anything, it was that fidelity to Shakespeare's language is essential. Cut the text, fill in the gaps with storytelling and gesture, but don't take apart the powerful speeches and exchanges of dialogue that make Shakespeare magical. Hearing Viola/Cesario speak, with conviction and a smile, "Excellently done, if God did all," provides much more pleasure than listening to a watered down version. And in this production, the echo effect of hearing two or three words spoken by the facilitator, then spoken again by the actor, allowed the words to submerge themselves in our minds:

> **Facilitator:** O,
> **Actor:** O,
> **Facilitator:** then unfold,
> **Actor:** then unfold,
> **Facilitator:** the passion,
> **Actor:** the passion,
> **Facilitator:** of my love.
> **Actor:** of my love.

Occasionally, an actor would anticipate the next words to come and would complete the line uninterrupted by the facilitator, which provided a thrilling reversal to the more common experience of hearing an actor lose a line.

Performing comedy is tricky under any circumstances, and even the most seasoned actors fear that audiences won't respond. Considering the name of the A.B.L.E. organization, "Artists Breaking Limits and Expectations," we might expand our notion of whose limits and whose expectations are being broken. Conventionally, we would think it is the artists' limits and the audience's expectations that are challenged through the work. But this group not only challenges expectations of what students with Down Syndrome can or cannot do, it also breaks the audience's limits regarding how we perceive Shakespeare's 400-year-old works. It calls into question who owns Shakespeare, who has the right to perform Shakespeare, and what makes Shakespeare appealing. I would suggest that the A.B.L.E. ensemble actors own Shakespeare on a personal level that I, having studied Shakespeare for over thirty years, cannot match. Actors in the company have developed a chemistry that transcends the play. They are serious, yet they display a sense of humor. They want their show to be a success, and they care about the story they tell.

It was nearly 50 years ago that Homer "Murph" Swander in California called on Shakespeare scholars and teachers to use performance as a way to immerse students in Shakespeare's texts. "It's a script, not a play!" Swander told his students, and he enlisted actors from the Royal Shakespeare Company to help spread his method. Getting students up on their feet and moving, speaking Shakespeare's language, mining the text for clues to unlock intention and meaning — Swander's teaching innovation has since become a well-known approach, carried forward by teachers around the world. Shakespeare's language comes to life when activated on stage. I can't help but think that Swander, now ninety-four, would have been moved if he had seen the A.B.L.E. *Twelfth Night*.

And who was this performance for? It was for the actors who would not have this opportunity without the grace of the A.B.L.E volunteers. It was for the families who got to experience their children performing Shakespeare on a professional stage. It was for the A.B.L.E. teaching artists and facilitators who believe in the power of theater to transform lives. Perhaps most of all, it was for the rest of us who were given the occasion to deepen our own humanity.

Katie Yohe and Lawrence Kern founded A.B.L.E. with the mission to provide "performing arts opportunities through which individuals with Down syndrome and other developmental special needs feel accepted and empowered to discover their own unique voices, and develop the confidence and skills to share who they are and what they are ABLE to do." In order to establish that confidence and the feeling of acceptance and empowerment, an audience is required, and the audience must be moved by what transpires on stage. I believe, having seen the A.B.L.E. group work their magic with *Twelfth Night*, that every participant in the program knows what an impact they had on their audience, which is what every serious actor craves. The joy with which the entire ensemble sang the closing song, having cast a spell and taken us to Illyria with Viola and Sebastian, positively radiated from the stage. The standing ovation they received was as authentic as their performance.

This experience convinces me even more deeply that all youth must be granted access to extracurricular programs that allow them to stretch their limits. The Individuals with Disabilities Education Act mandates that all students be afforded a free and appropriate public education in the least restrictive environment, with access to supports to help them succeed. Sometimes, evidently, the least restrictive environment for personal, academic, and artistic growth comes outside the confines of the school. We must pursue and support endeavors of this kind.

Bravo Colleen, Quincy, Marissa, Alena, Rachel, Jack, Benjamin, Samuel, Natalia, Fletcher, Andrew, Emily, Emily, Lucas, Mila, Claire, Sam, Sam, Hannah, Lucy, and all the A.B.L.E. teaching artists and facilitators. Bravo!

"One face, one voice, one habit, and two persons": A.B.L.E.'s *Twelfth Night*

Alexandra Bennett

It is a rare event indeed for any artistic production to elicit unequivocal delight from an audience. Yet that's exactly what happened on May 28 on the mainstage of Chicago Shakespeare Theater as Artists Breaking Limits + Expectations (A.B.L.E.) brought their engaging and—above all—joyful production of *Twelfth Night* to a near-capacity matinee crowd.

Founded in 2010 as the Teen Drama Troupe at Gigi's Playhouse Chicago, A.B.L.E. is a company whose mission is to provide performing arts opportunities for individuals with Down syndrome and other developmental special needs. Its productions focus on empowering these actors to discover their own voices and self-expression so that they can share both who they are and what they can do with a wide audience by developing confidence and skills in each production. The company has put on ten theatrical productions and a feature film so far, and the full engagement of the audience with the twenty young actors onstage for this show is a testament to just how well the company showcases the talents of its members.

In keeping with the comedy of shifting identities in *Twelfth Night*, each actor played more than one role, and each role was performed by more than one actor: simple costume changes clearly notified the audience as to who was playing whom at any given moment in the performance. In order to prioritize the playing at the heart of theater, A.B.L.E. cleverly did away with the need for actors to memorize lines or to be hidden from view by thick scripts: rather, each actor was accompanied onstage by a facilitator, who dropped the lines in piece by piece for the actor to interpret as s/he saw fit. Rather than getting caught up in remembering words, or in the possible complexities of Shakespeare's language, the actors could thus make full use of their voices and bodies to convey what the lines meant, resulting in some brilliantly vivid moments as an exasperated Maria expressed frustration with the dance-party antics of Sir Toby and his friends, an enamored Orsino emphasized his love for Olivia, and Malvolio gleefully and defiantly capered to show off his glamorous yellow stockings at the play's finale. The genuineness of each inflection and gesture made every moment absolutely true within the story being told, and implicitly provoked useful questions: why shouldn't Malvolio show off his stockings, after all, if he looks as wonderful in them as these actors do? In a play revolving around the changeability of human behavior, where Olivia can go from deep mourning to the giddiness of love in one scene, the diverse interpretations of each character by these individual performers made the topsy-turvy world of Illyria come brilliantly to life. The audience roared its approval and applauded the entrances and exits of each actor, sharing in the evident fun of the onstage action.

By the time the concluding ensemble song and accompanying dance was finished, my hands were red from clapping and the grin on my face mirrored those of everyone around me. Unquestionably, A.B.L.E.'s excellent and engaging production of *Twelfth Night* reminded us all that theater—and Shakespeare—is for everybody.

THE IMPROVISED SHAKESPEARE COMPANY
IMPROVISED SHAKESPEARE

Koury Angelo

Elizabethan Verse, Modern Jokes, Prostitution and Llamas
Lydia Craig

With other excited patrons, most clutching drinks from the theater bar, I joined a packed-out audience at the iO Theater on May 28, and waited to see why the Improvised Shakespeare Company is one of Chicago's most popular weekend theater acts. Part of this group's draw, of course, is the uniqueness of each performance. As the audience discovers prior to the show, this all-male acting company, suitably clad in white Renaissance laced shirts and breeches, improvises a play every performance night using "Shakespearean" language and plot devices. The title of each play derives from audience suggestions and neither plot nor dialogue can be recreated. Therefore, unless another critic went to see the same performance, this review is your only chance ever to read about the improbably titled play "Prostitution, or Llamas," improvised and acted by Matt Young, John Sabine, Asher Perlman, Brendan Dowling and Ric Walker.

How "Shakespearean" is this performance model? Obviously, Shakespeare's plays themselves were repeatedly performed and such performances relied on the play text, though the plurality of *Lear* versions, for instance, indicates the play text's adaptive fluidity.

However, just because Shakespeare's rhyming lines were already written does not mean that his comic actors recited them in that way, as I realized while watching this troupe connect with the crowd through their rhyming abilities. During this performance, the audience waited in suspense for the rhyme to be justified and usually burst into applause as each speaker concluded the second line of a couplet. Occasionally an audience member would suggest an ending ("ass" for "grass"), which the actor in rhyming difficulties would try to avoid using ("lass"). This jovial, bantering relationship between actors and audience evokes the role of the Shakespearean clown, or fool, who directly addressed and competed with spectators in wordplay.

The first scene showed farmer Henry (Brendan Dowling) and his loving wife Margaret (John Sabine) in the first of two subplots discussing how to improve their financial situation during England's drought. "Heaven unto me did you send/And you are my bank account, and my little dividend!" exclaimed Henry. "Aye, and you, be ever happy—I'm tired of seeing you pouting/And we shall have a number, a number most routing!" responded Margaret. After debating selling the plentiful llamas in their field, or writing a children's book about llamas, they decided that Henry must return to his old employment—moonlighting as stripper "Officer Mike" at the epic bachelorette party of Princess Elizabeth (Matt Young). There in the final act he met her friends: inexperienced Shauna, Sarah, Susan of the many ex-boyfriends, and perpetually dismal, milk-guzzling Deb, the girlfriend of a much older man ("When I stopped looking, I met Samuel. It's so great. We just talk"). To everyone's horror, Henry was unmasked as a *married man*, but pacified the girls by explaining his family's plight.

The main plot involved the King of England (Ric Walker) insisting against Princess Elizabeth's will that she marry the French dauphin, Prince Girard (played to coy Gallic perfection by John Sabine). Meanwhile, the Queen (Asher Perlman) and the dauphin carried on a passionate, secret affair. In a running joke, he constantly feared revealing France's most important state secret—the water cycle—that could end England's drought. "You are ze oxygen to mah fier, you are ze oxygen to mah wahter," said Prince Girard lasciviously to the Queen, then covered his horrified mouth and gasped, "Ah have zaid too much!" In a second subplot, virginal woodcutter and orphan Edmund (Matt Young) journeyed through London's streets to buy some love from ladies of the night. Having met the very weird courtesans "Beehive" (deep-voiced, slow-speaking), "Lydia, the Bat-Cave Dweller," and "Rock," Edmund began to get cold feet and eventually backed out: "I don't like the scary way that one talks...I feel like I went down the wrong street." Rhythmically stomping their feet in unison and converging around the terrified woodcutter in a wild dance that included swinging from the ceiling beams, they chanted, "You've got to make a choice! / Edmund, use your voice!" Several audience members were singing the catchy refrain at the bar during the intermission. After that impressive end to the first half, I felt that, were they ever to make an appearance, the llamas had no chance as rivals to the vivacious prostitutes.

A few problems emerged as the play concluded, but such is the comedic potential and license of the Improvised Shakespeare Company that these simply added meta-theatrical humor. The llamas dropped out of the plot almost entirely, but no one cared. A doubling nightmare ensued since Matt Young played both Princess Elizabeth and her suitor Edmund/Prince Edwardo of Spain, compelling him to constantly switch sides during "their" flirtatious conversation. In a rare listening failure, an actor mentioned the death of the King of France, to be corrected instantly by the dauphin and a few seconds later by a messenger entering to announce, "The King of Spain is dead." "Yes, we already established that!" exclaimed another actor, joining in audience laughter. Ends needed to be tied up, and so the wedding priest inexplicably revealed himself to be the dauphin's best friend Jean-Luc "in disguise!" Ultimately, Princess Elizabeth married Prince Edwardo (once Edmund), her mother married Prince Girard, and the couples' powerful loves brought showers of rain and herds of llamas (imaginary, unfortunately) pouring into the landscape.

Besides the delight of seeing twenty-first-century actors with great chemistry compose poetry and prose in Shakespearean language, hearing constant anachronistic references and modern slang mixed in alongside has an incredibly comical and doubly relevant effect whether you know the Bard's lingo or not. Past and present make beautiful comedy together, as Shakespeare himself realized. Just as his audience would have responded to the wild tavern scenes between Prince Hal and Falstaff during a king's reign occurring generations before while simultaneously "getting" contemporary allusions, so we also laugh both at the wit that parodies Shakespeare and the wit that mocks our own social behaviors and stereotypes.

Improv[ed] Shakespeare: The iO Theater's Improvised Shakespeare Company

Hilary J. Gross

On Friday, October 14, 2016, The Improvised Shakespeare Company performed the opening and closing night of "No Handlebars" to a packed house.[16] A year ago, on October 24, 2015, I saw the opening and closing night of "King Henry the 27th." The audience helps to choose the title, and, Shakespearean or not, each performance has been a joy. The Improvised Shakespeare Company's unique productions, each the opening and closing night of a completely new improvised Shakespearean parody, makes for a night out full of comradery and laughter.

The iO Theater moved in 2014 to a new larger location in Old Town, recreating their plain black minimalist set from Wrigleyville, providing both row and table seating, and expanding their bar into an independent space. I admit I missed some of the old theater's hole-in-the-wall ambiance, but the move also provided iO more space to work, and a location away from some of the complications of being a theater next door to the Cubs. As you enter the theater, you first pass the bar to stock up on whatever snacks or drinks you might need during the performance, though you can put in orders during the show if you are seated at one of the tables. Once you enter the space, and the show is about to begin, the mood takes on a celebratory feel, as the audience is amped up by multi-colored strobe lights and a sort of updated intense Elizabethan tune, all before the cast even enters to take suggestions.

What makes this "Improvised Shakespeare" and not just Long-Form Improv though? The cast takes nothing more than a title from the audience to begin their hour-long performance, with a break for intermission, and from that title, crafts a plot and accompanying dramatis personae using an arsenal of early modern performance tropes. On the most recent night I had the pleasure, the cast took a bike-related prompt, "No Handlebars" and twisted it to focus on an intense drama featuring a facial hair competition. A quick synopsis: two orphaned-sisters, Celia and Laurel live in a convent, under the care of Mallory Malcontent, and dream of the world outside. At the same time, the

---

[16] The cast on this night included Asher Perlman, Brendan Dowling, Ric Walker, Randall Harr and Tim Sniffen.

Duke's two sons, Orlando and Alonso, prepare for the Annual Festival and take into their guardianship a poor gardener, Betrando, and hijinks ensue, complete with love plots, reunited families, and unexpected twists. While "No Handlebars" included many recognizably "Shakespearean" characteristics, the Bard was fond of twin shenanigans, lost children, mentors in revelry, competition between brothers, and suspiciously reformed baddies, as well as impressive performative virtuoso moments of prologue and epilogue, which the ISC takes on in the form of improvised rhyming iambic pentameter, ISC's performance also featured elements of early modern court masques, as a catalogue of competitors in the facial hair competition paraded across the stage, and a nod toward Restoration Comedy with its penchant for on-the-nose alliterative names like Mallory Malcontent (her name later changes to Mallory Satisfied). While this may not make the performance strictly "Shakespearean," the Improvised Shakespeare Company brings together seventeenth-century performance methods and its recognizable genres, in order to create a night of modern comedic entertainment which also showcases an intense familiarity and expertise in the methods and practices of English theatre historiography and literature.

Perhaps the most enjoyable aspect of the show is watching the cast collaborate. Of course, this is true of any good Improv cast, but here, in a production named for the Bard, it harkens back to a method of highly ensemble performance, and makes a passing nod at "original practice" recasting Shakespeare in a modern genre. The actors must again hang on their scene partners' every word because they themselves don't know for sure what comes next, as they wait for their cue wherever it may appear. Long-Form Improv, though without the scripted "Parts" of a full *dramatis personae*, arguably has more in common to the theater as Shakespeare knew it than modern performances of Shakespeare's own plays sometimes do. Though the audience does sit in chairs, they react, call out, eat, drink, and generally enjoy themselves much like Falstaff and company do in *Henry IV Part 1*. ISC's answer to Falstaff's question "What, shall we be merry? Shall we have a play extempore?" (*1 Henry IV*, 2.4 280-1) is a resounding and joyous "yes," as is an especially fitting answer in the improv world.

The cast is always ready to play on stage, to support each other, and yes, to tease each other, especially when they've introduced a hyperbolic and complicated reference, as they did in "No Handlebars" on multiple occasions, putting each other on the spot to repeat the reference in full.

The cast also plays intensely with anachronism and specific call-outs for the audience. For example, when Ric Walker, playing Alonso, one of the Duke's sons, delivers a soliloquy describing his secret plan to beat his brother in the festival competition with his expandable wingspan handlebar moustache and win the love of Celia, he delivers an aside to note that he would not win her love without receiving her "consent enthusiastically." During this speech, the audience cheers and whoops and whistles their approval. In so doing, he manages to call attention to a major weakness of much early modern drama, a general lack of agency for female characters, and include a modern reference to education about consent as well.

It is somewhat odd however, that this skillfully presented critique of the dominant historic, and decidedly masculine, discourse comes from a man in a troupe of only men. Though it is perhaps significant that the moment cited above came from Ric Walker, the only PoC cast member that evening, and one of what appears to be only two black members of seventeen total players (the other fifteen of whom present as white cismen). In a city as diverse as Chicago, with as vibrant a theater and comedy community as this city boasts of, it seems, at least from the outside, like a problem worth the ISC's and iO's attention. This issue of diversity also comes up when considering that the ISC's cast is made up exclusively of individuals of the male persuasion.

I understand the reference to Original Practice performance in parody, and I understand the creativity and power of cross-gendered casting and drag performance. Though playing gendered stereotypes solely for comedic effect comes with its own baggage, I do feel the ISC, in general, is very respectful of their gendered performances and skillfully critiques the binary, as when Celia herself wins the facial hair competition in "No Handlebars." However, if the creative investment of the company is in cross-gendered casting, would not having actors perform genders different from their own but still within a mixed-gender cast also satisfy that concept? Or, if the investment is rather in the primarily single-gendered cast, why not have multiple casts? I would love to see female improvisers performing Shakespearean Improv with the ISC, and I don't think that I'm alone. Diversity of experience and identity in the cast will only improve an already strong show. Hell, I'd pay to see a double feature. Perhaps "No Handlebars, Parts 1 and 2" next time I'm in town.

TIM CROUCH
I, MALVOLIO

written + performed by Tim Crouch
presented by Chicago Shakespeare Theater

Greg Goodale

Malvolio and the Ethics of Spectatorship
Andrea Stevens

Staged in the intimate black-box "Upstairs at Chicago Shakespeare" venue, Tim Crouch's *I, Malvolio* retells the plot of *Twelfth Night* from the perspective of the puritanical steward of Olivia's household. Some of the play's earliest readers and spectators were likewise struck by the rules-obsessed Malvolio, who seems wholly out of place in a romantic comedy; in a diary entry describing a 1602 performance, for example, John Manningham ignored all other plotlines to focus exclusively on the steward's public shaming, and in his own copy of the Second Folio, King Charles II crossed out *Twelfth Night* and wrote in its place *Malvolio*. In Shakespeare, Malvolio is made to pay for his puritanism by being tricked into thinking his mistress is in love with him, after which he's locked in a "dark house" and treated as if he were mad. Crouch sets his production in the immediate aftermath of this 'notorious abuse.' As the audience files in we see him already standing onstage in a ridiculous hat, yellow stockings, and stained underwear, a sign reading "Turkey Cock" hanging off his back. And quite possibly a little bit mad after this poor treatment, although he keeps insisting he isn't.

The performance's central conceit is the character's adversarial relationship to the audience: if Malvolio is on the side of restraint, order, and moderation, we as theatrical spectators must necessarily be aligned with his enemies, the pleasure-seeking Sir Tobys, Festes, and Marias of the world. Throughout the roughly seventy-five-minute production Malvolio interrupts the narrative to sneer "you find this funny, do you," also reminding us that he'll eventually "have his revenge on the pack of us," one of the few lines drawn directly from the play. At times Malvolio's complaints seem eminently reasonable, if crankily delivered: it *would* be irritating to suffer a house guest like Sir Toby; it *is* odd that Olivia—having fallen in love with one person—happily accepts a substitute look-alike of the "appropriate" gender. As Malvolio, Crouch, moreover, movingly evinces the hurt and humiliation of being tricked into thinking that Olivia loves him.

Given its recurring threat of "revenge," *I, Malvolio* repeatedly asks its audience to reflect on the ethics of spectatorship—what exactly is funny about watching someone's humiliation? Behind this we might also consider the resentment of the actor who nightly walks onstage to solicit the approval of strangers. For the most part, however, I suspect the audience felt no particular qualms at all about watching what is an ultimately lighthearted take on the source material.

To be sure, those singled out for individual attention and abuse seemed to enjoy his improvisational banter very much. The majority of these "improvisatory" moments were clearly carefully scripted, for example appeals for members to come onstage to help him with various costume changes, but in no way seemed forced; Crouch is a dab hand at reading and interacting with his audience. Perhaps the closest the play came to eliciting more nervous, self-conscious, or complicit laughter was a bit of stage action that veered altogether from Shakespeare's plot: at one point it looks as if Malvolio is going to hang himself with the help of two spectators pulled from the crowd, one holding the chair, the other the rope, only for Malvolio to abandon the enterprise altogether. If he's going to get his revenge, it won't be this.

Instead, at the end of the play we see him literally reconstitute himself by stripping down to a thong only to don period costume, wig, and whiteface makeup, Malvolio once more his authoritative self (and if we laughed at the sight of his exposed buttocks well, more proof of what

Malvolio already believes about the moral probity of playgoers). Earlier in the play Malvolio had admonished the audience to sit up straight and pay attention while he briefly exited. He does the same again—only this time, he never comes back. Malvolio's revenge is thus to deny the audience the expected rhythms of theatrical closure—no real ending, no curtain call, just a trailing off, with the audience unsure as to what to do next.

I, Malvolio is the fourth in a series of solo plays that, in Crouch's words, "look at things through the eyes of Shakespeare's lesser characters." If these earlier plays were written with younger audiences in mind, the program notes tells us that *I, Malvolio* was designed to appeal to a broader age range, but I still thought it seemed to imagine younger audiences who may not be that familiar with Shakespeare—this show a gateway drug to the real thing, as it were. Given his talent for improvisation, I would love to see Crouch engage with riskier or edgier material and to push the idea of the audience's discomfort to an even greater degree.

Malvolio's Revenge; or, Disabusing the Audience
Elizabeth Elaine Tavares

Experimental thespian Tim Crouch's *I, Malvolio* is a study in what it means to laugh at another's sorrow. The play is part of a sequence focusing on lesser, unsung, and often unlikable characters from Shakespeare's oeuvre, including Caliban, Peaseblossom, Banquo, and Cinna. Comedies like *Twelfth Night*, from which Crouch draws for the roughly ninety-minute piece, were and are vehicles for compelling ensemble work, while tragedies often serve a celebrity front-man. Part of the ingenuity of this one-man Shakespearean comedy is to explore, in form and in content, where exactly that sweet spot between comedy and discomfort lies.

You find this funny, do you?

"You find this funny, do you?": Crouch's Malvolio asked this of us over and over as he subjected himself to a series of embarrassments. While cracking wise at the average age of the afternoon matinee audience, he summoned up three students to aid in his public shaming. One, a boy he nicknamed "Bluey" for his blue shirt, he had kick him in response to the signs on his back: the first read "turkey cock" and second "kick me." Another, "Pinky," for his pink shorts, was asked alongside a young woman to help facilitate an on-stage hanging. While at first the audience's laughter was immediate in response to these antics, by the time we reached the hanging scene the laughter was forced and uncomfortable—the audience uncertain of the script they were to follow. Routinely pointing at the audience to accuse us of sins varietal, as much as Malvolio inquired of our sense of humor he also intoned that he would certainly have "revenge on the pack of you."

Mourning, interrupted

Structuring the arc of Malvolio's interrogations of us was his re-narrativizing the plot of *Twelfth Night*. Crouch makes two particularly astute observations about the possible motivations compelling his character's puritanical attitude. First, he reminds us that Malvolio not only organized and served for the lifetime of Olivia's recently deceased brother, but also her father. Second, he reflects on the fast approach of Sir

Toby Belch, whose behaviors interrupt the fragile routine the household has barely had a chance to cobble together after these deaths. Aside from the interloping Sir Toby and Sir Andrew Aguecheek, arguably Malvolio and the Fool are the only male members of the household left— reorganizing the flow of power in the household into a matriarchy. Not only is Malvolio a Puritan trapped in the world of a play, but he is trapped in a household now run by women. Accosted by the constant interruptions of Sir Toby, Sir Andrew, the Duke Orsino and his household, Malvolio is unable to move through the natural progression of mourning.

Many a good hanging

In this light, the play quite literally adds insult to Malvolio's emotional injury when Sir Toby and his crew bait him with the forged letter. The letter makes an appearance on stage, crumpled at the outset and then orbited around by Malvolio as if it were the gravitational center of his injury—a site of trauma he can't help but rehearse. Rotating, he weighs his own sanity, insisting that despite the "ontological duality" of his presence in a theater—simultaneously in Illyria and in Chicago—he is "not mad." Working through this ontological duality with a speedy set of jokes of local color (no few references to the presidential race were made), Malvolio works through the sanity of his cross-gartered response to the letter. We are reminded briefly of the darkest moment in *Twelfth Night*, Malvolio's entrapment in a pit by the Fool to keep him from impeding the more procreatively and hierarchically suitable coupling of his lady to a mysterious twin she has only just met. (Again, his desire to slow that courtship seems anything but insane outside the world of Shakespeare's play.) More than the letter, the pit is the catharsis, the event that underscores the line where laughing at the ways in which the ego and the body will out crosses into schadenfreude. He concludes: we, the audience, are Sir Toby in this Chicago theater; we are the bully on which he must have revenge.

Malvolio's revenge

And he does get it. In the last act of *I, Malvolio*, our leading man rejects his noose and instead strips out of his soiled undergarments down to a leopard-printed thong. From there, he gradually applied face powder and period costume to reassume his position as rule-maker and -enforcer of the hierarchy that bullied him so. At the end of the first act, we were told to sit up straight and stay exactly as we were while he stepped off stage; he returned rather immediately from what seemed like an otherwise pointless exercise. Now re-dressed, we were instructed by Malvolio once again to sit up straight, keeping just as we were until his return. He left, and we waited. And waited. Awkward shuffling commenced. A clever member of the audience shouted out, "Come back, Malvolio! All is forgiven!" Crouch had sacrificed his applause so that Malvolio might have his revenge on the audience, and by extension, Sir Toby. We never knew when the play had ended—and still don't. We never knew when it had started, for that matter, since Malvolio had been on the stage waiting for us since we arrived and the black box space used universal lighting throughout.

By examining Malvolio's motivations for clues as to why he may have been such a target for abuse in the world of *Twelfth Night*, *I, Malvolio* confirms that this character is in fact deserving of dislike, but not for the reasons one might assume. While Malvolio spends the adaptation accusing and coercing the audience into playing the role of the bully, as the Puritan valet he has far greater bullying to answer for—in upholding the social norms and mechanizing aristocratic hierarchy—than his audience. By exploring the zone where humor transforms into hate, *I, Malvolio* asks us to consider what is to be gained by troubling the rule-makers.

CHICAGO HUMANITIES FESTIVAL
+ CHICAGO SHAKESPEARE THEATER
SILENT SHAKESPEARE

featuring Judith Buchanan

Still from "Romeo and Juliet" (Fox, 1916)

Silent Film's Visual Poetry
Regina Buccola

On Monday, June 6, Chicago Shakespeare Theater and the Chicago Humanities Festival partnered to bring Judith Buchanan, Professor of Film and Literature at the University of York, to the Music Box Theatre for a delightful 90-minute, multi-media presentation devoted to Shakespeare on silent film. In introducing Professor Buchanan, Chicago Humanities Festival Board Chair Clark Hulse observed that it might seem oxymoronic, given the emphasis placed on Shakespeare's language (as both poet and assiduous neologist), to consider his oeuvre performed in silence. Buchanan echoed this sentiment in her opening remarks, but assured us that the silent celluloid would have a poetry all its own, which proved to be true in her captivating collaboration with actors Erika Haaland and Joe Bianco, and musician Matt Deitchman.

Buchanan framed her lecture, part of the Shakespeare 400 Chicago festivities, by invoking the corresponding celebrations for the tercentenary in 1916, including dramatic readings by Haaland and

Bianco of excerpts from the ten special supplements in *The New York Times* that marked the occasion, and with discussion of a cluster of silent films from the year: *The Real Thing at Last* (J. M. Barrie and Edmund Gwenn), *Macbeth* (Sir Herbert Beerbohm-Tree), and two competing productions of *Romeo and Juliet* (Beverly Bayne and Francis X. Bushman for Metro, and Theda Bara and Harry Hilliard for Fox). Of the 400 silent Shakespeare films known to exist, Buchanan noted that only around forty survive today (though archival research does occasionally turn up another here or there). Barrie's *The Real Thing at Last* was one such casualty, but a sufficiently detailed description survived of the film's cheeky comparative study of a British and an American film production of *Macbeth* for Haaland and Bianco to give a spirited (and hilarious) rendition of the contrasts. The British film, for example, offered a prim Lady Macbeth, daintily dabbing at a spot of blood, whereas the American film was awash in blood and gore.

Fox and Metro went head to head with their *Romeo and Juliet*s in 1916. Buchanan wryly noted that Metro tried to get out ahead of the competition by advertising their film as the only one worth seeing, while Fox openly urged audiences to put the two films side by side, and judge for themselves which they preferred. According to Buchanan, Fox's marketing instincts proved correct: the reviews—and the box office receipts—for both films established that Shakespeare on film, silent or no, had all the makings of a blockbuster, particularly when the ingénue Juliet was played by the vamp Theda Bara.

Buchanan demonstrated her considerable skill as both a director and an archivist in her presentation. Noting that her research indicates that, at times, live actors voiced lines in accompaniment to the films, either next to the stage or from behind the screen, Buchanan put Haaland and Bianco through a similar approach to Richard's confrontation with the Lady Anne in Act 1 of *Richard III*, complete with rapier sound effects. First, the pair staged the scene for the audience themselves. Then, Buchanan screened the 1911 film of Frank Benson's performance in the title role at the Memorial Theatre in Stratford-upon-Avon, while Haaland and Bianco voiced the same lines (and scraped and clashed the rapiers at the appropriate junctures). The result was compelling, and demonstrated how effectively these films might have conveyed a rich experience of Shakespeare to early twentieth-century movie theater audiences.

Reaching back to 1907 for another lost film, Buchanan stitched together two completely different images from two completely different archives to offer a tiny glimpse into Georges Méliès's *Shakespeare Writing Julius Caesar*. She stumbled upon a still of a film set attributed in the lower right-hand corner to Méliès while working in one archive that looked familiar to her. "Watch the chair," she advised us, projecting the still, and then dissolving it into a still shot from the film from a totally different archive, in which Méliès, as Shakespeare, slouches in the chair, while the scene he has been struggling to write from *Julius Caesar* unfolds around him. This screen dissolve of one shot into the other was, she told us triumphantly, the first reunion of these two disparate images since they sank into the obscurity of their current archival homes.

Throughout, Matt Deitchman offered wonderfully sensitive scoring to accompany each film clip on piano. One of the more arresting performances in the evening's presentation came from Asta Nielsen's 1920 cross-dressed depiction of Hamlet. As Buchanan explained, the film establishes at the outset the conceit that Hamlet is a woman, cross-dressed as a prince (for whatever reason)—a sartorial fiction the truth of which is known only by Hamlet herself and Gertrude. The audience laughed as Nielsen swooned next to Horatio in scenes of their meeting at Wittenberg, and subsequent meanderings at Elsinore. As Buchanan tartly noted, Nielsen's cross-dressed performance choice gives Hamlet—who scarcely seems to need it—yet one more thing about which to wax melancholic.

Silent film buffs who missed the opportunity to see this wonderful presentation can access parts of it via Buchanan's book, *Shakespeare on Silent Film: An Excellent Dumb Discourse* (Cambridge University Press, 2009), or the British Film Institute's DVDs *Silent Shakespeare* and *Play On!*.

YO-YO MA WITH MUSICIANS FROM CHICAGO SYMPHONY ORCHESTRA
A DISTANT MIRROR

Todd Rosenberg

Once and Future Music:
Yo-Yo Ma's Not-So-Distant Mirror
Rebecca L. Fall

Yo-Yo Ma's *A Distant Mirror* began with a bang, followed by a jingle. The beat of a *riqq*, an Arabic tambourine, rang out from the back of the main floor. Percussionist Cynthia Yeh made her way through the aisle to the front of the hall, pounding a joyful, syncopated rhythm. When she arrived at the foot of the stage, Ma's voice boomed through the hall: "If music be the food of love," he started, before a chorus of voices shouted "Play on!" Answering their own directive, the rest of the ensemble burst into the hall. Alongside another percussionist, eight cello-players marched through the audience to the stage with instruments fixed to their chests on "Block Straps," an ingenious device (invented by Mike Block, one of *Distant Mirror*'s players and organizers) that allows cellists to move on their feet while playing. Finally, the ensemble took the stage to finish their processional piece, *Hanacpachap Cussicuinin*, a traditional Incan Catholic chant written in the Quechua language, arranged by Block for cello and percussion. This dramatic entrance set the tone for the rest of the performance, which mingled to spectacular effect the conventions of Western chamber music with performance traditions from around the globe.

A Distant Mirror would be best described as a celebration: of different cultural traditions, musical and otherwise; of percussive music, and of the cello as an instrument; of our pasts and of the present. The quatercentenary of Shakespeare's and Cervantes' deaths ostensibly inspired the program, but the concert itself went on to take a much broader view, holding up a mirror to a world that at times seemed more immediate than "distant."

Much of the music on the program was evidently chosen for its historical status, the first four pieces being more or less contemporary with Shakespeare and Cervantes. *Hanacpachap Cussicuinin* dates to the first decades of the seventeenth century and remains the earliest surviving example of notated polyphonic music in the New World. The three following pieces were gathered into *A Distant Mirror Suite*, each one representing a different early modern cultural tradition. Juan Arañés's joyful dance tune, *Chacona: La Vida Bona* (ca. 1624), saw both percussionists accompanying a cello quartet, who clapped and stamped and sang "To life, to life, come to chaconne" in Spanish, all while playing their instruments. Claude Gervaise's dances (ca. 1550s), also here arranged for cello quartet with percussion accompaniment, were decidedly Northern Renaissance in style, and highlighted a tradition in the midst of a major cultural shift: Gervaise was one of the first composers to notate secular dance tunes. *Nikriz Peşrev* offered an exciting example of early modern Turkish music, and allowed members of the cello octet to display their individual chops as they passed around short call-and-response solos. Its composer, Ali Ufkî Bey (1610?-1675), was an Ottoman musician and Muslim convert of Polish birth who notated two anthologies of traditional Turkish music and translated the melodies of a Calvinist Psalter for the Middle Easternmodal system.

Despite the historical distance of these compositions, they seemed strikingly modern in arrangement, instrumentation, and performance style. Blaise Déjardin arranged Gervaise's dances; *Hanacpachap Cussicuinin*, *Chacona*, and *Nikriz Peşrev* were all arranged by Block. Both arrangers up-dated the pieces such that it became delightfully difficult to distinguish old from new. *Hanacpachap Cussicuinin*, for instance, was composed well before celli were invented, but in its arrangement here sounded as if it were written specifically for marching cello octet.

Likewise, those pieces on the program written by living composers (one present on stage) bridged the gulf between past and present in fascinating ways. A recent composition, Colin Jacobsen's *A Mirror for a Prince* drew on early seventeenth-century Persian music, including Zoroastrian musical traditions. Mario Diaz de Leon's *Anima* evinced an eclectic mix of inspirations, including Buddhist chants and the hymns of medieval abbess Hildegard van Bingen; its use of quarter tones to express sorrow furthermore recalled Sephardic Jewish musical conventions as well as the heavy metal Diaz de Leon records as a solo artist. Shane Shanahan's percussion duet *Saidi Swing* offered an object lesson in the evolution of Middle Eastern rhythm—one reinforced with a brief lecture from the stage on Arabic drumming techniques. And Giovanni Sollima's *Guglielmo Scrollalanza*, inspired by an Italian legend that Shakespeare was a Sicilian emigrant, incorporated musical phrases reminiscent of Renaissance dance tunes while employing inventive performance techniques, such as playing cymbals with cello bows.

The program concluded with another Renaissance/modern-day hybrid, Block's arrangement of *Romance del Conde Claros* by Francisco Salinas (1513-1590). Two encore selections, however, ultimately wrapped up the concert: Déjardin's arrangement of Vaughn Williams's *Fantastia on a Theme by Thomas Tallis*, and a reprise of Block's arrangement of Arañés's *Chacona*. These selections made a particularly appropriate end for this performance of historical and cultural interchange. As a very recent arrangement of an Edwardian-era variation on a sixteenth-century theme, *Fantasia* offered a lovely example of transhistorical collaboration. The reprise of *Chacona* circled back to the concert's beginning, reiterating an exuberant melody encouraging listeners to celebrate "la vida bona" through music and dance.

As Ma explained from the stage, *A Distant Mirror* aimed to enliven the past not just to examine the global networks within which Shakespeare and Cervantes operated, but because looking backward can provide productive insight into our world today. The concert offered a means for far-flung cultures separated by space as well as time to speak to each other so that we might appreciate their contradictions and delight in their similarities. By teaching us to celebrate unity in difference, Ma insisted, such reflection can help us "do better and be better" as a people. This effort seemed particularly appropriate on the afternoon of the concert, in the dark aftermath of what had occurred overnight in Orlando. It was a hard day to feel happy or hopeful at all.

But the joy and compassion that *A Distant Mirror*'s multicultural, interhistorical performance evoked made it feel for a moment as if we just might be able to make things right someday.

STEPPENWOLF THEATRE COMPANY + SECOND CITY THEATRICALS
THE PEOPLE VS FRIAR LAURENCE, THE MAN WHO KILLED ROMEO & JULIET

book + direction by Ron West
music + lyrics by Phil Swann + Ron West
featuring Bruce Green as Friar Laurence

A Surrogate Vaudevillain
Casey Caldwell

I know that my fellow City Desk correspondent, Lydia Craig, is also reviewing this staged reading, so I've decided to focus on a very specific point of contact between *The People vs Friar Laurence* and Shakespeare's *Romeo and Juliet*: Friar Laurence's exit at line 170 in Act 5, scene 3 of *R&J* (as found in the 1623 First Folio). Written by Ron West, with music and lyrics by Ron West and Phil Swann, this incredibly well-directed staged reading was co-produced by Steppenwolf's LookOut and Second City Theatricals.

Writing about free will, the German philosopher Friedrich Schelling claimed that people will often prefer a decisive villain over an ineffectual moralist. That is, we seem to be drawn to people who actually *do* things, regardless of the moral implications. What Schelling is speaking to here is the fact that in "real life," we spend a lot of our time *not acting* on any number of impulses we have on a minute-to-minute basis, living a life of duties chosen over desires. And this can take its toll on us, regardless of the consolations of "ethics."

I think this insight says a lot about why audiences are able to enjoy Shakespeare's villains and tragedies. We can find a proxy release for our desire for action in stage villains—Richard III, Iago, Edmund, these characters *do* things, they don't allow themselves to be held back by petty social constraints, and they actually accomplish their goals. I think this can also help explain why we are able to enjoy tragic endings. Shakespearean comedies and tragedies cue us at the outset that they are setting out to *do* something: comedies set out to marry people, tragedies set out to kill people, and they tend to deliver. While it might be less confusing why we are able to take delight in comic endings, we can extend Schelling's point to say that tragedies are also able to harness our desire for *any* action to their own generic ends. Really good tragedy finds a way to show us this fact about ourselves, that our pent-up desire for action can even lead us to delight in the death of others (on stage or off).

Hamlet, Lear, Macbeth, these plays all perform this double function of entertaining and edifying, inviting us to reflect on our delight in carnage even in the very moment we are experiencing this delight. And contrary to the reductive image of the play that has resulted from the American primary education system, in some key ways *R&J* does this better than these "great" tragedies: most pertinently here, because it works us sequentially through a (Shakespearean) comic ending and then a tragic ending. We get to enjoy the comic delivery of Romeo and Juliet consummating their romantic desires, then we get to enjoy tragedy fulfilling its promise of their deaths. Friar Laurence is the mechanism behind both of these generic actions: he arranges their wedding, then he stages death in such a way that it becomes real.

West and Swann's *The People vs Friar Laurence,* by putting Friar Laurence on trial and claiming that he is responsible for what has happened, has located for us the character in *R&J* that acts as proxy for our desire. This musical comedy satire levels a series of accusations as to Friar Laurence's guilt, claiming that he is a villain. After enumerating the different bumbling maneuvers Friar Laurence enacts, the final accusation as to his guilt comes from the hangman immediately prior to Laurence's scheduled execution. In the final scene of *R&J,* Friar Laurence has entered the crypt where Juliet is supposed to awake from the death-counterfeiting potion he's given her, only to find that Romeo has killed himself because he mistook Laurence's theater of death for the "real thing." Then comes this very odd moment: in the space of nine lines, Laurence says he has just heard a noise and they should run away, informs Juliet that Romeo has died, says he will "dispose of" her (in a nunnery), and then starts leaving on the strange line, "Come, go, good Juliet." The whole bit is made more urgent and hurried by Laurence repeating that he has heard a noise. Here's the speech as it appears in the 1623 First Folio, including Juliet's first lines as she awakes:

> *Iul.* O comfortable Frier, where's my Lord?
> I do remember well where I should be:
> And there I am, where is my *Romeo*?
>
> *Fri.* I heare some noyse Lady, come from that nest

Of death, contagion, and vnnaturall sleepe,
A greater power then we can contradict
Hath thwarted our entents, come, come away,
Thy husband in thy bosome there lies dead:
And *Paris* too: come Ile dispose of thee,
Among a Sisterhood of holy Nunnes:
Stay not to question, for the watch is comming.
Come, go good *Iuliet*, I dare no longer stay.
                                        Exit.

In *The People vs Friar Laurence*, the hangman asks Laurence the important question here: why did he leave a teenager alone in that crypt with a dagger, knowing she has just learned her husband has killed himself, and that she threatened to kill herself to his face earlier in the play?

Why does he exit at this point? Part of the reason is that he kind of *is* the villain in this play, at least as I defined one above. He performs an action that leads immediately to Juliet's death, so in an odd way he is functioning as a proxy for our (tragic) desires. But the irony of "I'll dispose of thee" and the tension in "come, go," registers at the level of language contradictions in what Laurence wants that seem to be below the level of conscious thought, and his haste doesn't leave him (much?) time to think about how his exit in effect participates in killing Juliet. So it's a kind of tragi-comic, bungling action. He is and isn't making something happen. He couldn't possibly want her to die, yet how could he rapidly deliver all of that devastating news and then just run out? Is he a villain or just kind of dumb?

Why say all of this about Laurence, desire, sex and death? Because the American primary school education system really has ruined *R&J* for many of us, and audiences attending Steppenwolf and Second City's incredibly well-produced staged reading might, therefore, miss how smart the insights are that their show has to offer. This satire wisely saves its most insightful indictment of Laurence for the end, but audiences (and I include academics here) that have refused to return to the text or "traditional" stagings of *R&J* might just see this as pointing up one more funny incongruity in the plot, as well as an affirmation of an "oh well" attitude that can seem necessary to get past otherwise confusing plot twists in Shakespeare's plays. Putting Laurence on trial in general, then, puts our own violent delights on trial as well. The romping, satirical mode of West and Swann's musical comedy acknowledges and plays into how many Americans have come to feel about *R&J*—caricaturing Romeo as an insufferable, "one note" lover, or making multiple jokes about the mysterious origin of the Capulet/Montague quarrel—and at the same time educates us in the finer points of Shakespeare's tragedy. In this sense, *The People vs Friar Laurence* is a "gateway play" back into Shakespeare's *Romeo and Juliet* and the specific insights it has to offer. There isn't a moment quite like Laurence's hurried, bungling exit from the crypt in any of Shakespeare's other tragedies, and it shows us how even our goofy ineptitudes can be in service of "A greater power than we can contradict."

Lethal Divisions in ~~Chicago~~ Venice
Lydia Craig

I watched Ron West and Phil Swann's 2010 play *The People vs Friar Laurence, The Man Who Killed Romeo & Juliet* with my esteemed Shakespeare 400 colleague Casey Caldwell, whose review on its tragic violence appeared last week. Admittedly, *Romeo and Juliet* isn't my favorite Shakespeare play, due in part to Act 1, scene 5's unlikely love-at-first-sight scene. However, this staged reading convincingly met this and other difficulties by changing the characters' secret motivations. For instance, to frustrate their strict parents and experience sensuality, Juliet and Romeo mutually (and musically) agree at the Capulet's Masquerade Ball cum Fourth of July party to "USE EACH OTHER TONIGHT." More reasonably, they become infatuated after conversing further and singing several duets.

As hilarious of a dark comedy as this staged reading proved to be, the ideological takeaway felt extremely bleak. While West and Swann's play comically addressed many long-standing frustrations with Shakespeare's play, it also as a production provoked the following extremely grave questions of its audience: What does a society look like in which lovers commit suicide? Or that effectively destroys its own future, along with any possibility of happiness, fertility, and dynastic continuity?

Much like our own, as it turns out. In *The People vs Friar Laurence*, the things that divide, define, not those that unify. Lest the audience conclude that the rivalries between the two families and the political situation in the Prince's Venice has nothing whatsoever to do with our city of Chicago in the twenty-first century, the actors were outfitted at the start of the first scene in Cubs, White Sox, Bears, and (to my utter disgust) Packers sportswear. These are minor indications of deeper rifts to come between the families, the most notable of which occurring when Tybalt stabs Mercutio to death. Mercutio expires, groaning, "A plague o' both your houses!" (Act 3, Scene 1)

Especially given its constant insistence on anachronistically transposing American culture and nationalism onto early modern Venice to Friar Laurence's bemusement and vain protests, *The People vs Friar Laurence* speaks to current social issues in the US. Highlighted issues include street violence, hatred of the "other," failing family structures, abusive patriarchy, greed, and debauchery. A major reason for the constant violence erupting between the Houses of Montague and

Capulet is extreme boredom and affluence, as the cast explains in the first song, "It's a Beautiful Day in Verona":

> **FRIAR LAURENCE**
> I'VE GOT TICKETS FOR THE CARNIVAL
> JUST LIKE THE ONE IN FLORENCE.
> IT'LL BENEFIT THE UNDERPRIV'LEGED
> KIDS HERE IN VERONA.
>
> **EVERYONE ELSE**
> PARDON US IF WE DON'T CARE...
>
> **ALL BUT FRIAR LAURENCE**
> WE'RE YOUNG AND RICH AND BORED AND
> PRE-DISPOSED TO BEING JERKS!
> WHO GIVES A SHIT ABOUT THE POOR
> OR DOING VOLUNTEER WORK!

Despite Friar Laurence's own unabashed shenanigans with Lady Capulet, the Nurse, and most of Venice, his hapless struggles to unite two young people in love provokes sympathy, especially considering the Friar's cynical perspective on a corrupt society in which alcoholism, prostitution, and drug abuse are rampant: "I'VE NOT BEEN TO HELL, BUT I SURE KNOW THE WAY!" When Lord and Lady Capulet aren't hurling invectives at each other or their daughter, they bully, drink feverishly, and copulate with underlings. Romeo's Apothecary deals in "poisonous" drugs—of the heroin, hashish, and methamphetamine variety in addition to arsenic, morphine, and cyanide—and seems oblivious to the fact that his customer will actually go through with his expressed intention to commit suicide. There is no mercy or understanding in this world, much less true love.

Throughout Shakespeare's life he witnessed deadly conflicts between Protestants and Roman Catholics, English, Irish, and Spanish. In the midst of religious and racial conflict, a plague decimated London in 1592, causing upwards of 17,000 deaths, closing theaters, churches, and paralyzing trade. Scholars believe *Romeo and Juliet* was first staged after the theaters re-opened in 1594 or 1595, the first being the year in which Jewish doctor Roderigo Lopez was executed for the dubious charge of attempting to poison his patient, Queen Elizabeth I, while the latter is that in which Robert Southwell was hanged, drawn, and quartered for the crime of being a Roman Catholic, an execution that provoked much debate. When Shakespeare's Mercutio threatens a plague on warring houses, the playwright knowingly has his character condemn and abandon an entire civilization—the arts, friends, and all—to utter devastation, because its only produce is vindictive, endless death like his own.

Though both the Montague and Capulet families occupy the same city, their inherited hate, stemming from a mysterious originary cause, destroys the public peace and disturbs Prince Escalus's political machinations; hence the scapegoating of the Friar. The lovers' deaths can't possibly be the state's fault, since this conclusion would necessitate change and repentance as occurs in the last scene of *Romeo and Juliet*. No one repents in West and Swann's play. God (a character who never directly appears in Shakespeare's pantheon) pardons Friar Laurence just prior to his hanging, but politely declines to bring back the dead. Supplementing the "gaps" in Shakespeare's *Romeo and Juliet* and "updating" the story, West and Swann's additions indicate the startling degree to which Shakespeare's own play-text emphasizes the dangers of polarization, blind hatred based on difference, rigidly defined self-identity, and a corrupt society's inability to correct its own trajectory until far too late.

DAVID CARL'S
CELEBRITY ONE-MAN HAMLET

co-created + directed by Michole Biancosino
co-created, written + as performed by David Carl
presented by Chicago Shakespeare Theater + Richard Jordan Productions
+ PM2 Entertainment + Project Y Theatre, in association with Underbelly

Giancarlo Osaben

Oddball *Hamlet*
Andrea Stevens

David Carl's Celebrity One-Man Hamlet gives us *Hamlet* through the lens of the wonderfully weird and manic actor, Gary Busey. (The show ran eighty minutes and was staged in the black-box theater, Upstairs at Chicago Shakespeare.) Nominated for an Oscar for his portrayal of Buddy Holly in *The Buddy Holly Story* (1978), Busey's promising career was derailed by a catastrophic motorcycle accident in 1988 that left him with severe head injuries (he wasn't wearing a helmet and remains to this day an advocate against mandatory helmet laws). In interviews Busey claims to have passed over and "been to the other side" and, by dint of this near-death experience, considers himself something of a spiritual emissary-qua-motivational speaker: "...my brain has been altered... to a high dimension in the spiritual realm. And that's where I operate consciously and unconsciously."

Although he still acted in major films after the accident (*Lethal Weapon, Point Break*), lately Busey is more known for cultish roles in films such as *Sharknado 4*, cameos as himself in *Entourage*, and for his participation in a range of reality television shows including *Celebrity Apprentice* and *Celebrity Big Brother: UK,* which he won (and if you haven't seen his episode of *Celebrity Wife Swap* alongside disgraced evangelist Ted Haggard, you are not living your best life).

To be sure, Busey is also warmly energetic and engaging—like a friendly yellow Lab sent to earth to empower us with New Age words of wisdom that frequently take the form of initialisms: "You know what 'FEAR' stands for? It stands for 'False Evidence Appearing Real.'" "You know what 'FAILING' stands for? It stands for 'Finding An Important Lesson, Inviting Needed Growth.'" Carl incorporates similarly nonsensical Buseyisms throughout his show and—to great effect— within an engaging "talk-back" after the performance where Carl, as Busey, takes questions about his career and then makes slogans out of the letters of the askers' first names. The contrast, then, between the melancholic Hamlet and the defiantly exuberant Busey is pronounced— although the real-life Busey certainly shares Hamlet's penchant for gnomic utterances, in Hamlet's case spoken to keep people at bay, in Busey's case…less clear? Because he's Busey and/or because he's cannily embracing and exploiting the public's impression of him as unhinged?

Costumed in a Hawaiian shirt and board shorts and sporting giant dentures that capture Busey's distinctively large teeth, Carl-as-Busey breezes through each scene of the play, taking on all the roles and ruthlessly skipping over all the "unnecessary" bits (in structure and speed I was reminded of Richard Curtis's *Skinhead Hamlet*). To play each part Busey either voiced a paper cutout hand-puppet or embodied the role himself, his Polonius especially memorable (and irritating) for his cringing, Uriah Heep-like facial expression and posture. Some of the roles were also prerecorded and then projected on a screen so that the live Busey could play against his filmed self: Hamlet's encounter with the Ghost of Old Hamlet was conveyed in this fashion, as was one excellent, splendidly timed and choreographed action sequence where the onstage Busey fought in "real" time against a screen Laertes over the grave of Ophelia. One exception: Rosencrantz and Guildenstern appear as a projected film still of Gary Oldman and Tim Roth in those parts from the 1990 film *Rosencrantz and Guildenstern Are Dead.* (Carl-as-Busey:

"I knew Tim Roth before he got famous...we used to walk through the La Brea tar pits trading taco recipes.")

Very little of the actual text of the play makes it into the production, the "rogue and peasant slave" speech, for example, veering off-script into a brilliant set of acting instructions to the players covering the highlights of Busey's career. The production furthermore incorporated both live and prerecorded music, Carl is also a deft singer. One of my favorite moments was Carl-as-Busey-as-Ophelia singing the '90s Cranberries hit "Zombie" in the mad scene. For the deaths that rapidly accumulate in the fifth act, Busey unceremoniously popped the heads off of the paper cutout dolls before dying himself. Interestingly—and I don't quite know what to make of this—for the death of Polonius the "Busey" persona abruptly stopped the scene, telling us that he found it too painful to perform that particular death.

I loved the performance's closing sequence. Busey knows Benedict Cumberbatch (of course), and Cumberbatch told him that one ought always to close a Shakespeare production with a talk-back. In addition to the audience banter I mentioned above, Busey solemnly intones that he's learned something from performing this revenge tragedy. It's not wise to hold a grudge; maybe now he's ready to call up Jon Voight and finally forgive him for beating him in that Best Actor category back in '79.

Funny, silly, and consistently engaging, the only drawback to the production—as I learned from one of my students who was in attendance—would be a lack of familiarity with the Gary Busey of current popular culture. The show is more about Busey's current persona than it is a parody of *Hamlet*; to a spectator unfamiliar with Busey and his career, Carl's performance, if intrinsically comic, might also seem bewildering. I can't make up my mind whether this conceit—Carl performing celebrity one-man Shakespeares—could bear future installments; "Nicolas Cage's One-Man *Coriolanus*," perhaps?

Madness in Great Ones
Casey Caldwell

The first three shows I have reflected on for the City Desk 400 have been about America. The Q Brothers' *Othello: The Remix* mapped Shakespeare's tragedy onto the American hip hop industry, in order to raise questions simultaneously about *Othello* and this sector of contemporary music entertainment culture. Steppenwolf and Second City's staged reading of *The People vs Friar Laurence* was American in form and content—it was a satire of *Romeo and Juliet* in the American tradition of the musical comedy, and it consistently mapped early modern figures and dates onto American counterparts. *David Carl's Celebrity One-Man Hamlet* is about the rolef "celebrity" in American popular culture, but also more generally about what it means to "stick around"—something that *Hamlet* is also interested in.

Originally staged as part of the 2014 NY Fringe Festival, Carl's one-man show about Gary Busey's one-man *Hamlet* is at a surface level a joke about the place Busey has in American culture today. Especially his place as the Gary Busey of Donald Trump's TV show, *Celebrity Apprentice*—this is present-day Busey, not *Point Break* Busey. Carl's show opens with him entering in character as Busey, going straight into performing his one-man *Hamlet*. There's no framing device for this—Carl-as-Busey doesn't give us a pretense for why this show is happening, so Carl isn't interested in situating it in that way, he doesn't want to add a meta-layer of realism or at least backstory to this production of *Hamlet*.

So the show is more surreal for all of that. Busey moves back and forth between projection screen act and scene announcements, finger puppet shows, impersonations of various characters, pauses in the action for projection screen graphics of Busey-ism acronyms (made famous on *Celebrity Apprentice*), well-done famous monologues from *Hamlet* including "To be or not to be," and even a fight between Busey-as-Hamlet on stage and Busey-as-Laertes on the projection screen. Carl's show launches into its action very much in the way that Busey himself will suddenly launch into one of his famous unpackings of an acronym that wasn't already an acronym (FUN: Finally. Understanding. Nothing). There's something kind of mad about this show that's also what's kind of mad about Gary Busey.

And there's the rub. Or rather the rub that first got me thinking: why did Carl choose to bring these two things together, Gary Busey and *Hamlet*? I mentioned above that on the surface this show is a joke about Gary Busey. But there's more to it than that. Busey and Hamlet are both famously "mad" characters, but further than this there's a question with both of them of if and where there is method in't. One of *Hamlet*'s basic driving questions is: if one is performing madness, is there any difference anymore between "acting" and "really" being mad? That's the most famous question, but there's an additional one that's perhaps even more important/interesting: what political role can this performance of madness play? When enacted by one endowed with public, "celebrity" power as well? Is there anything meaningful this individual can accomplish?

There are famously two Gary Buseys, one that seemed sane as far as Hollywood stars go, and one that has seemed crazy. As with Hamlet, it gets complicated though. In 2011, Jezebel published a brief post entitled, "Is Gary Busey Just Pretending to Be Crazy?" The author of the post is essentially just raising the question, seemingly for the purpose of spurring on the comments section that followed. The debate in the comments section hashes out the broader questions that many of us in general who have followed Busey's career have been asking (and in this, I may be David Carl's perfect audience member: someone who is nearly as well versed in Gary Busey's filmography as he is in Shakespeare's oeuvre). The Jezebel post raises the possibility that Busey has just been performing his madness for the sake of keeping himself in the limelight, whereas several of the commenters suggest a well-known alternative theory: in 1989, Busey was famously involved in a motorcycle accident that nearly took his life, fractured his skull, required nearly two hours of neurosurgery, and may have left him with significant brain damage. The argument goes that this was the cause of his "madness," but then Busey put in performances and made public appearances after this where he did not seem to be so mad. A more nuanced theory suggests that Busey may be improvising upon the kernel of madness his accident introduced into his life, amplifying and making use of it through performance. I do not know where the "facts" really lie here, but David Carl is usefully engaging with this general "popular" confusion about Busey's sanity to not only make a joke but also some kind of point.

So if that's the rub, what is the point? I didn't used to like *Hamlet*. In fact, for a long time I didn't like Shakespeare's tragedies in general. The sense of affirmation I felt in the comedies spoke more to the dimensions of life I could relate to essentially up through college. I had to get out in the world and get beat up more by life—to learn how inexorably long rough and rougher patches or seemingly insoluble problems could be and what kind of sheer *patience* it takes to live through them—to see the truth in the tragic experience of life that plays like *Macbeth, King Lear,* and *Hamlet* speak to. That in raising the tragic experience of life to its height on stage, we can see more clearly that there is a heroism simply in endurance, and a comfort in the notion that "time and the hour runs through the roughest day." What I found I was able to like in *Hamlet* when I came back to it later in life was precisely this sense of endurance—Hamlet's enduring madness both as an effect of an event that was out of his control (his father's regicide by his uncle who then married his mother, the queen) and as an expedient for surviving the consequences of this event—perhaps even finding way to make a difference in its wake as well. Enduring this leads Hamlet ultimately to the realization, in the "To be or not to be" speech, that life in time involves, at least tacitly, a decision to remain. To stay, even if life and time in its most practical sense is making us crazy, and our only way to find some control is to embrace and perhaps outwardly perform, and so make use of, the madness of life.

I don't think I've ever heard anyone who was a fan of Gary Busey on *Celebrity Apprentice* express their admiration for him in these terms, but I do think that at some level it helps explain a deeper level of his enduring appeal, perhaps especially for older generations. The key moment in David Carl's production comes when Busey is performing a revision of the "original script:" Busey has chosen in his one-man *Hamlet* to perform the part of Polonius when he is spying on Hamlet while he confronts Gertrude in Act 3, scene 4, showing us Hamlet's stabbing of him from Polonius's perspective. Carl-as-Busey-as-Polonius is moving in slow motion, reaching out his hand to grab the invisible dagger that is slowing pressing towards his chest, and just as Polonius's hand is about to be pressed into his chest, Carl-as-Busey stops the show (the Busey show, not the Carl show), calls out to his imaginary (but maybe also the real) sound and light board operator to cut the sound and lights, and says he can't play this moment tonight. Busey leans over panting, recovering himself, and there is a palpable, slightly awkward moment of silence before Busey rebounds and skips over this moment to go on with the rest of the action of *Hamlet*. This is the biggest break in the action and the biggest stand-out moment in the entire show. Busey is visibly distraught for a moment, with Carl just approaching and touching upon a level of sincerity in his overall show before we see Busey rush back into his zany *Hamlet*. This moment is the real point of contact between the joke and the point of this show.

If Hamlet is the condensation of all the issues I noted in *Hamlet* surrounding madness, endurance, and life in time, he is a young man first facing these truths. Polonius is in this sense an old man who has been living with these truths for a long time. If Hamlet is Gary Busey on, say, the day he woke up from his motorcycle accident, Polonius is Gary Busey today having lived with its consequences—and perhaps performed them—for a long time. Polonius is a lot of things in *Hamlet*—doddering, digressive, and meddling being a few of his worst offenses—but he certainly doesn't deserve to die the way he does. In staging Polonius's death from his perspective, Busey shows a sense of sympathy for this. The fact that he can't bring himself to actually perform it in the moment shows how deep, and perhaps unacknowledged, that sympathy and ultimately identification goes.

Truly tragic events in life have an ability to seemingly wipe away our memories of what life was like before they happened. This is something Hamlet and Gary Busey both understand. When Hamlet's father demands that he avenge his murder and remember him, the young Hamlet says that he will wipe his memory clean of all else. But he also in this moment suddenly experiences time's attempt to make him old, that is, he suddenly feels his living in time:

> O all you host of heaven! O earth! what else?
> And shall I couple hell? O, fie! Hold, hold, my heart;
> And you, my sinews, grow not instant old,
> But bear me stiffly up. Remember thee!
> Ay, thou poor ghost, while memory holds a seat
> In this distracted globe. Remember thee!
> Yea, from the table of my memory
> I'll wipe away all trivial fond records,
> All saws of books, all forms, all pressures past,
> That youth and observation copied there;
> And thy commandment all alone shall live
> Within the book and volume of my brain,
> Unmix'd with baser matter...

It's an active decision here, but it performs the relation that tragic experiences and memory can have in life, including the break this relation introduces between youth and old age—it can threaten to make the sinews grow instantly old and erase from the book of the mind all "that youth and observation copied there." I'll leave you with a similar quote from Gary Busey on memory that might have a little more wisdom in it, or at least the benefit of time. Well into his Polonius phase, Busey appeared on *Jimmy Kimmel Live* promoting a new book of his Busey-isms. Once again he makes an aphorism out of a word, "memory," that wasn't already an aphorism, but perhaps his understanding of memory also contains a lesson or revision in it for the young Hamlet. Quoting from his book, Busey says, "Memory. M.E.M.O.R.Y. Stands for: Making Exciting Moments On Remaining Yours. When you write from your mind, you write with an invisible pen called, Memory."

CHICAGO SHAKESPEARE THEATER
CHICAGO SHAKESPEARE IN THE PARKS:
TWELFTH NIGHT

by William Shakespeare
adapted + directed by Kirsten Kelly

Courtesy of Chicago Shakespeare Theater

Out of the Text and Into the Audience:
Twelfth Night in the Parks
Anna Ullmann

In Shakespeare's *Twelfth Night*, after having quickly tricked Cesario into straying from Orsino's prepared speeches of courtship, the Countess Olivia triumphantly declares that the poor Viola-in-disguise is "Now out of your text" (1.5.204). This causes Cesario to abandon the "text" completely, so that Olivia receives passionate words directly from the heart, perhaps for the first time, and ultimately falls in love with this unwitting messenger.

Similarly, it was the extra-textual, intuitive nature of Chicago Shakespeare in the Parks: *Twelfth Night* that drew love from the audience at Welles Park. Before the show began, Will Mobley, the show's Feste, addressed an audience that professed to be about half newcomers to Shakespeare's works and advised them to use context to guide their experience when the text itself became too impenetrable. Flanked by the grand Welles Gazebo on one side and a group of elderly men playing bocce on the other, and preceded by a riveting presentation by the Old Town School of Folk Music that had many playgoers dancing in their seats, CST gave a performance that enabled the audience to use this context to enjoy a show that was true to the spirit of Shakespeare's words while updating and packaging them for a modern, casual setting.

Presented with a play that often rings with dark notes even as it is undoubtedly a comedy, director Kirsten Kelly and the performers were able to remove some of this ambiguity for an audience that included dogs, babies, and balloons, as well as attentive listeners. While some might say this detracts from the play's overall complexity and Shakespeare's artistic achievement, the beauty of theater is that it is adaptable to the context outside it in the same way that it is able to use onstage context to draw listeners in. For this particular show, the decision to turn Orsino's and Olivia's melancholy into melodrama was the right one. For example, Orsino made his entrance carrying an enormous portrait of Olivia done in lurid colors, which he then proceeded to dance with and eventually kiss rather emphatically, laying on it a large, wet smack that was audible over the "food of love" coming from Feste's piano. We were unquestionably in a comedy from the start.

The transformation of Feste, the "wise fool" originally created for the more satirical and serious clown Robert Armin, into a lively jester-turned-musician kept much of the more confusing dialogue at bay and consistently kept the energy of the show high. Feste often speaks in riddles that take us a moment to puzzle out. Some of these moments were kept, such as his logical proof that Olivia is really the fool and not he (1.5.61), but many of them were cut, rightfully I think, as it kept the audience's attention moving in this abridged, outdoor production. They had also composed an upbeat musical score for many of Feste's songs, particularly the finale known most often as "The Wind and the Rain," and incorporated this music throughout the show. Such decisions made for a cohesive, pleasant performance for a Sunday afternoon in the park.

Perhaps one of the most interesting ways in which the director and cast upheld the joyful arc of the show while making use of the context of performance was the overall treatment of Malvolio. This is often one of those dark notes already mentioned. While he is never exactly likable, in other renditions I have seen and in the text itself the other characters' trickery and humiliation of Malvolio can easily come across as cruel; the humor goes one step too far. This negativity is underscored by his final line, in which he vows to "be revenged on the whole pack of [them]" (5.1.365). The Chicago Shakespeare in the Parks show left none of this lingering doubt amidst our happily ever after, and this was achieved largely by the actors' full engagement with the audience and the brilliant characterization of the long-suffering, absurdly pedantic, and somehow endearing Malvolio by Jonathan Weir.

In *Shakespeare and the Popular Tradition in the Theatre*, Robert Weimann outlines the difference between what he terms the *locus* and *platea*. The *locus* is the upper, more focalized part of the stage where action is more separated from the audience, while the *platea* is the lower part, sometimes even spilling into the seats, where the action is more connected to the spectators and context of playing. Rather than place Malvolio, the focus of our ridicule, on the more separated *locus* of the stage, nearly all of his actions were given on the *platea*, either at the very front of the stage or on the ramp and grass in front of it. From the way he addressed the reading of "Olivia's" love letter directly to the audience, to his swiping of a snack from a playgoer in the front row, to his retreating after his declaration of revenge *not* backstage and out of sight but fairly deeply into the actual audience, Malvolio was clearly someone we laughed with, not at; an engaging character with his own kind of humor, who was reconciled back into the cast at the end and was never alienated from the silliness of the other characters or the casualness of the setting.

CST went quite far "out of their text" for this Chicago Shakespeare in the Parks performance, abridging many scenes and even translating whole speeches into Spanish, but the results were truly gratifying. By balancing their commitment to Shakespeare with their duty to their audience, Kelly and her cast and crew produced a show that sent both first-time viewers and seasoned veterans away laughing.

Would Will Approve of Bilingual Shakespeare?
Lydia Craig

On August 6, I went to Welles Park with hundreds of other Chicagoans carrying picnic blankets, food, and those little Shakespeare fans to see Chicago Shakespeare in the Parks' performance of *Twelfth Night*. It's worth the trek to your neighborhood park in terms of stage design alone. Without spoiling too much, one device that struck me as being highly original and humorous in this production was that of Viola/Cesario riding her bike in place on stage, while Malvolio races up, falls back, puffing, and finally overtakes her by overturning the bike and demanding that she take back the ring that she supposedly gifted to Olivia. Similarly, in the first scene of this production (the original play's Act 1, scene 2) the twins hurl themselves around the nautical stage's ladders and rigging, mimicking the violence of the wind and waves as their ship breaks apart and hurls them in opposite directions, movements rendered more striking by the sound of snapping timber and howling winds. Besides the fanciness of some of these more dramatic moments, Chicago Shakespeare in the Parks: *Twelfth Night* makes some interesting changes that speak to the question of translating Shakespeare's work to modern audiences. Adapted and directed by Kirsten Kelly, this production introduced Spanish translations of Viola and Sebastian's English lines when they spoke to each other, played up and updated the music in Shakespeare's original play, and eliminated Malvolio's Puritan antecedents, three significant changes that update and simplify the convoluted plot.

In particular, the first change provides a subtext to the story that would otherwise be lacking, juxtaposing the familiar with the unfamiliar, the domestic with the foreign. With two Spanish-speaking actors in the production playing leading roles, the brash, amusing Andrea San Miguel as Viola and Nate Santana as a dashing Sebastian, Kelly apparently chose to have the twins occasionally converse with each other in this language. This brief use of Spanish ironically had the effect of being intelligible to some bilingual members of an audience already straining to understand early modern English, while excluding others from the intimacy of the twins' relationship. Actor Will Mobley's pre-play adjuration, "Watching Shakespeare takes a few minutes before eyes and ears adjust. Watch the faces and watch what the actors do," applied perfectly to this scenario as well. Accordingly, this change did not obscure the play's sense at all. Through their corresponding actions, such as desperate reaching, crying aloud, or embracing passionately, the general sense of these words could be easily interpreted by viewers: A brother and sister torn apart...A brother and sister lovingly reunited. These few translated lines also stressed how such Spanish-speakers in a predominately English-speaking society could find intimacy, familiarity, and even privacy in conversing with family members in their mother tongue. But what would Shakespeare say to his English lines being translated into modern Spanish? Based on his track record with languages other than English and Latin, I think he would love it.

Though all of Shakespeare's lines in *Twelfth Night* are originally composed in English, the playwright also relished writing lines in other languages for diversion and show off his learning. Notably, he left spaces for Welsh to be spoken by the Earl of Glendower's daughter, (a part possibly enacted by a Welsh-speaking actor in his company) in *1 Henry IV* and in *Henry V* wrote the majority of Princess Katherine of France's lines in French to indicate the cultural and linguistic divides that separated couples transculturally wedded in a time of war and dynastic change. As for Shakespeare's use of ancient Illyria as the setting, this seems to have been motivated by a desire to choose a fantasyland for his shipwrecked travelers that would be culturally vague and exotic-sounding, not to pinpoint a specific setting. Dwellers at the sites of modern Montenegro and Albania, both the Illyrians and their native language remain lost to history, representing a convenient European geographical vacancy for Shakespeare to fill with a motley assortment of inhabitants inexplicably and haphazardly given English (Sir Andrew Aguecheek, Sir Toby Belch) and Italian (Olivia, Orsino, and Malvolio) names, regardless of interrelation or social class. As no indication is given in the original play as to Viola and Sebastian's parentage, country of origin, or station in life beyond its being "above [their] fortunes" (Act 1, scene 5) and their having had a father who had previously "named" Orsino to his daughter as an eligible bachelor (Act 1, scene 2), it may reasonably be assumed that these twins with Italian or Latin names are from an Iberian locale and of noble birth. Having Viola and Sebastian speak Spanish to each other in Kelly's adaptation ultimately emphasizes their secret foreignness in Orsino's Illyria, a single wistful echo of the familiar world lost to them through their journey, shipwreck, and perhaps even new marriages to local Illyrian nobility, in an otherwise outrageous comedy.

And yes, this comedy is outrageous, playful fun by an impressively solid cast. Devastatingly regal in nightcap and silk dressing-gown, Jonathan Weir plays an off-the-cuff Malvolio for all he is worth, flailing his long, yellow cross-gartered legs about, making absurd facial contortions, and persistently stealing Lays potato chips and white wine from the audience at the least excuse: "Can't eat just one!" Moping about Byronically with disheveled attire, Neal Moeller's portrayal of Orsino emphasizes the character's ridiculous oversentimentality while preserving the menace of his misogynistic diatribes against Olivia for spurning his advances. Further high points throughout the comedy were Dominic Conti's hilarious gaucherie as the clueless suitor Sir Andrew Aguecheek, the comedic timing of Ronald Conner's Sir Toby Belch, Nike Kadri's dignified, passionate Olivia, and Will Mobley's empathetic interpretation of Feste, Olivia's fool. The boxing scene and its choreography were utterly marvelous—but I'll say no more. Pack a basket, grab some congenial folks, and go see the play for yourself!

GRANT PARK MUSIC FESTIVAL
GRANT PARK CHORUS

chorus director Christopher Bell

Courtesy of Grant Park Music Festival

Bardic Lays: Music for All Time
Lydia Craig

The Grant Park Chorus performed at the Columbus Park Refectory on July 24, 2016, to an overflowing audience. So many eager attendees thronged into the hall that the performance was held up by the necessity of adding new rows of seats for the newcomers still streaming in after 3 pm. Choral member Matt Greenberg, who recently celebrated nearly twenty years of performing with the GPC, began by welcoming everyone. Participating in Chicago's Shakespeare 400 Celebration, he said, gave the chorus a welcome opportunity to stand out from The Grant Park Orchestra with which they usually collaborate. Moving chronologically through history, the chorus began with Shakespearean songs set to music by early modern composers before performing present-day renditions. First they sang two instantly recognizable songs from Shakespeare's *As You Like It,* the first being "It Was a Lover and His Lass," set to music by Thomas Morley (1557/1558-1602) in his *First Book of Balletts* (1595). Their united voices echoed throughout the rectangular space and Columbus Hall and its wooden rafters in a hair-raisingly lovely sound.

Pausing the performance after the chorus had imitated the harsh, gusting blast in "Blow, Blow Thou Winter Wind" by Thomas Augustine Arne arr. Radcliffe (1710-1778), Director Christopher Bell faulted the audience's applause for being too polite, "sounding as though we're here to entertain you on a summer afternoon!" After the audience obliged with greater applause, Bell made the first of several remarks on Shakespearean music and drama, pointing out that no main characters would be singing these songs in the plays. "Some lowlife, some wandering minstrel would sing the song, which would reflect in some way on what was occurring in the drama," he observed. Divorced from the cultural contexts in which Shakespeare's songs were originally performed, however, musicians are free to experiment with the playwright's words according to their own inclinations. In terms of why he himself chose these particular songs for the Shakespeare 400 program, Bell explained, "True, a wide variety of composers have composed Shakespeare arrangements. In my particular choices for this performance, my one criteria is—I have to like the music."

Fortunately for this critic throughout the next hour, Bell's musical tastes seemed to accord well with my own. As exemplified by the first two songs, the selections either tended to the rollicking comical, or the wistfully solemn, reflecting in a way the tenor and variations of Shakespearean drama in its two extremes. "Full Fathom Five" (*The Tempest*) was the first of the next set of three Shakespearean songs by composer Ralph Vaughan Williams (1872-1958), which seemed to me to, in conjunction, describe the different moods in which the playwright approaches Faery: in wonderment, in delight, and occasionally with somber respect and fear. Underwater bells tolled in a shimmering sound voiced by the female part of the chorus, giving way to a funereal, magical, very playful dirge as the male parts sang the verses in an undulating rhythm. The bells and words built up to a purpose and then just as intangibly slipped away into silence, ending on slow bells punctuating the stillness. Next came the joyous, lilting "Over Hill, Over Dale," (*A Midsummer Night's Dream*), an arrangement clearly influenced by English and Irish folk songs or madrigals in the style of John Farmer (ca. 1570—ca. 1601). Finally, "The Cloud-Capp'd Towers" (*The Tempest*) was slow and stately, carefully enunciated and held in choral unison, bass sinking meanwhile and soprano rising steadily and clearly above the middle parts.

Three songs from Jaakko Mäntyjärvi (b. 1963) followed, which all played with the power of the human voice to enact Shakespeare's jarring poetry in song. "Come Away, Death"(*Twelfth Night*) in F major was mysterious, grave, thrilling, and eerie. The adjuration "to weep" hung out impossibly. As for "Lullaby" (*A Midsummer Night's Dream*), any baby hearing that opening note would be as far from sleep as humanly possible regardless of waves of rhythmic intoning from the bass section! Chanting in unison throughout its rendition of "Double, Double, Toil and Trouble" (*Macbeth*), high-pitched shrieks from the alto and soprano sections mimicked the witches' frothing brew. As all parts joined, the slower recitation of the lines "Eye of newt, and toe of frog, / Wool of bat, and tongue of dog" soon escalated again into harsh and unrelenting cacophony. The choir transformed into a witches' Sabbath driven wild in gibbering excitement, emitting sliding yelps and occasionally expressing themselves. with outlandish physical gestures I can only describe as "magical jazz hands." Though only the female sections sang the concluding lines, a powerful ending stamp from all members imitated the opening door as Macbeth enters in the play itself. This song, obviously, was a big hit with the audience!

Two of the final arrangements hinted towards the future potential of re-envisioning and re-framing Shakespeare's verses within a variety of musical styles. At the start of Matthew Harris's (b. 1956) Who is Sylvia (*The Two Gentlemen of Verona*), soprano Corinne Wallace left the rest of the group and sashayed down the aisle while the choir and she engaged in a gospel call-and-response. In time with the beat, Director Bell often fist-pumped and excitedly bounded around as he directed the chorus, clearly "feeling it." For the penultimate song, tenor Hoss Brock sang Kevin Olson's (b. 1970): "A Summer Sonnet" (Sonnet 18), with its famous opening line, "Shall I compare thee to a summer's day?" in the style of a nightclub singer such as Frank Sinatra while the choir backed him up. Many similar musical projects have been done lately that aim to convert Shakespeare's Sonnets into pop or folk music using Elizabethan instruments such as the harp, flute, and viol. This kind of modern exploration of preexisting conventions and historical recovery injects twenty-first century sound into Shakespeare, allowing his words to be sung to music that has significant cultural meaning for us. The Grant Park Chorus's performance, in gesturing to past "interpretations" of

Shakespeare throughout history and incorporating contemporary renditions, both celebrates the expressive power of music and indicates the extraordinary flexibility and endurance of Shakespeare's verse in adapting itself to a variety of genres and purposes across every century.

SHAKESPEARE'S GLOBE ON TOUR
THE MERCHANT OF VENICE

by William Shakespeare
directed by Jonathan Munby
starring Jonathan Pryce
presented by Chicago Shakespeare Theater

Marc Brenner

Negotiating Jewish and Christian Society in
The Merchant of Venice: Jessica's Story
Verna Foster

The Merchant of Venice is an Elizabethan romantic comedy that time and changing mores, especially attitudes towards Jews and a post-Holocaust abhorrence of anti-Semitism, have transformed into a modern dark tragicomedy. Shylock, the comic blocking figure who, like Hermia's father in *A Midsummer Night's Dream*, stands in the way of young lovers, has become in most productions of *The Merchant of Venice* the play's tragic protagonist.

In the Elizabethan romantic comedy, Shylock's daughter, Jessica, and her Christian lover, Lorenzo, must circumvent the old usurer in order to marry; and before Portia and Bassanio and Nerissa and Gratiano may consummate their marriages, Portia in a thrilling cross-dressed performance as a brilliant young lawyer must save Bassanio's friend,

Antonio, from Shylock's murderous attempt on his life. She succeeds in a last-minute courtroom *tour de force* that uses Shylock's legalism against him: if in taking his contractual pound of flesh from Antonio's breast, Shylock spills a drop of blood or takes even slightly more or less than a pound, his own life is forfeit. Defeated and then "generously" ordered by Antonio and the Duke of Venice to convert to Christianity, thereby saving his life and his soul, Shylock leaves the stage to the lovers for the play's idyllic and humorous final act.

This modern darkly tragicomic *Merchant of Venice* gives us instead a sympathetic Shylock abused by Christians, especially Antonio, abandoned and robbed by his only child, and fighting back in the only way he can in an environment of intense and pervasive anti-Semitism: that is, by insisting on a strict interpretation of the law of contracts that Venice must uphold or risk losing its position as the most important commercial power in the Mediterranean. In this version, Portia's cunning interpretation of the relevant legal statute deflates Shylock's businessman's belief in the law of commerce, while the order for his forced conversion destroys his sense of identity as a Jew and as a human being.

Shakespeare's Globe's production of *The Merchant of Venice*, directed by Jonathan Munby and one of several international shows visiting Chicago Shakespeare Theater during this quatercentenary year, does the best job of balancing the Elizabethan romantic comedy and the modern tragicomedy of any production I have seen. After almost half a century I still vividly remember Laurence Olivier's acutely intelligent and heartbreaking Shylock in a production directed by Jonathan Miller that was marked by the anti-Semitism of all of its Christian characters. But by focusing on the tragedy of Shylock and allowing the Christians no redeeming features, this production, brilliant and groundbreaking as it was, lost some of what is or can still be delightful in the play's romantic comedy.

Jonathan Munby's *Merchant*, by contrast, gave to every character his or her due. There was no attempt to gain extra sympathy for Shylock by sentimentalizing his relationship with his daughter—at their first appearance together they were quarreling in Yiddish. And the Christian characters were a more morally mixed and nuanced bunch than in some productions I have seen. While excoriating anti-Semitism, Munby also presented the more complex and perhaps uncomfortable truth that idealism and intolerance, decency and bigotry, can exist in the same person and that being an outsider oneself (Antonio as homosexual) need not grant one compassion for another kind of outsider.

Chicago Shakespeare Theater's stage was dressed to evoke rather than precisely imitate Shakespeare's Globe in London, where Munby's production originated. Dark curtains covered the back wall; simple tables, chairs, and plinths were brought on as needed; actors entered through a large central opening, from the sides, and through the audience. The permanent architectural features, as in Shakespeare's Globe, were two tall pillars, whose capitals were lit up to resemble gold in the Belmont scenes. The period costumes also emphasized the contrast between Venice and Belmont. The Venetians wore dull colors highlighted by red; in Belmont blonde heiress Portia wore gold, and Bassanio and Jessica, too, exchanged their drab Venetian clothes for golden ones in Belmont. Sixteenth-century Italy was evoked, too, by bursts of Italian music and pleasing Italian songs that punctuated the production and provided a basis for Lorenzo's beautiful invocation of the power of music in act five.

The production opened with a noisy carnival scene that was already underway as the audience took their seats. This prologue set the tone for the action to come as the good-natured jollity of maskers, musicians, and courtesans gave way to a violent, unprovoked attack on two Jews as they crossed the stage.

In keeping with the spirit of performance at Shakespeare's Globe, the actors in the prologue and in the play proper interacted with the audience. In particular, Launcelot (an engaging Stefan Adegbola) brought up onto the stage members of the audience to play the "fiend" and his "conscience" as he debated leaving Shylock's service. At the performance I attended (August 14), the first "fiend" (a local Shakespearean perhaps?) to the great amusement of the audience left the stage at the line "use your legs," and a second had to be recruited. At other times actors drew the audience into their world by referring to particular spectators. Most interestingly, Shylock (Jonathan Pryce) spoke his early asides *to* the audience, at those moments incorporating all of us as fellow Jews in an anti-Semitic society.

The Christians in Munby's production were not uniformly anti-Semitic. I have seen worse: for example, the vicious Venetians of Chicago Shakespeare Theater's 2005 production, which featured Mike Nussbaum as Shylock. Most virulent of Munby's Christians were Antonio (Dominic Mafham) and Gratiano (Jolyon Coy). Antonio was initially a sympathetic and dignified figure in his impossible but generous love for Bassanio. When Solanio (Raj Bajaj) asked him if he was sad because he was in love, Mafham's vehement "Fie" spoke volumes about the pain of keeping his feelings private. But in his interactions with Shylock, this Antonio was exceptionally brutal, verbally and physically, and when finally he shook Shylock's hand to seal their bargain, he immediately wiped his own on his garment. Gratiano, immoderate in all things (he first entered the stage in the process of throwing up and later was accused of fathering a baby), equally displayed mean-spiritedness, not only baiting Shylock during the trial but also attempting—through gestural interjections—to dissuade Lorenzo from marrying Jessica.

To his credit, Lorenzo (Andy Apollo), while clearly one of the boys, stood up for his love for Jessica with some spirit. Allowing Lorenzo this grace paid off in the last act when Shakespeare gives this young lover the most beautiful lines in the play about the loveliness of the starry night and the harmony of the music of the spheres: "Such harmony is in immortal souls." In the Olivier production, the moment had to be subverted in keeping with the general degradation of the Christians—the foppish Lorenzo carefully put his handkerchief on the ground for himself to sit on. Apollo's Lorenzo put his jacket on the ground for Jessica. All the difference in the world. And an exquisite moment was preserved.

The most decent of the Christians was Dan Fredenburgh's Bassanio, the most likeable Bassanio I can remember. Unlike Antonio, whose excess he attempted to restrain, Bassanio did not wipe his hand after shaking Shylock's (admittedly a low bar). Despite his impecuniousness, he did not play Antonio, instead gently deflecting an attempted kiss on the lips, and he appeared truly to love Portia, not only her money.

Though more acerbic than her Bassanio, Rachel Pickup offered a somewhat nuanced portrait of Portia. The audience could sympathize enough with her wit and charm and her beautifully spoken love for Bassanio to enjoy the romance of the caskets plot while cringing at her racial prejudice towards the Prince of Morocco and later Jessica. The choice to make Morocco (a character whose eloquence has encouraged critics to see him as a trial-run for Othello) as ridiculous as the Prince of Aragon somewhat mitigated the bad taste left by Portia's racist abhorrence of this suitor. Both Giles Terera as Morocco and Christopher Logan as Aragon gave highly entertaining over-the-top performances of cultural stereotypes that brought the house down, leaving one to wonder perhaps whether it is, after all, any more acceptable to mock Spaniards (or Dutchmen or Englishmen, like Portia's other undesirable but unseen suitors) than Africans.

Portia was least sympathetic in her offhand attitude to Jessica. Both she and Nerissa (Dorothea Myer-Bennett) repeatedly had difficulty remembering Jessica's name (in the manner established by Joan Plowright's Portia in Olivier's production). And at one point Portia handed Jessica her wine glass as if she were a servant. In the court scene Portia really did not figure out how to save Antonio until the last possible moment, making this well-known episode something of a nail-biter. But though perhaps less calculating than some Portias in this respect, Pickup was nasty enough in her put-down of Shylock.

The show belonged to Shylock—and to a greater extent than is usual to Jessica. Advance publicity prepared audiences for this focus by foregrounding the real-life father-daughter relationship between Jonathan Pryce's Shylock and Phoebe Pryce's Jessica. Maintaining his precarious masculine dignity through a harsh self-sufficiency, Pryce's Shylock was as passionately prejudiced against Christians as they were against Jews, obviously with more cause. But though he intended retribution from the beginning in proposing the "merry sport" of his contract with Antonio, the savagery of his revenge was primed by his daughter's elopement with a Christian. Expecting to triumph in the court of law, Shylock was instead humiliated by Portia, who reduced this strong, passionate individual to a frail old man—"I am not well"—and eviscerated him, body and soul.

The keynote figure in Munby's production was actually Jessica rather than Shylock. The audience apprehended Jewish experience in an anti-Semitic society through Jessica's attempts to engage with Venetian culture. At first more reprehensible than sympathetic in running off with her lover and her father's money, Jessica gained the audience's sympathy when, as an outsider at Belmont, she was ignored by Portia and Nerissa. Later, tutored by Lorenzo in private moments, Jessica learned to dance and to speak in appropriately fulsome language about Portia, whom, understandably, she did not like. Her delight in her new art of dancing and her new golden dress was irresistible. And so the audience was drawn with Jessica into acquiescence in the tempting pleasures of Belmont—that is, until she learned what had been done to her father.

Shylock's exit from the court is his textual exit from Shakespeare's play, but not from most contemporary productions, which find ways to bring him back to disturb the comic harmony of Belmont. The Olivier production, for example, concluded with the offstage recitation of the Kaddish. The 2004 film of *The Merchant of Venice*, starring Al Pacino, showed the newly baptized Shylock being barred from the Jewish ghetto. In Munby's production, while Portia and Bassanio and Nerissa and Gratiano were amusingly resolving their quarrels about their rings, Jessica read with horror the letter that Portia brought to Belmont detailing events in Venice. Implicitly, she realized what she had done in abandoning her father for Lorenzo, Judaism for Christianity.

The play ended with a devastating coda as a procession entered to perform the ceremony of Shylock's baptism. In agony Pryce's Shylock could barely respond with the required "Credo" to each article of the Christian Creed. In counterpoint to the triumphal Latin chanting of the Catholic ceremony, Jessica kneeled at the side of the stage singing with passionate sorrow a Hebrew prayer of repentance, begging for forgiveness. The Christian procession exited, and Lorenzo returned to take Jessica into Portia's house. But just as the doors were closing, she turned to face the audience. She was trapped—like Shylock.

The exceptional darkness of this ending to what was in many respects an audience-pleasing production of *The Merchant of Venice* was both deeply moving and theatrically thrilling. And the discordance was by no means out of keeping with what Shakespeare himself does elsewhere in his drama, even in an early romantic comedy such as *Love's Labor's Lost*, which I look forward to seeing at Chicago Shakespeare Theater next February.

The Globe's *Merchant* a Somber Tragicomedy
Regina Buccola

On August 4, Chicago Shakespeare Theater welcomed Shakespeare's Globe for a ten-day stand with their touring production of *The Merchant of Venice,* directed by Jonathan Munby. Munby has directed for Chicago Shakespeare Theater before as well, most recently in the 2016 production of *Othello*, set in a modern military context. In counterpoint, his *Merchant of Venice* was staged in early modern costumes, neck ruffs and puffy pantaloons keeping company with red skull caps for Shylock and Tubal.

It is virtually impossible in the post-Holocaust era to stage *The Merchant of Venice* in the genre category in which it originally appeared on stage: comedy. Its ugly episodes of anti-Semitism and forced conversion of Shylock from Judaism to Christianity are anathema in modern cultures that strive for religious tolerance. In Munby's production comedy was localized to a specific group of characters, treating the main Shylock plot with somber seriousness. Two of the most significant comic foils were Stefan Adegbola's Launcelot Gobbo (the cut text dispensed with Old Gobbo) and Jolyon Coy's Gratiano, who made his first stage entrance following the protracted opening Venetian Carnival prologue drunkenly puking into a metal bucket. Unless I am mistaken, Rachel Pickup (Portia) and Dorothea Myer-Bennett (Nerissa) appeared in the long carnival prologue as masked courtesans, their hair twisted into cornutos, in a foreshadowing of their disguised stint as a legal scholar and a clerk. In addition to this courtesan stint being of a piece with the later jesting with their ring-surrendering spouses about having slept with the lawyer and clerk, Portia also had moments of onstage flirtation with Andy Apollo's Lorenzo, suggestively cutting in with him as he danced at Belmont with his wife, Jessica. Just as Munby's production eschewed any notion of a happy ending for Shylock, the final stage grouping of the trio of young married couples with Antonio as a heartbroken seventh wheel offered little promise of happily ever after.

The raucous prologue, with live musicians onstage egging on the excesses of the debauched carnival-goers, took place with the house lights up, patrons still making their way to their seats. The over-the-top nature of the revelry put a thumb on the scale in favor of Shylock's later castigation of the depravity of Venetian carnival before we ever heard him deliver it. The excesses of this opening, and the broad brush strokes delineating Gratiano's character—in a brief Italian interlude he was accosted by a woman with a baby, who was clearly taxing him with failure to support his out-of-wedlock child—were of a piece with the full house lights of the prologue, as gestures toward this production's original staging in the outdoor venue of the Globe Theatre in Southwark. Some of these broad gestures played less well in the more intimate, indoor setting of Chicago Shakespeare Theater, and set me to musing anew about the likely alterations that Shakespeare's own theater company might have made as productions migrated from the outdoor, open-air theaters to the dark, indoor spaces like the Blackfriars Theatre, patronized by a narrower cross-section of society than the Globe.

Continuing to sound the comic register from the bass to the treble, both of Portia's princely suitors—Giles Terera's Prince of Morocco and Christopher Logan's Prince of Arragon—were played as buffoons, Morocco a scimitar-wielding ass-grabber, and Arragon a mincing narcissist in love with his own shadow ... and reflection. Pickup alternated between arrogant disdain for men she clearly considered beneath her, and nervous fear that one of these idiots would choose the proper casket, tying her to them for life. She openly tried to guide Bassanio to the proper casket as a disapproving Balthasar (Colin Haigh) looked on, holding the three keys on a gilt and velvet platter.

A broad brush was also used in the characterization of Antonio (Dominic Mafham), though for darker purposes. Bassanio clearly had a sexual attraction to Dan Fredenburgh's Bassanio, who gently rebuffed Antonio's attempt to kiss him after the court scene, for example. Antonio's naked hostility to Shylock visibly appalled Bassanio when Antonio approached him for a loan on his friend's behalf; Bassanio looked on in horror as Antonio snatched a religious text from Shylock's hands and threw it to the ground at his feet.

Adegbola bridged these broad characterizations with his comic style, effectively bridging the comedic and serious plots, as the former servant of Shylock (and confidante of Jessica), who joins the service of Bassanio. As he debated the pros and cons of leaving Shylock's service, Adegbola brought up two audience members to stand in as his conscience ("budge not") and the fiend ("budge"). In Adegbola's expert hands, even this witty, fourth-wall-breaking scene (an aspect of it Adegbola broke with the text to point out) subtly underlined the production's taking of Shylock's part—it is "the fiend," after all, who counsels abandoning the Jew's service.

Jonathan Pryce brought a wonderful subtlety to Shylock; while the production tilted in favor of sympathy for him, he was no angel, treating Gobbo with vicious contempt, and entering for the first time with Jessica—sensitively played by Pryce's own daughter, Phoebe—heatedly arguing in Hebrew. Jessica's elopement—coupled with her theft of money and jewels from her father as a self-determined dowry for her marriage to Lorenzo—turned Shylock's long suffering sharply in the direction of vindictive revenge. Pryce's transformation from contempt of Antonio to open hatred of him was beautifully calibrated in the way in which he delivered his lines, sinking gradually from a rational resentment of an abuser to the fear of a cornered animal, which will attack in self-defense. In the court Shylock turned the tables on Antonio initially, eagerly whetting his knife on the sole of his shoe and producing a set of brass scales from his carpet bag.

In court, Antonio appeared as a broken shell of his former arrogant self, in a tattered shift. When Portia in her guise as legal scholar temporarily conceded that the bond was forfeit, the pound of flesh Shylock's due, a cross-beam with manacles on each end flew in from above, and the bearded and disheveled Antonio was affixed to it, briefly resembling Christ on the cross. However, given what we had seen of Antonio's conduct prior to this scene, he scarcely seemed an ideal Christ figure. By this point in the play, the image appeared more of a critique of Christian hypocrisy than an elevation of Antonio's suffering, much of which was the result of his own previous conduct.

Jessica emerged as a significant figure in Munby's production, with numerous stage moments indicative of the conflicted nature of her character. Her relationship with her father, Shylock, was initially tense and bitter; her interactions with Gobbo were tender and loving; Lorenzo defended his love of Jessica to his fleering friends, Solanio and Gratiano, vehemently, lending legitimacy to a relationship that has, in some productions, been depicted as opportunistic on Lorenzo's part. After the interval, Jessica had a silent, solo stage moment in which she seemed depressed; Lorenzo approached to offer her a present: a large cross pendant on a necklace. Jessica brightened at the gift, and turned to let Lorenzo put it on her. However, her happiness was soon undercut by the mistress of Belmont; Portia sailed in, handed her wine to Jessica as if she were a common servant, and cut in on her to dance away with her husband. Jessica was jealous of Portia, but Lorenzo, in his turn, was jealous of the friendly intimacy between Jessica and Gobbo. All of these conflicted emotions were conveyed by the actors in brief scenes punctuating the information provided in the actual text.

The most stunning effect, however, was reserved for the epilogue. Just as the play began with carnival stage business that is not overtly in the text, it concluded with stage business that is forecast in the play text, but not staged within it. As Jessica read the court order giving her possession of half of Shylock's estate, she became increasingly agitated, eventually breaking into a song of mourning in Hebrew. The upstage wall then parted, breaking the darkness of Jessica's stage moment with a blaze of light, as white-clad priests carrying censors accompanied Shylock in a white shift on stage, chanting "Credo" in Latin, as he underwent his forced baptism. Jessica continued her Hebrew lament, punctuating the Christian ceremony, the two religions colliding in the epilogue in see-saw fashion, the daughter who had willingly converted now returning to the religious tradition—and, by extension, the father— she had spurned, as Shylock reluctantly followed his daughter into Christianity.

No one died in Munby's *Merchant of Venice*, making it no tragedy, but the community created via marriage and religious conversion in the final scenes scarcely seemed a happy one. The Globe brought a tragical comedy to Navy Pier, the emphasis on the tragic, the comedy reserved, on the whole, for characters who flitted through the production, tragedy the register for the central ones.

THEATER ZUIDPOOL
MACBETH

by William Shakespeare
composed by Mauro Pawlowski + Tijs Delbeke
presented by Chicago Shakespeare Theater
at Thalia Hall

Daniel Ribar

No EXIT: The Sound and Fury of Macbeth's Descent into Madness
Aaron Krall

Zuidpool's *Macbeth* begins with a witches' song. Six performers, stylishly dressed in black and white, approach a collection of instruments and microphones. A droning harmonium, feedback, sampled loops, and jagged percussion frame Femke Heijens's ethereal opening lines: "All hail, Macbeth!" After several repetitions, the tempo increases, and the song shifts into a chanted chorus of "Thou shalt be king hereafter!" punctuated by chilling witch cackles.

Framed by the elegantly decaying proscenium of the stage at Thalia Hall, set in front of the graffitied brick of the backstage wall, and drenched in red lighting, the show opens very much like a rock concert. The sometimes-sung, sometimes-spoken language of Shakespeare's play feels at home in the musical setting. Like a mashup of *Macbeth* and Pink

Floyd's *The Wall*, the play becomes the story of an ambitious singer/warrior/king confronting the tragic costs of his success.

The production's compression of the text supports this reading, as all peripheral plot is cut away. Macbeth's story—his ambition, his isolation, his horror—is elevated here. An audience member unacquainted with Shakespeare's play certainly couldn't follow the nuances of the Scottish royal succession, and even Lady Macbeth is reduced to a supporting character. Instead, Macbeth's experiences, his inner word and external expressions, are heightened through the words, the sounds, and the images of this production. We are offered a visceral experience of his descent into madness.

Theater Zuidpool, a Belgian theater company with a reputation for formal experimentation, offers a version of *Macbeth* that deliberately blurs the boundaries between theater and rock concert. Their version of the play was adapted by the company and features a score composed by Mauro Pawlowski and Tijs Delbeke, members of the Antwerp rock music scene. The production skillfully balances music and text, but the eclectic music played by the cast and featuring diverse instruments and influences, carries the show.

Jorgen Cassier plays Macbeth as a man too much in his own mind. For the first half of the performance, he is tightly wound, contemplative, and controlled, a spring under tension. He grapples with his ambition, the witches' prophecy, and his wife's prodding. The show's concert concept effectively highlights Macbeth's isolation as Cassier delivers his lines into a standing microphone directly to the audience. He does not physically engage with the other characters; his voice is mediated by the technology and the space at the front of the stage. His Macbeth is tormented and very alone.

A turning point comes when Wouter "Koen" Van Kaam performs the Porter's song as a creepy honky-tonk, late-night revelry. Playing a banjo and accompanied by harmonica, fiddle, and acoustic guitar. Van Kaam conjures Tom Waits as he growls a repeated "Knock, knock, knock! Who's there?" The song is played with a mixture of comedy and horror, and it stands out as a light moment in a very dark show. The darkness quickly returns at the end of the song, though, as Heijens voices Macduff's horrified and enraged discovery of Duncan's murder and stabs of electric guitar feedback replace the banjo plucking.

After this song, Macbeth's slow descent into madness becomes a sprint. Cassier's coiled spring explodes as the play becomes louder, faster, and even more focused on his isolated character. While we wait for the Great Birnam Wood to march against Macbeth, the music relies more heavily on electric guitar and bass, feedback, percussion, and sharp strings, echoes of the Velvet Underground's early sonic assaults, sludgy contemporary heavy metal, and even thudding Euro dance music as Banquo haunts the banquet. And more lines are shouted, screamed, and shrieked. This is a very loud show. The sound becomes physical. Only when Macbeth dies does the noise quiet and the play end.

By the time Macbeth despairs that life "is a tale / Told by an idiot, full of sound and fury, / Signifying nothing" it sounds like a mission statement, or a confession. Zuipool's *Macbeth* is undeniably full of sound and fury. The question is, what does it signify? The production gives us a glimpse of the tempest in the title character's psychology and his soul. And it asks us to experience it, emotionally and physically, through the music. It's an exhausting experience, but it feels true to Shakespeare's play. Throughout the show, a red emergency "EXIT" sign hung above a door in the backstage wall, complementing the show's lighting design and providing commentary on the action. We want Macbeth to find a way out of his tragedy, but for the character, and for the audience, there is no escape.

said anything) landed brilliantly when she, a bit behind on her dictation, made Oberon repeat "Athenian garments" several times as the Fairy King was describing who should be dosed with the love potion.

> **Puck:** Athenian what?
> **Oberon:** Garments!
> **Puck:** Right, got it! (*Scribbling. Pause.*) And…garments are clothes?
> **Oberon:** Yes!
> **Puck:** Athenian clothes, got it. That's it? Nothing else?

Of course, when the potion goes in the wrong eyes, and Oberon begins to blame Puck, she still has the words "Athenian garments" scribbled on her forearm to show to Oberon, to the raucous laughter of the crowd.

The topical references that, by Brook's account, are a vital part of the rough theatre were there: the "Ass's head" that Puck put onto Bottom was, of course, a Donald Trump mask. The joke was so obvious that it seemed almost too easy, but nonetheless it connected with the audience, many who have probably seen practically nothing else on their social media since the GOP convention the week before.

The audience relationship is the primary focus of the Project, but it is in service to the play. The actors are telling the story because the story is important to them. What they do with the story is often funny, often self-referential, and often a departure from the text, but their performance results in an audience experience that allows for thoughtful consideration of what the story is saying. In this production, the genders of the characters were assigned as if at random; all four lovers were played by women, while Hippolyta was played by a man. But on reflection, it is not random. Audiences for *Midsummer Night's Dream* regularly feel that they cannot tell the lovers apart or remember who is supposed to go with whom, and in this performance, it seems like that is part of the point of the play. At the opening of the play, Demetrius and Lysander both love Hermia, but the play take valuable exposition time right at the beginning to make it clear that the lovers have always been switching roles. Not long ago both men loved Helena, and first one and then the other changed allegiances. If the four lovers are all the same gender, then the mixing and matching between them is even harder to follow; we in the audience are led to understand that there might be less "true" about "true love" than a surface reading of the play would indicate.

As evidenced by this performance alone, The Backroom Shakespeare Project is worth seeing. In a way, the Project is a testament to the strength of Shakespeare's plays: there is room in Chicago for every kind of adaptation, performance and treatment, from the flagship productions of Chicago Shakespeare Theater, to the gritty storefront theaters, to the many Shakespeare in the Park productions this summer. Each has something to offer, some new insight into the Elizabethan world.

SONG OF THE GOAT THEATRE
SONGS OF LEAR

directed by Grzegorz Bral
composed by Jean-Claude Acquaviva + Maciej Rychły
presented by Chicago Shakespeare Theater

Z. Warzyński

Essentially Lear
Ira S. Murfin

Performed by an ensemble of twelve singers and musicians dressed in black on a bare stage, save for ten chairs and some musical instruments, Song of the Goat Theatre's *Songs of Lear* proposes that there is an essence of tragedy in *King Lear* that is not beholden to the formal expectations of modern theater, something powerful that predates and remains independent of the play. The performance intends to tap into that force and release it, without regard for intellectual analysis or understanding, through song and movement. Voices echo one another, clashing then merging, gestures are passed between members of the ensemble in an almost unconscious way, the performers keeping a constant sonic and kinesthetic awareness of one another, a result of the company's group training regimen. They function as one finely tuned instrument. A performer might embody a character for a moment and then let that identity dissolve back into the chorus of voices. The songs, composed by

Jean-Claude Acquaviva and Maciej Rychły, draw on Gregorian chant, the Gospel of Thomas, even an Emily Dickinson poem, in addition to language from *King Lear* itself. Though these sources, save a traditional Tibetan tune included at the very end, reveal a largely Christian and Eurocentric framework for the supposedly elemental and universally translatable capacity of music, the range of texts nonetheless make the case for a common thread running through many different sources of poetry from at least Biblical times.

This is the enduring tragic impulse that Song of the Goat, whose name is the literal translation of the term "tragedy," picks up and preserves, just as Shakespeare seized upon and shaped that same impulse to his own purposes. *Songs of Lear* suggests that this essence of tragedy may best be revisited not by endlessly restaging and reexamining the same text, recounting the same plot century after century, but rather by stepping into the emotional center that tragedy embodies and tuning into it together, as the ensemble begins its performance by tuning bodies and voices to the room, the audience, and to each other. In order to know firsthand the passions, desires, grief, and rage shared by humans in tragic circumstances across time—fictional and otherwise, noble and otherwise—we might need to discover our responses together in a theater, a place that should be devoted not to dull repetition or the recitation of literature, but to experiencing, directly and in the present, something very old in a new and unexpected way.

This potential for language to evoke a visceral response that transcends logic and meaning and touches something universal and ineffable is almost always described via metaphors of musicality. Where ordinary prose aspires to do more than merely communicate, we say that it becomes poetry, or becomes equal to poetry; and where the beauty of poetry exceeds its literal meaning, we can only compare it to music. Certainly the popular veneration of Shakespeare takes on these terms— he is not merely a dramatist, but a poet, and where his poetry reaches its expressive apex, it is the musicality of his language that we remark upon. But what does that mean? It certainly does not mean that the words are necessarily to be sung, in fact consigning words to the status of song lyrics can only emphasize the distance between language and music. Instead, our hyperbole suggests that the right words in the right order at the right time might literally *become* music, break free from the stifling container of syntactical meaning and express themselves as music does, through tone, melody, harmony, and rhythm, and so touch us in the way that music does, that is profoundly and beyond reason.

It is this act of cross-disciplinary translation that Song of the Goat Theatre attempts to realize with *Songs of Lear*, to take *Lear* and render it in music. *Songs of Lear* does not try to tell *King Lear*'s story through music, but rather to do with music what *King Lear* does, to invoke the effects of *Lear* without staging or recounting its plot, distilling to its most concentrated form the animus at the center of Shakespeare's play. In doing so, they mean to move the audience's apprehension of *Lear* from one filtered through theatrical representation into a more shared, lived, firsthand experience that embodies the energy of the drama rather than the specifics of its story (a weighty rebuke, perhaps, to Ira Glass's now infamous Tweet that *Lear* is "not relatable.")

Song of the Goat Theatre was established twenty years ago in Poland by Grzegorz Bral and Anna Zubrzycki. Both are alumni of Gardzienice, the remote Polish theater center founded by students and collaborators of influential teacher and director Jerzy Grotowski. Like Grotowski and the work done at Gardzienice, Song of the Goat Theatre creates work through a collective process based in sustained and ongoing training practices that incorporate voice, movement, rhythm, and energy. They perform as a single choral body engaged in polyphonic song and ensemble movement, aimed at the most concentrated expression of the very human desires, passions, and grief that have defined dramatic tragedy since classical times. In the process, they largely leave behind Shakespeare's language and the play's plot. Certainly a few lines from the play find their way in, both spoken and sung, and Bral himself narrates some of the plot, but in many ways Shakespeare's play, as we know it, is absent. *Songs of Lear* becomes not a staging of *Lear*, but a staging with *Lear*, in relationship to *Lear*, because of what Shakespeare's play makes possible.

Bral starts the performance quite non-musically, explaining rather informally and without irony to the audience that "theatre is about telling stories," and declaring that the performance begins with one. Instead of music or theatre, though, his story turns out to be about painting. Bral recalls an exhibition at the Tate Modern museum in London that traced the early career of pioneering modernist master Wassily Kandinsky from the pastoral landscapes and folkloric scenes with which he began to his discovery of the abstract techniques for which he is best known. The exhibition came together for Bral in a large gallery where he could see the progression of Kandinsky's painting style from the early landscapes toward ever-increasing levels of abstraction, until he arrived at an entirely black painting with some geometric lines cutting across it. Pure abstraction, it seemed. But in context of the gallery, Bral could perceive the relationship of the black painting to the landscapes, even though they had such clearly divergent representational fates, they shared a common origin and the same instigating impulse.

This relationship between representational and abstract forms is what Bral promises for *Songs of Lear*—*Lear* in twelve paintings, with sound as color and himself, the director, as docent, explaining the paintings as we go. The dozen songs that comprise *Songs of Lear* are meant to occupy the living heart of Shakespeare's play, to locate the dramatic impulse *Lear* embodies, and to remain there, tracing the psychic inner life of the play in absence of recited text and enfleshed portrayal of character. Bral's commentary provides a tenuous connection, tethering his production to Shakespeare's play so it does not float off into pure abstraction, just as Kandinsky's black painting could only be a landscape in relation to his earlier, representational works. By breaking *Lear* down to song, Song of the Goat Theatre seeks to clarify the play. Not to analyze and explicate it to the point of coherence, but rather to cook it down until it is at its most concentrated and transparent—a stock of *Lear*, *Lear*'s flavors with none of the meat left behind, a homeopathic preparation of the play. A *Lear* not to be seen, but to be seen through, heard and felt and understood in the moment of apprehension not as the play, but as an essence that remains of the play after the performance disappears, an essence that can permeate the boundaries between performers' bodies, between actors and spectators, and that can flow on into the next embodiment of tragedy in any of our lives or on that, or any, stage.

"See better, Lear"
Lori Humphrey Newcomb

Months after Song of the Goat Theatre (Teatr Pieśń Kozła) brought their *Songs of Lear* from Poland to Chicago Shakespeare Theater, their performance continues to teach me, as King Lear himself is taught, to "see better."

The first lesson was to widen my own vision of innovation. In the studio theater, rows of playgoers looked directly on an open area occupied by a dozen bentwood chairs arranged in a semicircle. The setting promised collaboration and improvisation, in line with the program statement by the troupe, citing "the need and search for connection...as the root of authentic experience." I thus was disconcerted when a man with directorial bearing walked alone to the front of the space. He earnestly apologized to the audience. He had, he said, no icebreaking joke for tonight's show; he was to guide us, as Virgil guides Dante. He wanted to describe an art show he had seen at London's Tate Modern, of the paintings of Wassily Kandinsky, which had spurred him to consider how a series of abstractions might capture a landscape as no single image could. (Presumably this show was the 2006 retrospective called *Kandinsky: The Path to Abstraction*.) This man was the company's director, Grzegorz Bral, and he explained that *Songs of Lear* would be twelve songs, or paintings, or "landscapes of sound."

As much as I liked Bral, his intervention puzzled me. Did we need to be told that performance could refract and abstract, or that an experimental troupe might present discontinuous scenes? Why invoke a painter, and a defendant of artistic isolation at that, to introduce a troupe that aims to "integrate movement, voice, song and text"?

The language of the performance became clearer as a group of performers occupied the arc of chairs. They were dressed not in dancewear or actor-casual jeans and sneakers, but in strict black: dress shoes, black sheaths on the women, black trousers and shirts on the men. The uniformity suggested a chorus, or, less literally, with the dark attire setting off the warmer curves of the bentwood, a string ensemble. We were not witnessing a rehearsal, but a concert, made up of twelve pieces. The program listed compositions, attributing lyrics to Shakespeare, the Gospel of Thomas, Gregorian chant, and Emily Dickinson, and music to the troupe's composers, Jean-Claude Acquaviva and Maciej Rychły. Yet we were to hear these compositions as theater, with the director guiding us much as a docent would guide viewers to read paintings as landscapes. The ensemble would indeed "integrate movement, voice, song and text" into an art form, but one that was consciously multimodal, not a totalizing art. The constant was that this art form was fundamentally choric: an ensemble of singers, largely *a cappella*, in tight harmonies and in solo, often with one of the actors (not always the same one, and not the director) as their conductor. The actors' bodies and chairs alike were instruments; at one point all the male actors drummed on their round chair seats like the tambourines used in another number. The half-circle of chairs itself invoked Lear's crown and its breaking.

Less like an opera than like Shozo Sato's kabuki-inflected Shakespeare adaptations, this was not the text of *Lear* set to music, but *Lear* with its text compressed to distinct, separate musical lines for different scenes from and around the play. The first scene, surprisingly, emphasized the calm before the storm. Other scenes gradually brought forward a consistent, but not insistent, case of main characters: the only jacketed, bearded actor as the impetuous Lear; a spare bespectacled man as Gloucester; a tall, dark woman of coiled energy as the Fool. Shakespeare's English texts were used amidst other evocative texts and wordless chants: the play's accusations and curses were interspersed with multilingual promises of peace. In one unforgettable sequence, after the director told us that the division of the kingdoms was not Lear's first rejection of Cordelia, we witnessed one female actor repeat Cordelia's words of grief as, at the ages of 4, 7, 11, and 14, her voice, facial comportment, and seated position evoking with dreadful specificity the stages of girlhood and the intensification of emotional pain.

As the play moved from betrayal to total war, the pieces became increasingly collective, percussive, urgent, mobile, and wordless. The company was tapping the wellspring of tragedy: a howling grief that preceded speech and yet compelled the search for words. What we heard might be an early Christian liturgy, an eastern European folk harmony, a Gregorian or Tibetan chant; what we saw was all-too-familiar scenes of damaged institutions and collectivity: divided juries, gridlocked parliaments, warring troops, thrusting mobs. The docent became a commentator, guiding us across an apparently orderly landscape devastated by the sight and sound of human anger and loss, and the production's many cultural referents reminded us that such conflicts erupt endlessly, are never fully averted. What I learned in the course of this performance was that although I am a teacher of texts, the power of a text like *King Lear* precedes and outlives any language, and yet that language must continue to intercede. I learned to be grateful, then, for the gentle guidance of the director's narration, for the hope that this unspeakable pain could be named and understood.

At the end of the performance, the director spoke of the troupe's stance against war, oppression, cruelty, and tyranny. He turned to the audience and offered his company's support against the "war going on now." The lights came up; audience members turned to each other in wordless appreciation. Was I the only one wondering which war he meant? There were so many to choose from, and I thought of Syria, and Palestine, and endangered European unity; but this offer seemed addressed to us as Americans. And thus it is that the full lesson of *Songs of Lear*, the full intimacy of its landscape, did not become clear to me until after Election Day.

PRITZKER MILITARY MUSEUM & LIBRARY
+ CHICAGO SHAKESPEARE THEATER
SHAKESPEARE AND THE CITIZEN SOLDIER

Courtesy of Pritzker Military Museum & Library

Constructing the Theater of War
Richard Gilbert

In fall 2016, The Pritzker Military Museum & Library filmed a series of in-depth interviews with scholars, artists, and military veterans entitled *Shakespeare and the Citizen Soldier*. In partnership with Chicago Shakespeare Theater, the four episodes explored the role of soldiers and warfare in Shakespeare's work and the role of Shakespeare in informing our understanding of soldiers and warfare.

I went to the Museum to watch the live taping of the last episode, and while touring the collection beforehand, I was struck by the fact that the Pritzker is an art museum. Not, of course, *only* an art museum, but the two major exhibits on display during my visit were both exhibits of Vietnam-era art. One was of photographs taken by the Department of the Army's Special Photographic Office (DASPO) of the day-to-day lives of American servicemen. The photos are alternately chilling, inspiring, beautiful, awful. They convey a sense of the war that brought home a kind of reality that was unavailable to me through reading books about it. The other exhibit was a collection of Viet Cong propaganda posters. Again, I was given a view of the war from the point of view of the North

Vietnamese that any amount of statistical and historical information about "the enemy" could not convey.

For me, the most intriguing through-line in *Shakespeare and the Citizen Soldier* was exactly how reciprocal that relationship between art and history is. The series featured actors, directors, soldiers, and scholars, all working together to bring stories of war to the stage in responsible, evocative, and truthful ways. The knowledge exchanges were surprising in many ways, but one after another, participants claimed that the value of the exchange had been in their favor—that is to say, most seemed to feel that they learned more from their involvement with their collaborators than they contributed.

The four sessions focus on different aspects of the larger topic. The first episode features Chicago Shakespeare Theater Artistic Director and Founder Barbara Gaines alongside Fordham University Professor Stuart Sherman. Sherman collaborated with Gaines on *Tug of War*, CST's flagship double production chronicling the foreign and civil wars from *Edward III* to *Richard III*. Gaines and Sherman discuss how they went about telling this story of war, using Sherman's historical knowledge to inform the art. Gaines had many advisors on this project, including a handful of veterans whom she interviewed personally in an attempt to bring onto the stage something like the experience of having been at war. Interestingly, Gaines repeatedly states that it is not possible for a civilian to truly understand what being a soldier in wartime is like. While such a claim responds to the mystique that surrounds war and soldiers, it is an odd claim for a theater artist to make; an important aim of the project of *Tug of War* is to convey that very experience—to allow audiences who are not veteran's insight into what war is like. Gaines describes a very powerful image that has stuck with her and which she used in conceptualizing the play. The image is from an adaptation of *The Odyssey* in which a river speaks of the bodies that have floated down it, the death that it has seen. Sherman—who also at one point claims that veterans have understandings which are unavailable to civilians—responds to Gaines that the theater *is* that river—the river that "knows the costs, the collective costs of killing." Such a sentiment is compelling; one hopes that art can, at its best, bring that knowledge to its audience.

For Stephan Wolfert, a veteran-turned-actor who was featured in the second episode, "Shakespeare wrote veterans perfectly." Wolfert served as an infantry officer for eight years before leaving the Army and eventually becoming an actor and director who works with veterans, using Shakespeare to help veterans re-integrate (or, as he calls it, "decruit"). Not only does Wolfert claim that Shakespeare (who was not a veteran) understands veterans, but that as a consequence, Shakespeare wrote characters who veterans understand easily. Wolfert's account of his first experience with *Richard III*'s opening speech is illuminating; for Wolfert, the story of a soldier lamenting his inability to fit into civilian society, and his sense of being deformed by his experiences in war, rang perfectly true. So true that he uses that speech, amongst others, to introduce veterans to Shakespeare, using theater as a kind of therapy.

The third episode features CST actors James Vincent Meredith and Jessie Fisher as well as Lieutenant Colonel Matthew Yandura, chair of Military Science at Loyola University. Meredith and Fisher played Othello and Emilia respectively in CST's 2016 production of *Othello*. Yandura worked with the cast to help them better portray soldiers. The production was set in modern day, and Emilia was also a soldier, so the two actors worked closely with the LTC to develop both a sense of soldiering based on both physical and psychological training. Learning actual drill from Yandura (in what he described as an abbreviated "basic training") was, according to the two actors, incredibly valuable to them and the rest of the cast. Theater ensembles are used to developing a group identity and esprit de corps, but doing that through military drill was both inspiring and educational. Meanwhile, Yandura felt that he learned more than he imparted; his exposure to the stories of the actors and to the play gave him new ways to think about how he might use theater skills to train his own students at Loyola. Yandura said that he found the actors, with their attention to detail and their willingness and their professional training in the ability to submerge their own egos in order to emulate the behavior of others, were amongst the quickest candidates he had ever trained.

Fisher's experience was particularly fascinating, as she learned both from Yandura and Yandura's wife (also a veteran), who came to rehearsal and was willing to discuss what it was like to be the wife of a soldier. Fisher's Emilia being a soldier created a very interesting reading of the character. As a soldier, her first loyalty lies with her commander, Othello, and her comrades, including her husband Iago. Assigned to "babysit" the civilian Desdemona, she is at first resentful of the woman who has no place in a military zone, and who is keeping her from "more important" duties. It is only as she realizes that the men are behaving poorly, and that Desdemona is demonstrating the pure loyalty which she believes she has a right to expect from Iago and Othello, that she comes to sympathize with her charge. This exciting new reading would have been difficult to create without the help of LTC Yandura.

In thinking more about the way that art and history inform each other, I am reminded of the vital importance of both as the foundation of a free society. According to the staff of the Library, there were protests by American servicemen when the exhibit of North Vietnamese propaganda art opened. These veterans were angry that posters showing our soldiers being killed and our planes being shot down would be displayed. Apparently, those protesters mostly changed their minds after actually seeing the exhibit. I wonder if their minds were changed about more than just the appropriateness of the exhibit; perhaps their perspectives on the war itself might have been shifted slightly, too.

CHICAGO SHAKESPEARE THEATER
TUG OF WAR: CIVIL STRIFE

adapted + directed by Barbara Gaines

Liz Lauren

When Jacks Are Trumps
Regina Buccola

In this election season, what could be better than a marathon march through Shakespeare's history plays devoted to the Wars of the Roses? *Tug of War: Civil Strife* romps through parts 2 and 3 of *Henry VI* and *Richard III*, with cynical modern dress and raucous song and dance numbers for the court crowd (contrasted with more somber musical interludes for a common soldier and his wife), and a pointed take on our baser tendencies to become enamored of anything that can be made to look good on TV.

The would-be usurper the Duke of York and his son Richard emerge as two peas in a pod in Chicago Shakespeare Theater's production. York's semi-psychotic song and dance routines in which he gleefully anticipates the havoc he will wreak on the Lancastrian court presage the maniacal power-madness of his son, who proves far more bloodthirsty and—perhaps, consequently—far more successful than his father at rebellion and usurpation. When it came his turn to use Pink's lyrics to demand that we "Get the Party Started," Timothy Edward Kane as

Richard mimicked the hip-shimmying dance of his father, played by Larry Yando. These extra-textual song-and-dance moments forged an interesting connection between them that I have not seen in other instances in which I have seen these plays staged sequentially.

In his own time and place, Shakespeare would have had much direct experience of the kinds of social unrest that is depicted among the commoners in part 2 of *Henry VI*. Stephen Greenblatt's introduction to the *Norton Shakespeare* tallies up thirty-five riots in the last two decades of the sixteenth century, a whopping twelve of them taking place in June 1595 alone. Shakespeare likely wrote the play featuring Cade in the early 1590s, but his history plays about the struggle for the throne during the reign of Henry VI (1422-1461, with a brief reprise from 1470-71) were popular on the London stage throughout the 1590s, when riots by the working classes swept the city outside of the theater.

Some of these riots were occasioned by frustration over the consolidation of political power in an aristocratic class seen as woefully out of touch with the life circumstances and needs of the working classes. Some were occasioned by fury at the encroachment of immigrants fleeing religious persecution as Protestants on the Continent into London and its workforce. Sound familiar? Director Barbara Gaines thought that it did, too. Kevin Gudahl does a star turn here as a Jack Cade made over in the image of Donald Trump.

It's topical, and wicked good fun, but it's more than that: it's an insightful read of Cade's role in part 2 of *Henry VI*. The crafty Duke of York privately encourages the rebel Jack Cade to foment rebellion against the aristocracy among the commoners. In our present day, these behind-the-scenes political machinations parallel conspiracy theories of early 2016 that Trump—who once lent financial support to the Clintons, who, in turn, attended his wedding to his third, current wife, Melania— had been suborned by the Clinton campaign to run against her as a straw man. The Duke of York, after all, never intends to make Cade king. Cade is a means to York's own ends. He's a troublemaker and a distraction from the real threat to the crown, York himself. Paradoxically—and hypocritically—Cade styles himself a man of the people, *and* a scion of the royal blood. He simultaneously demands that anyone with a whiff of education, good breeding, or wealth about them be summarily executed, but dubs himself "Sir John Mortimer," heir to the English throne. The riots that he incites in London swell to such a dangerous head that the king and court are forced to flee.

Both York and Richard take turns in the gilded tire that has served as the throne in both halves of *Tug of War*, which began last spring with *Edward III*, *Henry V*, and part 1 of *Henry VI*. The tire is a synecdoche for the throne and the power that comes with it, but also a constant reminder of the wars we currently wage over oil. Tires are petroleum products also used, paradoxically, to consume other petroleum products via the vehicles that roll on them. They are also toxic, leeching their poisons into the water table.

Never depicted with the gilded throne, Cade makes his first appearance descending from the fly space on a tire throne of his own devising, painted like a Union Jack. The gilded tire is garish, but the Union Jack tire protests too much; it's the Fourth of July parade attendee who is wearing a flag t-shirt with flag shorts and baseball cap, while also waving a flag. It telegraphs Cade's nominal, over-the-top allegiance to the very national entity he intends to disrupt. Cade and his followers sport Union Jack buttons summarily stamped with the single, all-caps word: CADE.

Determined to root out everyone whose pretensions to education mark them out as elite, Cade fulminates against grammar schools, and issues the dismissive assessment of all educated people: "intellectual degenerate." (A t-shirt slogan that should be made available in the theater lobby immediately). In a grim re-enactment of Trump's vicious, parodic imitation of *New York Times* reporter Serge Kovaleski's arthrogryposis, Gudahl's Cade lampoons the shaking of the palsy sufferer Lord Say once his goons have taken him into custody. If the precept that we should learn history in order that we do not repeat its mistakes has merit, we would all do well to consider how comfortably the Cade shoe fits Trump.

Trump became a household word—or, rather, his catchphrase "You're fired" did—as a result of his stint on the reality TV show *The Apprentice*. *Tug of War* delves into this terrain, too, not with Cade, but with Richard. Richard and Buckingham's series of collaborative performances becomes a television program in which Richard first accuses Queen Elizabeth of practicing witchcraft to give him birth defects everyone knows to have been congenital, then kills Lord Hastings for having the temerity to assert that she will be punished in a conditional phrase ("If they had done this deed, my noble lord..."), and, finally, persuades the Lord Mayor of London that he killed Hastings in self-defense before being begged by Buckingham to take the very throne he has been attempting to steal from his own nephew. A green screen descends, as Buckingham (James Newcomb) reads from a clipboard like a television producer while Richard's henchmen drape the red capes worn over bishops' cassocks over their military garb for the camera. In a gesture of true cynicism, Richard reads from the Bible he took from the hands of Henry VI when he killed him, as the camera offers—on video monitors flown in for the audience's benefit—a tight shot of his contemplative face framed by the faux devout ministrations of his bodyguards. While in her 2012 production of *Richard III* Barbara Gaines gave the Scrivener pride of place in an isolation spot, the Scrivener is entirely cut from *Tug of War*, perhaps because we need no one to ask, "Who's so gross that sees not this palpable device?" (3.6.10-11).

Follow the money to ferret out political corruption, *All the President's Men* admonished us. In *Tug of War*, one can follow the props. I have already noted Richard's cynical recycling of Henry VI's Bible for his own godless agendas. Margaret (Karen Aldridge) rises from an adulterous sexual tryst with Suffolk (John Tufts) in Lancastrian red bra and slip. As she prepares to put her game face back on, she pulls a stylish silver rosary bracelet from her bosom, wrapping it around her hand like brass knuckles. The tiny silver cross that dangles delicately across the back of her hand matches the simple silver cross worn in religious sincerity by her husband, the King (Steven Sutcliffe), but hers is merely decorative, while his is a genuine mark of devotion.

The props in Scott Davis's austere scenic design are minimal; thus, when they do appear, they are noteworthy. Despite its documentation of violent civil conflict over, and over, and over again, *Tug of War* uses no weapons of any kind in battle scenes. The glaring exception to this no-weapons rule is Richard. Moreover, his weapon—a knife—paradoxically appears in the context of his amorous pursuits. Richard courts Lady Anne, widow of the Lancastrian Prince Edward, while she is engaged in a lament over the corpse of King Henry VI (whom Richard killed) at the beginning of *Richard III*. In a twisted marital proposal, Richard asks Lady Anne to kill him if she will not marry him. In *Civil Strife*, he presents her with an actual knife as he makes this proposition.

In a sickening foreshadowing of the way their short-lived relationship will end, he then offers her the ring that signifies their betrothal on the blade of this same knife. Catesby (Kevin Gudahl) silently communicates to Richard that Anne has been killed once it has ceased to be politically expedient for him to be married to her by offering their marital ring back to Richard on the blade of Richard's knife. The knife drops out of the equation, but Richard gives the same betrothal ring to Queen Elizabeth when he sends her to court her daughter—his niece, and sister to the royal nephews Richard has had killed—on his behalf.

The media circus, the rock music soundtrack, the forced patriotism and the faux religious devotion—it all seems uncomfortably familiar. Shakespeare wrote these plays with the descendant of the king ascendant in the final act—Henry VII, grandfather to Queen Elizabeth I—on the throne. Bush, Clinton, Bush, Bush, Obama, Obama...Clinton? And Trump ran in the primaries against another Bush? Plays about a medieval, family political dynasty are of greater relevance to America's twenty-first-century democracy than the Founding Fathers might ever have imagined that they could be.

New Rule
Clark Hulse

New Rule: Those who do *not* repeat history are doomed to *not* learning from it. By *repeat*, I mean on the stage. Don't try it in real life.

Every performance of history is a kind of rehearsal for life. We glimpse in the passions of the past the tune we may dance to in the future. Hip-hop founding fathers spellbind us in the Chicago Loop, while indie-rock Plantagenets cavort at Navy Pier.

The effect of *Tug of War: Civil Strife* is arguably very different from the effect of an individual Shakespeare history play all by itself. *Richard III* is about, well, Richard III. *Henry VI Part 2* is about Richard, Duke of York and Queen Margaret. But when you add in *Henry VI Part 3* and weave them together over six hours, the individuals recede, and larger patterns emerge. York, Margaret, and Richard remain enthralling and appalling as stage figures, to be sure, but their singular domination over history itself is less, because each rises and falls so fast.

History is of course not what happened, but a story about what happened. Too much happened to too many people to recount every detail. So history is an art of subtraction, selecting out what can produce a coherent story that still suggests the "too much." Theater in turn makes its own selection. It picks out a few individual people and forces to confront and entwine with one another. Theater re-sequences their world and seeks for emotion as the fulcrum of meaning.

Civil Strife is story upon story upon story upon story: Barbara Gaines reworking Shakespeare reworking the chronicles reworking something that maybe happened. What comes to the fore are emotional choices gone bad: hate over love, faction over common good, mine over ours, domination over decency, service and duty over just staying at home.

Sometimes the pathway from English history to our history is short, as when Kevin Gudahl as the demagogic rogue Jack Cade mimics Donald John Trump adorned with what might be taken for a Brexit button. As Gina Buccola says in a previous post, "The media circus, the rock music soundtrack, the forced patriotism and the faux religious devotion—it all seems uncomfortably familiar."

At other times the connection of past to present is more oblique, or admits of a possible contrast. Is political murder quite so easy anymore? Are there no laws? But the step is never large from medieval to modern, from endless war to endless war, from endless ambition to endless ambition, from chaos to chaos.

Shakespeare on stage gives abstraction a local habitation and a name, whether the character is the Duke of York or of Gloucester or simply First Soldier. Even minimalist settings, as in *Tug of War*, have an inherent naturalism, for the bodies of the actors are a mere few feet away from us, or right next us in the aisle. Yet Salman Rushdie has argued that naturalism in the right hands becomes so overwhelming that it breaks through to a dreamlike mystical surreality or even magical realism.

Something like that happens halfway through *Tug of War: Civil Strife* as Queen Margaret issues her half-mad curses and prophecies. As her fantasies begin to come true, the remaining warriors are seized with dread and are haunted by ghosts. Margaret's words become apparitions, rash deeds, and neurotic mental states.

Magical reality in theater takes us closer to history, not away from it, moving us toward the other history below and beyond politics or economics or warfare. This is the interior history of human suffering. As York says when his enemies have foolishly provided him with soldiers: "You put sharp weapons in a madman's hands." In opposition to those weapons stand our knowledge of the past, and the power of theater to reproduce it. We pray they are the tools of sanity.

FORO SHAKESPEARE
ENAMORARSE DE UN INCENDIO

written + directed by Eduardo Pavez Goye
presented by Chicago Shakespeare Theater

Roberto Blenda

Fire and Distance: Star-crossed Love
Aaron Krall

The title of the play *Enamorarse de un incendio*, which roughly translates as "falling in love with a fire," comes from the final scene of the play, in which a group of screenwriters play a version of Pictionary and discuss their plans for a television script. One character describes a painting of pyromania as "like being in love with forest fires." The association of love with fire, and all of its wild, motivating, and destructive connotations, signals the play's relationship with *Romeo and Juliet*. This play, written and directed by Chilean playwright Eduardo Pavez Goye, is inspired by the themes of Shakespeare's play, but it is not a direct adaptation. Instead, we are offered three new interwoven stories of star-crossed love.

Over the course of ninety minutes, the production, imported from Mexico's Foro Shakespeare, follows these lovers through desire, commitment, and heartbreak. The narrative that frames the play concerns three screenwriters tasked with revising a script at the home of their assistant. They are telling a love story, and their personal lives intervene. Two of the writers, Vicente and Viviana, are former lovers who separated after a domestic tragedy, and the latter is now romantically involved with the third writer, a younger man. As the tensions between these writers mount, two other stories are spliced in: Julián, a young artist, falls in love and elopes with the wife of an art dealer and Renata, a young woman in financial and emotional distress, dies, leaving behind a suicidally devastated lover.

The individual performances are a highlight in the production. The cast of four brings an emotional intensity to their characters across the three stories, each performer playing multiple roles and exploring many shades of love. Verónica Merchant and Luis Miguel Lombana give particularly impressive performances as the pair of older lovers, communicating a shared history and unfinished business. Hamlet Ramírez plays several versions of the young lover, emphasizing restraint and never falling into cliché. Itari Marta, though, anchors the production with commanding performances as Celeste, the screenwriter's manic assistant, Renata, the dying young woman in debt to the mob, and Marlene, an artist's muse. Swinging between tears and laughter, Marta's characters are emotionally raw and exposed. In a scene where Renata confesses her failed dog fighting exploits to her mother, she is frightened, guilty, and unhinged. In another scene, playing Celeste, she stands in the foreground silently reacting to a phone call while the other characters argue behind her. A range of emotions wash over her face as she hears devastating news, crystalizing the heightened feelings of the play.

The production features three simultaneous performance spaces: a box set of a small living room; a large screen above the set that displays live video of the performance filmed by two camera operators; and a "backstage" space off right with a prop table and a costume rack. The performers are nearly always visible to the audience as they move on and off stage and as they are filmed and projected on the screen. This spatial arrangement reflects and reproduces the screenwriters' narrative as they discuss the writing of a love story for television, while also being transformed into a simulation of television during the performance. The audience is constantly reminded of the actors' work as actors in addition to the reality of the characters they portray. It also encourages the audience to consider the differences between live and filmed performances. While the screen offers the heightened intimacy of close-ups and guides the viewers' focus, it also flattens and distorts the bodies that are visible below. It allows the play to roam between versions of love as real or artificial, expressed or enacted, literally three dimensional or two dimensional.

The projected images that double the performers, the camera operators who move in and around the performance spaces, and the visible backstage emphasize the performative and mediated nature of the play. Throughout the production, we see characters whose interactions are refracted through external objects, including a television script, a painting, and numerous cell phones. The characters feel intense emotions, but their conversations are often halting or one-sided. When the audience sees the performers' bodies enlarged and flattened on the screen, or when we see them change costumes, dab makeup, and mentally and emotionally prepare for the next scene, it calls attention to love as an internally felt emotion and love as external displays for others.

As a mostly English-language-monolingual member of the audience, I have to admit that I found much of the Spanish text of the play inaccessible. Captions, displayed stage left on a flat screen monitor, summarized and commented on the action of the play, but torrents of expressive language washed over me. This had an effect similar to seeing a non-English opera performance, where emotion, movement, and spectacle are heightened and privileged over the discursive content. The actors' vocal and physical performances conveyed the relationships and conflicts of the play in ways that felt precise, but also broad and archetypal.

The language barrier also added a dimension to the themes of the performance. In each of the stories, we see divisions between insiders and outsiders. Viviana and Vicente share a past that the other characters cannot access; Julián exploits his relationship with the art dealer as he separates him from his wife; and Renata's parents play largely unspeaking mirrors to a love story they only hear about after the fact. My experience of *Enamorarse de un incendio* highlighted the ways audiences are always outside of a performance, voyeuristically experiencing the lives, actions, and emotions of the characters. In this way, the production allows the audience to explore the contours of love, while also recognizing that, like Romeo and Juliet, lovers always create their own worlds.

SHAKESPEARE IN THE CRIMINAL JUSTICE SYSTEM: A PANEL DISCUSSION

presented by Chicago Shakespeare Theater

Chuck Osgood

Building Caring Communities (plus Shakespeare) Behind Bars
Katie Blankenau

At the recent panel discussion on "Shakespeare in the Criminal Justice System," Haisan T. Williams described the patience and self-reflection critical to his experience as a participant in the Shakespeare Prison Project at Racine Correctional Institution. If something in a play strikes a chord—or opens a wound—in an inmate, the company takes time to talk about it. After all, he said, "We'll get to the script. The book's been written." Williams's comment distilled my experience of the discussion, which I left with a renewed sense of the book—of Shakespeare, written and waiting and richly rewarding. More important, though, was the reminder of just how much the arts can *do*, and how tragically restricted access to the arts is in this country. The men and women on the panel discussion are working to improve that access in the most restrictive of places: prisons.

As was probably the case for most of the audience, I was familiar with some of the panelists' work through the film *Shakespeare Behind*

Bars (2005), which focuses on Curt L. Tofteland's Kentucky- and Michigan-based program, and through "Act V" (2002), an episode of *This American Life* that follows Agnes Wilcox's production of *Hamlet* in a Missouri prison. Both the film and the podcast are deeply human explorations of theater; the *This American Life* episode, which I first heard years ago but has never lost its impact, includes the most understated yet powerful performance of Claudius's speech in 3.3 ("O, my offence is rank...") that I've ever heard. I was thrilled to see both Tofteland and Wilcox on the panel, but was surprised—and then intrigued—by the difference between their approaches. That difference centered on the emotions of the participants. Tofteland, explaining why he directs Shakespeare in particular, said that Shakespeare identifies traumas and speaks eloquently about them. Inmates, who are often struggling to work through violence in their past and present, can use Shakespeare's language to aestheticize and analyze their trauma. In contrast, Wilcox remarked that she encourages participants to put their angst on hold, to leave it at the door. This creates a space devoted to the individual's artistic life, separate from their incarceration.

The conversation moved on from this discussion more quickly than I would have liked, but it reminded me obliquely of debates about trigger warnings and the place of emotion in the classroom. Williams's descriptions of the effects of Shakespearean characters and situations— his matter-of-fact assertion of their relevance to inmates' lives— highlighted how emotionally demanding an encounter with a play can be. This reminder of the plays' visceral power was exciting; for a scholar, it's always nice when someone recognizes the relevance of one's object of study. But as an educator, I found his descriptions also illustrated the complexity of channeling that power, of respecting the emotional difficulty (in addition to the intellectual complexity) of both text and performance. Williams spoke of expanding horizons but also near fistfights among participants. In classrooms as well as correctional facilities, lively discussion, subtle violence and emotional truth are jumbled together. How are we to respond?

Tofteland's focus on trust and self-analysis gives participants freedom to reflect on their personal histories. But is the academically rigorous opportunity lost? At the same time, Wilcox's process shores up participants' confidence, discipline and focus. But can one really leave one's angst at the door, even when inhabiting another character? Ultimately, both programs turn out performances and performers that are deeply engaged with the text. And where comparison to the classroom is concerned, both approaches share an inspirational emphasis on *care*. Describing the group's response to performers who cannot read polysyllabic words, Wilcox stressed the generosity and patience extended by the other inmates who orally guide their colleagues through the script. The consideration for others' fears and struggles, integral to the programs, was especially evident in Williams's description of the cast as an organism, caring for its component parts. The panelists' Shakespeare productions, facilitated with attention to the needs of cast members, thus create some measure of safety in an uncaring environment.

Other panelists, including Itari Marta of the Penitentiary Theater Company in Mexico and Kate Powers of Rehabilitation Through the Arts at Sing Sing, dove into the practical side of Shakespeare in the justice system. Describing her efforts to organize and provide for performance as a process of constant improvisation, Marta spoke eloquently about the lack of resources, despite which she manages to pay actors with the remainder of hard-won ticket sales. Powers also evoked the need for adaptability, anecdotally recounting her attempt to secure some kind of swords or even sword-adjacent props to stage *Twelfth Night*'s fight scene in a maximum-security prison. She also testified to the tangible results of arts programs in the justice system, pointing to the drastically reduced recidivism for participants in her program and the high rate of former members who go on to pursue college degrees.

Discussion of how to defend inmates' access to the arts sparked some of the most applauded conversation on the panel. Powers described the pragmatic, humanist argument for the arts, which, she pointed out, are wrongly treated like a luxury. To those who question her work, she said, she responds with her own question: "Who do you want coming home?" Williams concurred, reflecting that the most formative experience during his participation in the Shakespeare Prison Project came in his first role, when he was cast as an ancillary character. Although he went on to play Othello and Kent in *Lear* (whom he quoted with more facility than most professors), he said that his bit part helped him grow out of self-absorption and into leadership roles in real life.

"Shakespeare in the Criminal Justice System" was among the most powerful and I think important events hosted by Shakespeare 400 Chicago thus far. After all, as we reflect on Shakespeare's cultural impact throughout 2016, we have to ask who owns Shakespeare. It's easy to assert that the works we celebrate belong to everyone, but as we know that is far from the case. The panelists not only demonstrated that Shakespeare *should* be made accessible, but also illustrated the literal and figurative bars to widespread access. And yet they work to open at least a few doors. As Powers said when explaining "Why Shakespeare?," inmates' response to culture at large can shift, once "Shakespeare belongs to them."

Dramatic Rehabilitation:
"Who do you want coming home?"
Richard Gilbert

On Saturday, September 24, Chicago Shakespeare Theater hosted a panel discussion on the practice of teaching and producing Shakespeare with incarcerated populations. The audience, who filled the theater Upstairs at Chicago Shakespeare at its Navy Pier home, was an eclectic mix of academics, activists, and artists who were all eager to get out of the beautiful fall weather and into a windowless theater to hear what the panelists had to say.

The discussion ran for two hours, and then at least another hour informally in the lobby for those who chose to stay. Many aspects of this work were discussed, and my intent here is only to explore a few of them that have particular interest for me; other discussions that I overheard in the lobby went in completely other directions, which I feel is the hallmark of a very successful panel.

One of the first issues that moderator Lisa Wagner-Carollo raised was what the relevance of Shakespeare is to incarcerated individuals and to the criminal justice system itself. Both practitioners and participants in prison programs described how Shakespeare speaks to them specifically. Panelist Agnes Wilcox, the founder and former artistic director of Prison Performing Arts in St. Louis, explained that prisoners see themselves in many of the characters Shakespeare writes. Doing *Julius Caesar*, the cast recognized in Cassius a "con man" — conning Brutus into doing a job that he did not want to do: the murder of his close friend. Wilcox told of a guard who, watching a rehearsal, started pointing to the conspirators without knowing the characters' names, but recognizing them nonetheless: "We have one of him, a couple of him.... definitely one of him..."[17]

That is, of course, a testament to the general applicability of Shakespeare—the fact that he writes characters which everyone can see themselves in is one of the most commonly cited reasons for his

---

[17] Throughout this essay, I am using quotes from the speakers, but those reflect my own notes taken in real time, and so are not necessarily verbatim. Where I have italicized words within the quotes, those reflect my perception of emphasis put there by the speaker. A final complication is that Itari Marta spoke in Spanish, which I do not speak, through a translator who was performing consecutive translation, not simultaneous.

enduring appeal. But Shakespeare also writes a surprising amount about justice and law. Even in his comedies, incarceration and legal action are constant elements. Kate Powers, who directs the Rehabilitation through the Arts program, discussed her recent production of *Twelfth Night* at Sing Sing maximum security prison. When I expressed surprise to her in the lobby after the panel, she elaborated on the choice. In that play, Malvolio is imprisoned in a tiny, dark room and tortured by characters with whom we have generally sympathized. Presumably that scene was funny for an early modern audience, but contemporary audiences often find it uncomfortable. According to Powers, however, her cast and audience loved it. They, more than anyone, understand what it is to be put in solitary, and to be abused by guards.

The prisoners take their work on the plays very seriously. Powers related a story about a rehearsal game where the ensemble working on *Hamlet* had put Claudius on trial. The rules were that the actors could only introduce evidence from the text. The actor playing Horatio was being cross-examined and answered every question about the ghost and about Hamlet with the same answer: "I don't know anything about that." Kate finally asked him why he was not relating what he knew, and he looked at her in mystification. "I swore to Hamlet I wouldn't say anything!" Panelist Haisan T. Williams, a past participant in the Shakespeare Prison Project at Racine Correctional Institute, told of a fellow prisoner who turned down parole because he would have been paroled before the performance for which he had been rehearsing.

This work is clearly important to the participants, but one of the most compelling issues raised at the panel is what the value of these programs is to society. It is worth, I think, interrogating the instinct that makes us think of these two questions as if they were different; that is, why do we think that something could have value to prisoners but not to society? Itari Marta, founder of the Penitentiary Theater Company, at Santa Martha Acatitla penitentiary in Mexico, made an observation that begins to offer an answer. "Prison" says Marta, "is a reflection of outside society." She said this in the context of a discussion of the particular challenges that she faces in her work; in this case, the corruption that is endemic to Mexican government and that has become normalized by Mexican society, which makes resource management very difficult for her. But this idea of prison as a reflection of society has remarkable explanatory power in several arenas. At the simplest level, if Shakespeare and prisons can both function as ways for a society to better understand itself, then the appeal of one within the other is not surprising.

Marta's observation, however, is also a call to think about *what* we see reflected in our prison systems. By her account, her challenges as an artist stem from the way her society thinks about prisoners and about crime: "Our country is corrupt and our government wants it that way. As a people, like anyone would, we have become used to the way things are and so the worst thing is that we cannot imagine things differently, so we have become infected. So when there is a chance for change, we reject it, either because we don't trust the authorities or because we don't trust the possibility of change." Participants in the Penitentiary Theater Company struggle for resources that often get diverted elsewhere. However, perhaps because of the way prisoners are considered, they have access to a source of income that is unavailable to American prisoners. Marta's project puts on performances for the general prison population, but they also do performances that are open to the public, and for these they charge admission. The proceeds of the public performances pay for the production, and whatever is left over goes to *pay the actors*. That may seem innocuous, but it would never occur to American programs that the work of rehearsing and performing a play is *work*, or more to the point that prisoners might be entitled to reap the fruits of their labor. According to Powers, her program is not even allowed to bring cookies for the actors. I see in this startling difference (and it was startling to every one of the Americans on the panel, according to discussions I had with them after the event) an important reflection of the different views of incarceration. Where Marta's challenges revolve around corruption, ours revolve around the perception of prisoners as sub-human.

In discussions of criminal justice system reform, the question we asked earlier about the value of these programs to society is usually asked in a way which implies that the questioner, intellectually concerned about limited resources, wants to make sure that those resources are being spent wisely. But hidden beneath the question, all too often, is the emotionally charged challenge: why do prisoners "deserve" Shakespeare? This is the issue that incarceration as a very concept struggles with. We talk about rehabilitation, but deep in our hearts many people look to the prison system for vengeance. Kate Powers gets asked at least once a week, "Why are these murderers getting free Shakespeare?" The question is indicative of the way

Americans have been trained to think about the incarcerated. Why indeed should prisoners be treated like people at all?

But if the goal of incarceration were actually rehabilitation, that question should answer itself. Who needs Shakespeare more than prisoners? Powers argues that that the values that prisoners develop while working on Shakespeare's plays are an important aspect of the programs. "These are human plays, and they teach us to be human." Curt Tofteland, founder of Shakespeare Behind Bars (a twenty-two-year-old program with twelve active prison programs) adds that the themes and characters found in Shakespeare's plays reflect the trauma that incarcerated men have experienced. For him, trauma and shame are part of the human experience, and he finds that the prisoners he works with find the characters whose particular traumas match their own, as a way to come to terms with their own lives. "As actors, they have to analyze and dissect the characters, building the actor's tools for self-reflection." Both Tofteland and Wilcox discussed the way such work trains the actors to develop empathy—that quality which is essential to play someone else on stage, but also, as Martha Nussbaum has argued in *Not for Profit*, essential to the role of citizen in a democratic society. Exactly the role that rehabilitation purposes for those who have served their time.

Put in terms of societal self-interest by Williams, the question becomes, "Who do you want coming home?" Because prisoners do come home. And when they do, the question of what happens to them is, or ought to be, of vital interest to civilians. Williams offers fairly stark options—either programs like these teach the values of our society, or men return to society with only the lessons that one might imagine are taught by being stuck in a box for seventeen years.

The effectiveness of the programs is unquestionable; recidivism rates amongst alumni of programs like those run by Tofteland and Powers are less than five percent, a tiny fraction of the fifty to sixty percent that is the national average. One can only hope that this is seen as a worthwhile goal by anything calling itself a *justice* system.

COMPANY THEATRE MUMBAI
PIYA BEHRUPIYA (TWELFTH NIGHT)

directed by Atul Kumar
presented by Chicago Shakespeare Theater + Eye on India

Courtesy of Company Theatre Mumbai

Love, Music and Playing on with *Piya Behrupiya*
Katie Blankenau

Piya Behrupiya does what the best adaptations do: it turns the original into a canvas on which to make something vibrantly new, and simultaneously makes conversation with the original. *Piya Behrupiya* is a particularly skillful, sparkling conversation. In their adaptation of *Twelfth Night,* the Company Theatre of Mumbai plays with Shakespeare like a loved and versatile toy, addressing the author by turns as an old favorite, a popular celebrity and an irritating competitor. The end result is hilarious, exuberant and, in my case, somewhat inaccessible. As a non-Hindi speaker, I couldn't follow the intricacies of the rhyming wordplay, cultural references and jokes that by the second act had the Hindi-speaking audience helpless with laughter. A fellow audience-member near me who kindly supplemented the surtitles often turned, laughing, to say she couldn't translate—but that it was funny. Although the actors make sure that the show is enjoyable regardless of language, for me, missing the joke was part of the fun, because it highlighted the production's brilliant riffs on the very ideas of adaptation and translation.

The most explicit comment on the play's status as an adaptation is embodied by Sebastian (Puranjeet Dasgupta, charismatic and witty in the double parts of Sebastian and disgruntled actor-translator). Striding down front to make his first speech, he comments on the character's shabby treatment by the author, counting his lines in comparison to Sir Toby's, and summing up his subplot with Antonio in a few one-sided exchanges. His belief that he deserves better grows throughout the play until he eventually claims to be the one who translated the play into Hindi in the first place. But, he complains, everyone who praises the play attributes his efforts to Shakespeare. In doing so he both acknowledges Shakespeare's cultural cachet and calls attention to *Piya Behrupiya*'s innovative flair. His irritation as a translator underscores the production's achievement, its skillful absorption and redeployment of *Twelfth Night*'s tale and themes. His comments unsettle the relationship between the performance and the author implied by the gigantic picture of Shakespeare that frames the Chorus. While everyone congratulates Shakespeare, he's also just a backdrop against which the adaptors play.

It's hard to overstate just how much *fun* the production has with adapting Shakespeare. Sometimes the meta-commentary on the play's status emerges in Shakespearean references, as with the many shout-outs to *Romeo and Juliet* in the play's first half. Comparing their lovers to Romeo and Juliet, the characters archly nod to the tragic potential embedded in Illyria's love stories, even as they highlight their own comic performances. Throughout the play, brilliantly mixed elements of Indian entertainment culture absorb *Twelfth Night*'s plot points. The fight between Sebastian and Sir Toby and co., for example, becomes a qawwali singing competition, Bollywood-style. At another point, devotional music is repurposed to comic effect for a love song. Due to the limitations of supertitles and my own ignorance, I could only pick up on the most obvious examples. Yet the language barriers among the audience focused attention on the limits of translation while also accentuating the extra-linguistic aspects of the performance, most obviously, music and dance.

Music is integral to *Piya Behrupiya*, both as a key element in *Twelfth Night* and of course in the play's adaptation into a musical comedy. When not required for a scene, the rest of the cast sit behind the musicians, facing the audience, and play the double role of choric commentators and chorus singers. Their participation ties the plot and songs together (especially for audience members who can't follow the lyrics). Orsino's "If music be the food of love, play on" is a clear statement of purpose: love songs make up the core of the music in the play, with each song depicting a different variation of desire. Throughout, the songs distill the emotion of the scene or the characters, sometimes in contrast to the rhyming poetry. In fact the efficacy of poetry is a point of debate in the play, with characters like Orsino trying to write love poems only to meet with Olivia's exasperation and derision. The songs, however, are presented as a more successful tactic, wooing the audience as well as the onstage beloved.

That's not to say that poetry is dismissed; the skillful adaptation of poetry and music allows the production to hit its most serious emotional note. Viola (Geetanjali Kulkarni) delivers a portion of the "Patience on a monument" speech as a soliloquy. "She never told her love," she begins, suggesting an alternate, unhappy ending for her character, and asserting that despite its comedic nature hers is "love indeed." The mournful, aching solo that follows is a beautiful culmination of the emotions in the speech, and grounds the lightheartedness of the rest of the production. With tones ranging from poignant to raunchy to giddy, *Piya Behrupiya* never stales—no surfeit here—but exudes confidence from first to last.

From Mumbai to London to Chicago, by Way of Illyria
Regina Buccola

In collaboration with the Eye on India Festival, Chicago Shakespeare Theater brought India's Company Mumbai Theatre to their main stage for a short, two-night-only stand with a rollicking adaptation of *Twelfth Night,* which premiered at the Globe in London in 2012. In Hindi, with projected supertitles in English, *Piya Behrupiya* put the music with which *Twelfth Night* so famously begins front and center, along with spirited dancing, raucous audience interactions, and a script in rhyming couplets that killed any and all suspense with its blithe disregard for the original plot's chronology. For example, Puranjeet Dasgupta, who portrayed Sebastian, began his stint on stage by running out to assess Olivia's physical appearance during Viola/Cesario's first encounter with her (unseen by either), and then escalated to metatheatrical commentary on the limitations of the role Shakespeare had written for him, and his perceived need to absorb Antonio's role to make showing up to perform worthwhile—all in hilarious rhyming verse, along with Hindi adlibs that kept an audience filled with festivalgoers who understood the language in stitches.

The entire cast—consistently referred to as a "Chorus"—joined the three musicians on a red platform upstage center for the entire performance, watching the action (and the audience) from the rear of the platform, under a gorgeous red-washed portrait of Shakespeare's head emerging from a vibrant lotus flower in a gilt frame. In addition to Dasgupta, Gagan Singh Riar, who portrayed Uncle Toby, also repeatedly broke character to alternately flirt with and taunt the audience. In a characteristically deflationary couplet, he damned Sir Andrew (Aadar Malik) with the faint praise that he "speaks with such flair, you'll scour the dictionary for his words in despair."

Orsino (Sagar Deshmukh) repeatedly directly invoked Shakespeare, and his interactions with Cesario/Viola (Geetanjali Kulkarni) looked wittily ahead to their ultimate union from the outset. In the first scene between them, they hugged one another; as they broke apart, she self-consciously adjusted her breast binding while he grabbed his own chest in clear recognition of her breasts, turning to face the audience with mouth agape in over-the-top consternation. In addition to physical comedy such as this, the song titles foretold much later outcomes in the play, as when the first introduction to Toby and Maria (Trupti Khamkar) bore the supertitle, "Love Song of Toby and Maria."

Olivia's willing suspension of disbelief in the face of Cesario's lame cross-dressed disguise reached its zenith in uproarious physical comedy after the intermission. Seductively singing her heart out, Mansi Multani (Olivia) made the most of her substantial height advantage over Kulkarni's Cesario, gripping him/her into an embrace that planted his/her face squarely in her bosom. A make-out session with a prone Cesario produced the hilarious cosmetic malfunction of a full layer of Cesario's drawn-on moustache transferred to Olivia's face, which Olivia then smeared back onto Cesario's temple.

The "duel" between Sebastian and Andrew was staged as a sing-off, with each combatant backed by half of the Chorus: Orsino, Feste, Olivia and Viola were initially Team Sebastian, while Toby, Maria and Malvolio backed Andrew, but Orsino switched teams at the height of the musical battle to end up with Andrew. The musical comedy replacement of the play's physical fight was of a piece with other production choices, including the decision to retain lines about sending the yellow-stockinged Malvolio to an asylum, while his scene of torture by "Sir Topas"/Feste was completely cut. Choices such as these produced an entirely sunny performance, for although Malvolio was still wounded when the deception practiced upon him with Maria's crafty letter was revealed (along with Olivia's marriage to Sebastian), he still got the opportunity to offer a marital garland of flowers to women in the audience during the closing "Wedding Song" for the three couples celebrated in the finale. In the end, musicians, chorus, and audience were all in it together in *Piya Behrupiya*.

SHANGHAI JINGJU THEATRE
THE REVENGE OF PRINCE ZI DAN (HAMLET)

directed by Shi Yukun
written by Feng Gang
presented by the Harris Theater for Music and Dance
+ Chicago Shakespeare Theater

Liu Haifa

A Single Ghost Wandering in the Chaos
Casey Caldwell

"The world is in chaos." This is the phrase that replaces Hamlet's famous, "The time is out of joint," in Shanghai Jingju Theatre Company's Peking Opera-style adaptation of *Hamlet, The Revenge of Prince Zi Dan*, performed at the Harris Theater. References to chaos become a refrain running through this production, with Zi Dan (Hamlet) demanding during his confrontation with Ophelia that she should "let me be a single ghost wandering in the chaos." As a complete outsider to the *Jingju* (also known as Peking Opera) style, the conjuration of chaos in this production was in tension with its performance style in inspiring and delightful ways. After summarizing some of the basic elements on this production, I'll take this chance to simply meditate on my own experience as a deeply invested outsider to a performance tradition that has adapted a source I am, by contrast, extremely familiar with. Like one of Barnet Newman's immense, cloud-dark paintings with a single, precise white line passing across it, *The Revenge of Prince of Zi Dan* produces a looming, abstract sense of chaotic doom out of a minimal set and tightly controlled, physical technique. Also like those Newman paintings, the immense darkness and the tightly controlled passage through it each bring the other into definition and clarity for the viewer, making the power in both manifest as well.

Shanghai Jingju's production opens with a long duration of darkness in the theater, then two figures on stage, a very minimal set, and a digital display above the stage showing the spoken lines in English. At first I thought these were the two guards that start off Shakespeare's *Hamlet*, but it becomes obvious as time passes that these are in fact Hamlet and Horatio. The significant majority of the dialog is sung, in the distinct *Jingju* style, and there is a group of musicians off stage playing constant musical accompaniment. As the opera progresses, it moves through much of the familiar storyline from Shakespeare's *Hamlet*, with some famous monologues truncated, rearranged in their order, or even combined at times (e.g. it seemed to me that "To be or not to be" had been combined with "How all occasions do inform against me"). Large portions of the *Hamlet* are skipped over—for example, we go straight from Hamlet's encounter with the ghost, to Polonius telling the King and Queen that Hamlet is mad. All of this was done with discernment, in the service of producing a coherent show that utilized *Hamlet* as it material.

The role-type tradition in *Jingju* is very reminiscent of Italian *commedia dell'arte*, an extremely felicitous parallel with the theatrical tradition behind *Hamlet* (the character-type based performance style of *dell'arte* had a strong influence on England's emerging professional theatre in the early modern period). The ghost, Claudius, and Polonius each felt very much like dramatic types adapted to this particular story—the ghost and Claudius both wearing masks the entire time, for reasons I was both not aware of and very curious about. Ophelia, played by a woman, had a naturalistic sounding voice (relative to this operatic style), whereas Gertrude was played by a man and portrayed with a very high pitched voice that to my ears sounded like a parody. The very useful history of *Jingju* included in the festival program for this production notes the history of men playing women in the earliest stages of this performance style, so I suspect that what to my untrained ears sounded like a man *parodying* a woman's voice was in fact the product of a vocal tradition passed down from its earliest beginnings (but this is again my speculation, reflecting upon my experience as an audience member completely unfamiliar with this style). The virtuoso performance by Polonius highlighted most directly the acrobatic tradition threaded into the other strands making up *Jingju*. Wearing age makeup and a fake beard, the actor was crouched down on his legs to the point that his knees were against his chest, covered over by his official gown, leaving his feat exposed at the bottom and creating the illusion that he was about one- quarter the actor's actual height. Simply walking across the stage was a physical feat, performed with mind-boggling naturalness and ease. The production capitalizes on this in maybe my favorite moment in the performance: when Hamlet stabs Polonius, Polonius is given a frenetic, comically extended, acrobatic, Nick Bottom-as-Pyramus-like-death scene that ranged across the stage, and that frankly I never wanted to end. It is difficult to even understand how the actor accomplished it.

The female characters in the play get solo "monologues" that they are denied in *Hamlet*, giving us time alone with them to hear more of their own thoughts about what is happening to and around them. Gertrude knowingly drinks from the poisoned cup in the final fight scene, which itself features excellent fight acrobatics by Hamlet and Laertes, wearing resplendent ceremonial armor. As someone who has seen so many *Hamlets*, it was in fact refreshing how quickly we got to the final scene in *The Revenge of Prince Zi Dan*—the various scene cuts and monologue shrinkages getting us to the end fast.

As an early modern scholar unfamiliar with *Jingju*, what the concision in the storytelling helped me do was to focus on the feat of the style itself, and its effects on me. The singing style works in a tonal way that was strange at first for my ears, and there was tendency to stretch out words and phrases as they are sung. Everyday physical movements often felt ritualistic, the body's movements tightly controlled and rigidly, incrementally progressive in a manner that, paradoxically, produced a sense of fluidity much as a role of film in a projector can produce the illusion of movement on a movie screen. The music itself had a "traditional" sound to it for my uneducated ears, but also sounded "upbeat" to me as well. Not comically so, but in the way that a song about heroin addiction by a band like Wilco can be up-tempo—it doesn't minimize how devastating the lyrics are. That up-tempo feel to the music also helped with the sense of sweeping momentum in the advancing of the plots. The set itself was quite minimal—there were a few set changes, but these were often large abstract compositions. Even when banners were hung or furniture placed on stage, as physical objects they seemed very alone up there on stage, serving as much to highlight the formless void surrounding the lives of these characters as to give a visual anchor for a scene.

When I think back on this production, my memories of the scenes are like Barnett Newman's *Cathedra* or Jacques-Louis David's *The Death of Marat*. A very clearly defined strip or section—on the level of the stage— of brightly lit characterizations produced by intensely refined technique, and a dark cloud of chaos—above the stage—brimming around these characters. Saying that the world is chaos, rather than that the time is out of joint, puts an emphasis on the spatial rather than the temporal—but a space filled with unstructured movement, rather than a time that cannot move properly, maybe at all, because it has been dislocated. *The Revenge of Prince Zi Dan's* substitution of this phrase is extremely apt, precisely in terms of the point where form and content intersect in this show. The content of the words in this show conjure a failed civil order, but the physicalization of how these words are expressed is so disciplined (*not* chaotic) that the contrasts serve to highlight each other—the failed world conjured by the success of a performance style resulting, for this naïve audience member, in one of the best nights he has had in the theater in a long time. My main critique is that they have not come to Chicago more often.

East and West Meet in *Prince Zi Dan* (*Hamlet*)
Cynthia Rutz

The internationally renowned Shanghai Jingju Theatre Company brought a production of Shakespeare's *Hamlet,* performed as a highly stylized Peking opera, to the Harris Theater for a two-night run on September 28 and 29. The opera, *The Revenge of Prince Zi Dan*, was sung in Chinese with English supertitles. The company follows the strict rules of Chinese operatic tradition, including specific types of singing for such roles as a clown or a serious tragic heroine. (Gertrude sang in a high-pitched, warbling voice, for example.) Each type of role also has its own particular style of dress, movement, and vocalization. Some actors, for instance, performed in whiteface, while others had elaborate masks. A small band just offstage played music traditional to the Peking Opera throughout the performance, with the tempo and style of music changing to fit the scenes and to accompany the actors as they sang arias. The libretto was a stripped down but recognizable version of the main events from Shakespeare's play.

The intricate costumes and stylized acting made this production of *Hamlet* an intriguing blend of traditions that sometimes worked well, and at other times may have puzzled a Western audience. For instance, actors sometimes moved in extremely acrobatic ways that did not always seem connected to the events in the story. In one instance, when Hamlet (Prince Zi Dan) tells of his father's ghost, he raises one leg up flush with his ear. At other times, however, the acrobatic movements worked splendidly, as in the highly stylized duel in the last act between Hamlet and Laertes. Another intriguing cultural choice was to portray the Polonius character as a clown figure. He walked about exclusively on his knees for most of the show, but during his death scene he sat cross-legged, pulled up his knees, and rolled around on the floor like a roly-poly toy.

Both the ghost of Hamlet's father and his brother Claudius were portrayed by actors in elaborate masks, so we never see their faces. The frightening mask worked especially well for the ghost, who appeared out of a mist, rendering him even more supernatural. Claudius's mask also seemed to fit with his formal role as king, making him seem less human and more distant from the other actors. One could not help but be reminded of ancient Greek theater, where all the actors performed in masks, with audiences trained to recognize whether it was the mask of a king or a young girl.

Another feature of the Chinese opera tradition is minimal settings and props. Actors mimed some actions, such as riding a horse. And instead of formal sets, the troupe used three simple backdrops throughout most of the play. These backdrops were reversed for the final scene, to reveal a single red dragon. Simple chairs used in many scenes were later tipped over and turned backwards to represent gravestones during the gravedigger scene.

The formality of the costumes and movements probably worked best in the final scene; a formal setting at court with the masked Claudius presiding in the center. For the duel in this scene between Hamlet and Laertes, the two combatants entered in Chinese warrior costumes. The duel itself was choreographed as an elaborate acrobatic dance.

Overall, this was a production that challenged the audience with its blend of Eastern and Western traditions. But our familiarity with the *Hamlet* story allowed us to notice how this production both honored the familiar story and also made it strange and new by adding these formal elements of Chinese operatic tradition.

ONE STEP AT A TIME LIKE THIS
UNDREAMED SHORES

conceived + created by one step at a time like this
commissioned + presented by Chicago Shakespeare Theater
+ Richard Jordan Productions

Chuck Osgood

When Was a Long Time Ago? (A Walk Down Navy Pier)
Ira S. Murfin

On a hot summer night a couple of years ago, I arrived at a certain designated corner in the Loop and waited. After a few minutes my phone rang and the caller spoke to me by name even though we had never met. She patiently guided me down the street until suddenly the doors of the grand Cadillac Palace Theatre, which I happened to be passing, were swung open to me and I was ushered inside its vast, empty lobby. There a woman in an evening gown descended the staircase and sat beside me to explain how to work the special smart phone she gave me as a guide through the rest of my evening. From that point on, the city opened to me in the most remarkable ways as I moved through it: People emerged from alleyways and crevices between buildings to give me secret messages. In a luxury high-rise apartment I found myself climbing into bed with an anonymous stranger. I was driven, blindfolded, down Lower Wacker and through downtown and when the blindfold was removed I found that I was on the stage of another grand historic theater, dozens of blocks from the one where I'd started, with blinding stage lights glaring down on me. This was *Since I Suppose*, an immersive audio and video tour of downtown Chicago based loosely on *Measure for Measure*, which was created by the Australian company one step at a time like this, and commissioned by and developed with Chicago Shakespeare Theater and Richard Jordan Productions in 2014.

So when I arrived at Navy Pier on a cold and windy afternoon not long ago for the newest audio-guided tour from one step at a time like this, *undreamed shores*, I was ready for Navy Pier to similarly come alive once I put my headphones on and started walking. But *undreamed shores* was a decidedly more atmospheric and solitary affair, a moody wander for one in which, as the sole audience member, I was encouraged to pretend that the people around me were not really there and to move through a world inhabited only by myself and the disembodied voices in my headphones. There was a twinge of disappointment when I realized the pier was not going to become a responsive, immersive, fictional world the way the Loop had two years earlier. I imagined being beckoned onto a gondola as I approached the Ferris wheel and being lifted into the sky. I hoped, as the audio track instructed me to pause near the entrance to a seafood restaurant, that I might be invited in for a specially prepared *amuse-bouche*. I wondered, as I approached the doors of Chicago Shakespeare Theater, if they would be flung open to me for a special command performance for one in the Courtyard Theater. But none of that happened. Navy Pier had not been stocked with carefully planned encounters and surprises, it remained itself, a place to be discovered and observed as it is. This made for a more furtive and subdued, though perhaps no less strange, experience. Instead of riding the Ferris wheel, I was instructed to lie down on a ledge beneath it and look up at it turning against an ominous sky while the voice in my ear talked to me about the mechanics of the universe.

I remembered then that some of the most effective moments in *Since I Suppose* had occurred just between myself, the soundtrack, and the city: a pause on a bridge over the Chicago River as music swelled in my ears; the view from a rooftop poolside balcony of fireworks going off over the lake across downtown, tiny but visible; collaged fragments from *Measure for Measure* enveloping me as I walked down the street. These quiet, reflective, essentially internal moments, when the strategically composed audio overlaid and altered the ordinary environment, recruiting the city into a private and subjective spectacle, best made the case for the unique potential of the immersive audio tour, or sound walk, as a theatrical form. *undreamed shores* was made up of such moments. Framed simply as a journey down Navy Pier, it comprised a series of opportunities to notice the pier and its environs, including parts of it one might never visit—lovely and decidedly unlovely, both. What each lone audience member made of that journey was ultimately up to each of us. "Take your time," the person who had handed me the headset at the beginning of *undreamed shores* had told me, "whatever that means to you."

Even though it took an abstract, fragmentary approach, *Since I Suppose* had *Measure for Measure* as a structure and reference point, but the structural device for *undreamed shores* was markedly less well defined. Its themes and ideas washed over me along the journey like the concept of water that vaguely flowed through the piece. The voices guiding me wanted me to think about the pier itself, particularly its history at almost 100 years old, and about the city that surrounds it, and about the relationship of that city to the lake it sits beside. And they also wanted me to think about Shakespeare and his time 400 years ago, and how people then thought about the world and bodies of water and the universe and death. And still more, they wanted me to think about aquatic ecosystems, and pollution, and climate change, and the loss of sea life, and the environmental changes evidenced by the water. They wanted me to think about all of these things together—mortality and longevity and relative lengths of time. A walk down the pier of an hour or so is vanishingly brief from this perspective, but it is nonetheless time passing, just as the years that make up my life are time passing, or the 100 years since Navy Pier was built, or the 400 years since Shakespeare's death, or the 14,000 years since the lake was ice, are all passages of time at the end of which we are each located. When was a long time ago? Before I was born? When the pier was built? When Shakespeare lived? The last Ice Age? And when is a long time from now? What will this all be like then?

It was difficult to put my finger on any of this, though, as I climbed stairs, rode elevators, walked through closed doors, lay down on benches, and gazed out windows. Philosophical musings on facts about the lake, the pier, the city, Shakespeare, and the environment paired with snippets from Shakespeare's plays—some about water, some about death, some about cities—floated in one ear and out the other. There was a lot from *The Tempest*, unsurprisingly, though surprisingly not only about water and islands and shipwrecks, plenty of love and death, too; the description of Ophelia drowning from *Hamlet*, of course; and the Chorus in *Henry V* envisaging the sails of ships as a city on the sea; but there was also Macbeth at his metatheatrical bleakest. The quotes were tossed in incidentally, riffing tangentially on a particular nearby feature—window, city, ship—as much atmosphere as anything else. Sometimes they washed over me, at other times one hit and stuck, capturing something meaningful between the physical place and my subjective headspace. But the factoids and Shakespeare snippets hardly seemed to be the point.

The point was that the point was the journey. Emerging onto the north side of the pier midway through the tour, I was guided to a particular bollard and instructed to tie a bit of rope I found in an envelope I had discovered secreted in a little mailbox on top of the parking garage half an hour earlier to the chain running along the water. I tied it beside all the other lengths of rope tied there by each successive audience of one who had made their way along the pier before me. I paused and looked down at the water. There was no significance to this sequence of actions other than having gotten to the same point as everyone who had come before me. I found something one place and I left it another, where I saw evidence that others had been there and had done the same thing. Now someone else would come along and tie their length of rope next to mine. No need for a narrative or metaphor, this was life being lived, making connections and hitting milestones and seeing evidence that I am in the world with others, some of whom have gone before me, and doubtless some who will come after. And because I took this journey and was curious and attentive and followed signposts and the advice of those who showed up to guide me along the way, I found many things I otherwise would not have, and saw things that I did not expect to see.

By the time I reached the very end of the pier, I did feel as if I had been on a journey. It was not exactly strenuous, but I had been in motion almost the whole time (I found myself aware of the privilege of having a relatively able body—there were many places where someone with impaired mobility would not have been able to go, and no alternatives were offered.) Reaching the end, I got to sit down and rest and look out at the lake, reflecting on where I was and where I had been. It helped that in many ways I had literally gone back in time, from the shiny new and getting newer layers of redesign and renovation on the west end of Navy Pier to the east end, where the solid brick buildings remain seemingly unchanged from the pier's original construction almost 100 years ago. It was a cold and blustery afternoon, and the benches at the end of the pier were empty except for me, and the bronze statue of Bob Newhart (check it out)! In the ballroom just behind me, though, an elaborate graduation ceremony for new firefighters happened to be taking place, and young people dressed for the special occasion hurried in and out of the hall, eager to see their loved ones embark on a grand new adventure. Excitement was in the air as the sky darkened and the ballroom emanated the kind of golden light that made me think of wintertime parties, flushed cheeks, warmth from food and drink and dancing, pleasures that could have been indulged at any time during the pier's 100-year history.

I had reached the end of my journey. I sat on my bench and looked out at the gray expanse of lake and sky and listened as the voices that had guided me all that way asked me to imagine myself, the pier, the lake, the world 100, then 400, years from now. What would still be here? The pier? The city? The birds? The lake? I felt myself fading into insignificance, just a blip on the horizon of all that time passing, a brief jaunt down a short pier, before their voices stopped. I remembered the advice to "take my time" with which I had begun and, as I sat there, looking out at the lake, I felt that was exactly what I was doing, taking time—this time, the only time I had. I remained there, even after I had pulled the headset off and someone had come by to collect it, even after *undreamed shores* had ended I remained there for just a little while longer, taking my time.

"As one upon a rock, / Environed with a wilderness of sea"
Regina Buccola

Australia-based performance group one step at a time like this has returned to Chicago Shakespeare Theater for a third time, with a specially commissioned audio exploration of Navy Pier and its environs for Shakespeare 400 Chicago. In 2011, one step at a time like this brought their pedestrian-driven exploration of a series of cities, *en route*, to Chicago, and, in 2014, collaborated with Chicago Shakespeare Theater to produce another ambulatory, immersive interaction with *Measure for Measure*, entitled *Since I Suppose*. A departure from both of these previous immersive experiences, *undreamed shores* confined itself to a smaller geographic area, even as it ranged across a wider array of Shakespearean texts.

Participants in the audio-guided journey were directed to convene at the large, orange letter "P" at the easternmost edge of Polk Bros. Park, across from the main entrance to Navy Pier. Once there, a guide took the participant off to a mosaic-decorated concrete banquette to the north, (I noticed the word "walking"—a key part of the experience—in the mosaic near where we sat down together) to orient them to the use of a Motorola hand-held audio device and headphones. Once oriented, the participant was on their own, with only the audio, the sensory input of the Pier, and their own thoughts for the next seventy minutes.

The Tempest and *The Comedy of Errors*, both of which use shipwrecks as plot points, loomed large in the audio pastiche that directed the journey. One of the earliest quotes, however, came from *Titus Andronicus*: "For now I stand as one upon a rock, / Environed with a wilderness of sea" (3.1.93-94). As participants stood at the western edge of Polk Bros. Park, facing the main entrance to the Pier to the east, they were invited to contemplate the fact that the place where they were standing did not exist a thousand years ago. A thousand years ago, it would not even have been a rock, environed by an inland sea, but the inland sea itself. The audio narrative reminded us that we were standing on landfill, the silver lining pulled from the dark cloud of the Chicago Fire, and an isthmus of land (re?)claimed from the water as the debris from that disaster was shoveled in, clearing out the old, burned city to make way for the new, modern one. The rock environed by the lake is manmade: concrete.

And there are shipwrecks in this inland sea, too. As the participant progressed east, onto the Pier, the audio guide discussed the thousand shipwrecks—some as yet undiscovered—strewn across the bottom of the lake. Zigging and zagging through the Pier, the participant started out like a slightly eccentric tourist: climbing stairs outdoors, lying down beneath the Ferris wheel to contemplate its breathtaking sweep from the maximal angle, going in glass doors that give onto the interior pedway, pausing outside of the Chicago Shakespeare Theater lobby. Eventually, the journey became less conventional: the participant was directed onto elevators that took them to abandoned corridors where they were eerily advised to try all available elevator buttons for the return journey since "at least one of them never works"; concrete service stairs in which your footfalls echoed in the empty, uninhabited space, spray-on insulation overhead, banquet tables stacked to your left with the haphazard remains of some social event; two wine glasses incongruously sparkling in the gloom.

Outdoors again, on the northern side of the Pier, the participant was asked to contemplate the lake as a living thing, sending distress calls through its changing surface. The audio guide included an interview with someone unidentified explaining that people in Chicago (including me) exult in the lake's color shift from briny green to "Caribbean blue." However, this color change, while perhaps pretty, actually conveys grim news about the state of life in the lake. The lake was green when the plankton that lived in it were thriving. It turned blue when the invasive zebra mussels, who hitched rides into Lake Michigan on cargo vessels from Asia, gained the upper hand and ate their way to dominance.

"All the world's a stage" (*As You Like It*, 2.7.139) the participant heard Jaques explain, describing the seven stages of man, as they stood in an empty meeting room overlooking the Skyline Stage. I amused myself as I listened by trying to match the seven stages of man described in the audio to the hula hoop performer, juggler, and living statue scattered across the square below me, tourists photographing them and/or themselves with them, and Navy Pier staff in reflective vests and nametags actually approaching the charcoal gray living statue to knock on her face, tap on her hat, to see if they could disrupt her silent, still performance with their antics, but they could not. She remained immovable as the concrete slab of the Pier beneath her feet.

The performance ended outdoors, at the easternmost edge of the Pier, facing the lighthouse, and the breakwater that separates the harbor around the Pier from the deep blue wilds of the lake. Midway through the experience, however, the participant was asked to stand just east of the Ferris wheel, on the upper level of the parking deck, and take in the skyline to the west. Here, we heard a description of Tarsus from *Pericles* applied to Chicago:

> A city on whom plenty held full hand,
> For riches strew'd herself even in the streets;
> Whose towers bore heads so high they kiss'd the clouds,
> And strangers ne'er beheld but wondered at.

(1.4.22-25)

In the old English elegiac verse form *ubi sunt*, the poet offered a lyric catalog of personal connections and material possessions in order to record their loss. An *ubi sunt* lyric in reverse, *undreamed shores* asked us to contemplate the riches strewed in our streets, the cloud-capped towers, the almost obscene opulence of natural and manmade beauty all around us, none of which was here a thousand years ago. What will be here a thousand years hence? Turn, now, and look at the deep blue of the lake. Full fathom five nothing remains but what suffers a sea change into something whose strangeness we would do well to contemplate, lest we, too, fade into the blue.

JOFFREY BALLET
ROMEO & JULIET

choreography by Krzysztof Pastor
music by Sergei Prokofiev

Cheryl Mann

The Joffrey's *Romeo & Juliet* and the Dance of Politics
Anna Ullmann

Joffrey Ballet's 2016 production of Prokofiev's and Pastor's *Romeo & Juliet* opens upon a scene of stark contrasts, not just the obvious black and white of the costume and set design or the unexpected stillness of the dancers upon the stage as old newsreels play in the background, but what these visual contrasts represent—the age-old conflict between the Capulets and Montagues. These two families must share a stage world where everything is black and white, and here we are no longer talking about visuals. Family, politics, worldview separate the two groups, and group choreography scenes at the beginning of acts 1 and 2 make this clear. Costuming clearly articulates the families, and the choreography itself is a striking mixture of dance and stage combat, movements somehow both graceful and stark that express the tension and violence beneath the surface. The climactic street fight between Mercutio (Derrick Agnoletti) and Tybalt (Temur Suluashvili) in particular has such a sense of both regimented movements and chaos that the audience is left stunned when it is over, even those who knew the deaths were coming. This is a world and a stage where both nothing and everything is shocking, where black and white and harsh reds combine with militaristic music and sometimes jerky dance steps to convey a sense of animosity that is barely, and sometimes not, concealed.

In the midst of this world, Romeo and Juliet: star-cross'd lovers clearly demarcated by their pale blue dress and peaceful but passionate movements. The performance of Amanda Assucena in particular as Juliet on the night of October 14 was masterful, both in Assucena's execution of notated choreography but more importantly in her embodiment of the struggling spirit and nearly inexpressible grief of the heroine as she mourns not just for her lover but her family and her entire world. It is a role needing to be both danced and acted, and Assucena excelled at both. Our Juliet and her Romeo, Alberto Velazquez, drew tears and a standing ovation from the audience on this particular night. The tragedy of the plot and the triumph of the performance were quite clearly theirs.

The lovers and their families and friends are set, in Pastor's version, in a twentieth-century Italy; moving between the acts, the action moves forward in time, drawing a thread between the Fascism of Mussolini's 1930s, the violence of the Red Brigade 1960s, and the right-wing political parties of contemporary Italy. The political implications of the production are clear, with the Capulets as the dominant, autocratic Fascists and then the right-wing traditionalists, and the Montagues as the leftist opposition. The conflict is far larger than the two families, the forces with which the two lovers must contend almost insurmountable in scope. While an interesting interpretation that brings relevance for the audience into the performance, such a depiction does have its drawbacks. In Shakespeare's play, the Capulets and Montagues get no more description than their brief introduction in the Prologue as "two households, both *alike* in dignity" (line 1, emphasis mine) who are consumed in an "ancient grudge" (line 3) of which no one seems to remember the origins. Shakespeare gives us two nearly identical foes. The audience sides with no one but the lovers, who seem caught up in a pointless struggle that ends easily enough at the end of the play, when the two families reconcile over their shared tragedy. In the Joffrey's performance, the all-black, military-style costumes and borderline goose-stepping of the Capulets leave no room for ambiguity: the audience is clearly meant to side with the Montagues in this ongoing battle. Their vibrantly colored costumes in the second half and the lovable antics of Mercutio underscore this. Such an interpretation tends to remove Romeo from danger and shift the audience's sympathies wholly onto Juliet, who might be happy living with her Romeo and his family if only she could escape her own. While the political dimension may add depth and emotion for a modern audience, it is not very true to the spirit of Shakespeare's text, where both lovers are equally victims and where their deaths, though tragic, seem not to have been in vain when their fathers make peace.

But the presence of the modern audience is key, as the audience is to any performing art. While a Shakespearean scholar may take slight issue with the recasting of the Montagues and Capulets as good and evil, the significance of Pastor's version for our contemporary world is clear. Italian politics are not the only ones under scrutiny: the timelessness of the performance is matched only by its timeliness, in an American election cycle where we seem as starkly divided as the two families. The Joffrey's performance highlights not just the never-ending cycle of violence and war between two Italian families, but the perpetuation of conflict everywhere in our world. It is telling that the performance ends without the reconciliation scene that Shakespeare's text provides; both families simply march away from each other bearing their dead, heedless of the other's pain, in a display reminiscent of two hardened politicians who refuse to shake hands. The imagery and performances offered in the Joffrey's *Romeo & Juliet* may depart from the text, but they are yet another example of how fully the stage is capable of bringing the text to life.

Pessimism, Violence, and Love across Time: The Joffrey's *Romeo & Juliet*
Rebecca L. Fall

It has not been long since the Joffrey Ballet last staged Krzysztof Pastor's unapologetically modern take on Sergei Prokofiev's ballet of *Romeo and Juliet*. Pastor's production saw its US premiere at the Joffrey only two years ago, in 2014. Yet, in a year of great divides—not least among them, a US election cycle of unprecedented partisan hostility, the Brexit vote, and the large-scale displacement of refugee populations around the world—this *Romeo & Juliet* seems to be a particularly appropriate production to revive. Pastor's interpretation of Shakespeare's play and Prokofiev's score boils both down to one core theme: the devastating conflict between individual feeling and group authority. In exploring this theme, the ballet twists the logic of time itself, stretching one brief moment of love across a century of conflict.

Act One takes place in Italy in the 1930s. As the act begins, devastating video footage from World War II is projected onto the painted streetscape that serves a backdrop throughout the performance. Lord Capulet, a Mussolini-like dictator clad all in black, evidently runs Verona with an iron fist. The Montagues, wearing white, amount less to a rival family and function more as a rival ideological community: a democratic-minded populace suffering under Capulet's fascist rule. Capulet's absolute control is borne out in his treatment of staff and family: he manhandles Juliet at the ball and directs his guests' movement with military precision. The music here, particularly the score's famously sinister "Dance of the Knights," amplifies his dominance. Pastor's choreography for this dance is angular and muscular, exuding strength and control; it is all the more imposing in the hands of Fabrice Calmels's 6'7" Lord Capulet.

Romeo and Juliet romance each other at the ball, but their connection is hardly secret. Lord Capulet takes pains to keep them physically separated while maintaining order among his guests. Eventually, the lovers steal away to meet in private for the famous balcony scene—here set in a mirrored elevator that gives us several Juliets in reflection, suggesting that this young lover represents many others. Even during this intimate scene, though, the lovers are not alone. As they dance an ecstatic *pas de deux*, other dancers hover silently at the back of the stage. Much as Romeo and Juliet would like to imagine the possibility, the scene implies, they will never inhabit a world to themselves; they remain very much in the world of their families, a world of violence and social control. As their dance comes to an end, the bulk of the cast reemerges onto the stage to surround the lovers before dividing again into their pre-existing factions.

While taking place in the same location and involving the same characters, Act Two is set in the 1950s. The Capulets evidently remain an influential family in town, but the Montagues have come to dominate Verona. It's a time of freedom, commerce, and the *dolce vita*. Video footage at the beginning of the act shows happy, mid-century Italians eating gelato and smiling. The streetscape backdrop is updated to include rows of Vespa scooters, and the stark black and white of the lighting and costuming gives way to warm sepia color tones. But deadly conflict still dominates life in Verona: Lord Capulet, surrounded by foot soldiers, urges the younger generation to fight, egging on the quarrel between Tybalt and Mercutio that will leave both dead. When the fight begins to wane, he presses a knife into Tybalt's hand and directs him to stab Mercutio in the back. The appalled Montagues pressure Romeo to take vengeance, and he murders Tybalt under the eye—and approval— of his community.

Act Three opens to projected footage of car bombs and terrorist attacks. Set in the 1990s under the Berlusconi government, the color has cooled to a bloodless, icy blue. The cold, watery lighting feels appropriate when Capulet forces Juliet to dance for a group of suitors, then demands she choose one to marry. The score here swells and sways, evoking the sensation of being trapped under a cycle of crushing ocean waves.

It is this sensation of being dragged along—even crushed—by an overwhelming force that characterizes the whole of Pastor's ballet. Romeo and Juliet try in vain to defy the fates that their families have determined for them and create a new world of possibilities, but their efforts are doomed to failure. In a heartbreaking final scene, Juliet awakes in her tomb to find Romeo dead beside her and attempts to revive him through dance. She tries to drag him around the stage, to coax his corpse back to life with her own movement. There is no hope, though, and no possibility to make a new life. In the end, she wraps Romeo's lifeless hand around a knife and uses it to stab herself in a gesture that recalls Lord Capulet's physical control over her body in earlier scenes. At last, her life ends not with a bang but a whimper. In a score otherwise characterized by imposing motifs, full-throated strings, and dissonant brass, Juliet dies to the sound of a *tremolo pianissimo*. Afterwards, nothing changes. The Montagues and Capulets return to the stage to find the dead lovers, and in a moment reminiscent of the balcony scene's ominous end, carry away the two bodies separately, without acknowledging each other at all. There is no reconciliation in this *Romeo & Juliet*, no "statue[s] in pure gold" raised in tribute to the tragic couple, no unifying "talk of these sad things." The rest is silence.

Pastor's is a deeply pessimistic—and deeply moving—*Romeo & Juliet*. The couple's love transcends decades, generations, and governments. But so does the violent enmity between their two houses. Even in death, Romeo and Juliet cannot escape control by their families or the community. They may bend time itself, but cannot break the authority of the society that has made them.

GEORGES BIGOT + THEATRE Y
MACBETH

by William Shakespeare
directed by Georges Bigot

Devron Enarson

Underground Nightmare: Georges Bigot's *Macbeth*
Alfred Thomas

This production of Shakespeare's *Macbeth* is the fruitful culmination of a yearlong collaboration between Melissa Lorraine's Theatre Y and the French actor-director Georges Bigot, a major figure in Ariane Mnouchkine's famous Théâtre du Soleil. Mr. Bigot brings to this new staging of *Macbeth* an unapologetically dystopian vision of our contemporary political reality: "In this very fragile moment in the USA, I propose in the city of Chicago to share an underground nightmare. The [US] election is a time where we can [approach] a lot of themes.... Manipulation, power, truth, lie, shadow, light.... And also fear."

Macbeth was written with a kind of frenzied haste during the nightmare of the Gunpowder Plot of November 1605 and its bloody aftermath. The failed attempt by a group of disaffected Catholic gentlemen to assassinate King James I of England (James VI of Scotland), his family, government, and the entire political establishment by blowing up the parliament house was an exercise in terrorism *avant la lettre*. If it had succeeded, the plot would have killed hundreds of people and destroyed all the buildings within a 500-yard radius of the parliament house, including Westminster Abbey and Westminster Hall. The horror of 9/11 inevitably comes to mind.

But if the plot itself was nightmarish, the fallout was even more so. The surviving plotters were captured, tortured, and executed in two batches, hanged, drawn and quartered in a grisly public ritual that haunts *Macbeth* from beginning to end. "Till he unseam'd him from the nave to th' chops" (1.2.22) was the way the plotters were eviscerated while they were still alive, their bodies slit open and their entrails pulled out and burned in front of their very own eyes. The severed heads of the condemned were then mounted on poles and displayed on London Bridge for the purpose of public deterrence, as echoed in Macduff's jeering threat to Macbeth:

> Then yield thee, coward,
> And live to be the show and gaze o'th'time:
> We'll have thee, *as our rarer monsters are,*
> Painted upon a pole, and underwrit,
> 'Here may you see the tyrant'

(5.8. 23-27)

What makes these lines so subversive is that they effectively switch the roles of perpetrator and victim: instead of the plotters' heads placed on display, Macduff imagines that of a tyrannical king being held up for public mockery and scorn. This equivocal treatment of words—saying the same thing with directly opposite intention—goes to the very heart of the play. *Macbeth* is not just about violence; it is above all about the violence enacted on language in which opposites (foul/fair, truth/lie) collapse inward on each other and how language and violence are interconnected. Equivocation is the key to the play's obsession with doubling and double meanings. It was a word that resonated throughout Shakespeare's London after the failure of the Gunpowder Plot. The trial and execution of the Jesuit leader Henry Garnet, who was accused of being an accessory to the plot, brought to light his infamous *Treatise on Lying and Dissembling,* which justified the use of equivocation in the extreme cases of interrogation and torture so that the suspect could sidestep incriminating himself and others.

What a close reading of the play yields is that equivocation is not the exclusive practice of the Weird Sisters but of all the characters, including "gracious" King Duncan who promises to promote Macbeth in one breath ("I have begun to plant thee, and will labor / to make thee full of growing") and designates his son heir to the kingdom (Prince of Cumberland) in the next. Equivocation, Shakespeare seems to suggest, is the inevitable default position of everyone in a society where telling the truth can be dangerous, even fatal and where lying has become the modus operandi of all and sundry.

All this makes *Macbeth* both universal and topically applicable to our current world of political spin and cover-up. The e-mails hacked by WikiLeaks have revealed Hillary Clinton's double-talk of saying one thing to Corporate America and the exact opposite to the American public, while the threat of real post-election violence lurks below the surface of Donald Trump's bombastic speeches. Political discourse has become seemingly polarized. Both presidential candidates trade insults back and forth, pivoting away the moment they are put on the spot. Evasiveness and deceit from politicians and the mainstream media outlets alike are on constant display as naked techniques for the cynical manipulation of power. An increasingly restive and disillusioned electorate is confronted with spin and counter-spin. Subterfuge trumps substance, rhetoric usurps reality.

This is what Georges Bigot means by the "underground nightmare" of *Macbeth*, a play in which language and violence are never far apart. It is a nightmare that has its historical origins in the religious politics of Shakespeare's England in which a propaganda war was waged between a beleaguered Protestant government and Catholic dissidents spearheaded by underground Jesuits. But it is a nightmare that is still with us, played out discursively in the endless spin and partisan punditry of CNN and Fox News. Bigot brings to these topical concerns a visceral power by giving us a vibrant modern-day dress production of the Scottish Play in which politics, language and sex go hand in hand. Powerful women loom large in this world where fragile masculinity is under constant threat from empowered femininity, personified by the Witches and Lady Macbeth. Like Hillary Clinton in debate with her Republican opponent—most recently, likening Trump to a puppet of Russian President Vladimir Putin—Lady Macbeth taunts and goads her husband by questioning his manhood: "When you durst do it, then you were a man" (1.7.48). The Weird Sisters are similarly gutsy, emancipated young women in torn jeans with female gender symbols painted on their bellies. They are more anarchic than scary, devil-may-care feminists who revel in their diabolical mischief. Even the drunken Porter (perhaps the most subversive character in the entire play) is cast as an inebriated corporate party girl holding a champagne bottle in one hand and her high-heel shoes in another. As Macduff chides her with the line, "Was it so late friend, ere you went to bed that you do lie so late?," we see her relieving herself behind a wall, a clever example of the triple meaning of the word Elizabethan word "lie" (tell an untruth, be recumbent, urinate).

The epitome of the feminine control of language in the play, Lady Macbeth (Katie Stimpson) is a tall, powerful *femme fatale*, who enters smiling and dancing in a Japanese kimono to the sardonic strains of the classic song "Que será, será." There is a wonderful resonance here of Christopher Marlowe's *Doctor Faustus*, a similar drama about an overreacher who reads words too literally:

> If we say that we have no sin
> We deceive ourselves, and there's no truth in us.
> Why, then, belike we must sin and consequently die.
> Ay, we must die an everlasting death.
> What doctrine call you this? *Che serà, serà*?
> What will be, shall be? Divinity adieu! (*Puts down Bible*.)[18]

The heavily ironic implications of this song ("The future is not ours to see") prepare the ground for the internally conflicted monologues of Macbeth (Brendan Mulhern), trapped between free will ("We still have judgment here") and predestination, lingering doubts about the Witches' prognostications and a desperate need to take them at literal face value. In the end, like Faustus, Macbeth rejects the Catholic faith for Calvinist fundamentalism—with the inevitable violent consequences of taking truth too literally.

New to the classical repertory, Mr. Mulhern brings his background in comedy and improvised theater to bear in an impressive, high-energy performance shot through with moments of grim humor—whether he is leading his guests to the coronation banquet in a song-and-dance routine or strapping on his armor and then taking it off again in a fit of comic indecisiveness. His soliloquies constantly transform him from a smiling self-confident man of the world into a grimacing, anguished monster, the inevitable Janus face of power politics. The Banquo ghost scene is a model of choreographed ensemble acting as Mulhern/Macbeth veers

---

[18] A-Text (1604), 1.1. 43-48.

violently between a carefree hedonist and an anguished victim of his own nightmares. I have never seen a more convincing portrayal of power unraveling before our very eyes, the nightmare that lurks below the smiling brittle facade of the *homo politicus*.

Other strong performances were also on display: Héctor Álvarez as a diminutive but indomitable Malcolm; the physically impressive Arch Harmon as King Duncan, and Katie Stimpson as a terrifying yet sympathetic Lady Macbeth. Mr. Bigot's prodigious experience as an actor in the French theater makes for a tightly controlled, cohesive production. He has harnessed the creative energy of these young Chicago actors and transformed what might so easily have been an uneven set of performances into a disciplined ensemble cohesion. Enhanced by witty musical interludes and the creative use of chiaroscuro lighting and dramatic sound effects, this vibrant new production of *Macbeth* highlights the play's inexorable downward spiral from military triumph to political ruin, from the dream of worldly success to the nightmarish reality of tyranny in which lies have usurped truth and equivocation seems to be the only means of survival.

A Nightmare Reality in Theatre Y + Bigot's *Macbeth*

Rebecca L. Fall

Walking into the Chopin Theatre to attend a performance of Theatre Y's *Macbeth* is a bit of a trip. In addition to the Scottish Play, the Chopin is currently home to a production of *The Nutcracker*, that family-friendly holiday classic. In keeping with *The Nutcracker*'s holiday theme, the lobby of the Chopin is decorated in ribbons, glitter, and evergreens for Christmas; when I arrived on the Friday after Election Day, the pleasant pop tones of the *Jackson 5 Christmas Album* floated through the lobby's festive air. Amid all of this holiday cheer, though, was a prominent display covered in dripping blood to advertise Theatre Y's *Macbeth*.

That audience members must walk through a dizzying Christmas scene to enter the dark black-box theater where *Macbeth* is being staged may amount to nothing more than a scheduling coincidence, but the resulting sense of cognitive dissonance perfectly matches Theatre Y's disorientating take on Shakespeare's Scottish Play. The product of a yearlong collaboration between Theatre Y's independent, mission-driven company and French theater luminary Georges Bigot, this *Macbeth* imagines Shakespeare's bloody tragedy as a surreal nightmare. Amplifying the text's major themes—How do we know what we know? Can we trust our own senses? Are we in charge of our actions, or is control an illusion?—the production offers a deliberately "non-realist" take on the play that fundamentally blurs kitsch and high art, comedy and tragedy, audience and actor.

The play begins, of course, with witches. In this production, these three sisters are truly *weird*. They add substantially to the sense of unreality, of time out of place. As a spectator, it is difficult to know whether one is meant to laugh at them or cower in fear. They roar and screech and twist their bodies into unnatural shapes, but also dance flirtatiously to a doo-wop tune while displaying their bodies provocatively—for in a nod to Europe's radical FEMEN activists, these witches appear nearly nude from the waist up. They wear bikini tops that reveal female symbols painted across their torsos (at the post-election performance I attended, the word "nasty" was scrawled across the ribs of one weird sister). Like members of FEMEN, though, these women expose their bodies not to entice but to terrify men. They wear sloppy cut-off jean shorts and long, unkempt hair that they gleefully twist across their chins into beards when Banquo insults their looks.

In Act 1, one of the witches is heavily pregnant, making it all the more shocking when she smears blood across her mouth and body. When the weird sisters reappear in Act 4, she has evidently delivered the pregnancy, signaling the "delivery" of Macbeth's malevolent ambition into the world. In a horrifying parody of maternity, the witches in this act proceed to use a baby carriage as a cauldron in which they stew such ingredients as the "maw and gulf / Of the ravin'd sea-salt shark," the "liver of a blaspheming Jew," and the "finger of a birth-strangled babe / Ditch-deliver'd by a drab." They take turns showing their "apparitions" to the increasingly desperate and violent Macbeth in this carriage-cauldron, thrusting pagan statues puppet-like out from under the pram's bonnet and ventriloquizing them in voices that are alternately silly and scary. The confused combination of Halloween horror-kitsch, aggressive sexuality, twisted violence, and total unpredictability makes these witches all the more frightening—and advances the disorienting atmosphere that infuses the whole play.

The production further amplifies its sense of nightmarish unreality by conscripting the audience into the performance, framing the viewer not only as a participant in the play, but also as responsible for its outcome. While the performers do interact physically and verbally, acting out *Macbeth*'s political and interpersonal drama according to the dictates of language and plot, they deliver most (indeed, almost all) of their lines in the form of direct address to the audience. Accordingly, we as viewers are treated as complicit in the play's bloody conspiracies and strange turns. Upon receiving her husband's letter near the end of Act 1, for instance, Katie Stimpson's captivating Lady Macbeth stretches luxuriously on her bed and speaks to the audience as if we are the absent Macbeth, staring directly into the eyes of the closest viewers to engender a powerful sense of intimacy. In the staging of the scene, *we* become her spousal co-conspirator. Yet when Macduff passes Malcolm's test of loyalty, the prince speaks to the spectators, not his thane; instead of murderous conspirators, the audience become saviors of "good truth and honor." By the end, it becomes difficult to discern if we spectators have been cast as heroes or enemies. We have, it seems, taken on both—even all—roles at once. Indeed, in the final battle scene, Macbeth and Macduff deliver not only their *lines* to the audience, but blows as well. Rather than battling each other, the two actors perform their fight choreography side by side, aiming each violent strike and every vengeful word at the crowd of viewers.

The feeling of being responsible for the play's events but unable to respond—whether by talking back to Lady Macbeth or defending oneself from Macduff and Macbeth's blows—augments the nightmarish unreality of the play as a whole. After all, if we cannot even be sure what role we play as mere audience members, how can we trust anything we see, hear, or otherwise perceive? By means of this disorienting effect, Theatre Y and Georges Bigot's production foregrounds one of *Macbeth*'s most unsettling questions. The play doubts not merely whether we can control the reality we live in, but whether we can identify what is "real" at all. Theatre Y refuses to give a straightforward answer either way, suggesting instead that there may be more power—if less comfort—in the asking.

CHICAGO SHAKESPEARE THEATER
+ CHICAGO YOUTH SHAKESPEARE
BATTLE OF THE BARD:
HIGH SCHOOL SHAKESPEARE SLAM

Liz Lauren

Battle of the Bard: Teenagers, Shakespeare, Community, and the Power of Narrative

Timothy J. Duggan

On November 14, I attended Battle of the Bard: Final Bout at Chicago Shakespeare Theater on Navy Pier. The atmosphere was electric, even in the lobby before the show began, as diverse groups of high school students moved to find their friends and their seats. I was handed a program on my way into the Jentes Family Courtyard Theater and noted the first sentence on the back panel: "Battle of the Bard builds a culture of community spanning the Chicago region." As I settled into my seat near the stage, a former graduate student of mine, Patrick Escobedo, approached to say hello. I asked him whether his students from Fenton High School (Bensenville, IL) were performing, and he said, "No, we didn't make the finals, but we didn't want to miss this." He went on to explain what a positive experience the Battle had been for his students, detailing what they had learned about Shakespeare and about each other in the process of competing. I looked around and realized that several other schools not among the nine finalists had also come to cheer, to snap their fingers, and to feel a part of this culture of community.

The show included two emcees, Donovan Diaz and Sarah Ruggles, with Patrick Budde serving as DJ. They focused the crowd with some amusing repartee and music, then introduced the five judges for the event, including television stars Eamonn Walker and Joe Minoso, popular Chicago actor Ronald Conner, Chicago Shakespeare Theater's casting director Bob Mason, and Carol Jago, author and national leader in English education. Prior to the competition, the audience was treated to a warm-up act, chosen from the 30+ schools that did not make the finals. A group of young women wearing "Battle of the Bard" tee-shirts, and matching salmon-pink hijabs filed onto the stage, stood together, and pronounced: "We are Islamic Foundation School, and WE OWN THIS SPACE!" The audience, mostly high school peers, but also teachers, parents, and friends, applauded as the performers launched into a powerful montage of lines from Shakespeare, beginning with the words "She is ... ," accompanied by various movement around the stage. Lines such as "She is fierce" and "She is made of truth," rang through the theater in succession, and then at some point, almost imperceptibly, the lines changed to "I am ... ," with each actor proclaiming, "I am," "I am," "I am," "I am," and then, in unison, "I am ... a woman!" After a split second of silence, the crowd erupted in cheers. The competition itself had not even started, and yet a powerful culture-spanning moment had already taken place.

Battle of the Bard is a collaboration between Chicago Shakespeare Theater and Chicago Youth Shakespeare. Following the warm-up act, Marilyn Halperin, Director of Education and Communications for CST and Manon Spadaro, founder of CYS, addressed the crowd and spoke briefly about the program's philosophy. Spadaro founded Chicago Youth Shakespeare a few years back with the idea of "bringing kids together who would never otherwise meet each other and find common ground." She designed the first Battle of the Bard competition in 2014, and nine schools competed. When she teamed up with Chicago Shakespeare Theater in 2015, the number grew to thirty and it reached over forty schools in 2016. Although the event is a competition, the overriding philosophy, as stated several times by the emcees and hosts, is, "The points are not the point!"

This year's Battle of the Bard involved two competitive rounds, the Scene Round and the Ensemble Round. The Scene Round required each school group to construct a five-minute scene from Shakespeare, without the benefit of costumes and using only chairs for props. Every school began each scene with the name of their school, the title of their scene, and the pronouncement, "We own this space!" Four of the nine schools interpreted scenes from *A Midsummer Night's Dream*. Kenwood Academy (Chicago) performed a hilarious take on Puck and the fairies, leading to the meeting of Titania and Oberon in the forest. Senn Arts (Chicago) took on the lovers' quarrel between Helena, Hermia, Lysander, and Demetrius, with well-coordinated movement. Both Prosser Academy (Chicago) and Niles North (Skokie) performed excerpts from the "play within a play," with very different takes on the scene.

Teams constructed their own scene titles, such as "Viola's Weird Day" from Lindblom Math and Science Academy (Chicago) and "Don't Take Love for Granted," for a scene from *The Winter's Tale* performed by Christian Liberty Academy (Arlington Heights). A team from Oak Park and River Forest High School did the blinding of Gloucester from *King Lear*, which they titled, "The Eyes Have It." The group from Mundelein High School did the forgiveness scene in *The Tempest*, and Elk Grove High School offered a lovely duet scene between Juliet and the Nurse. Whenever a scene picked up energy, the finger snaps popped in the audience. Likewise, on the rare occasions when an actor struggled, the snaps rang out in support, to guide the actor through it. The judges perhaps had the most difficult job, as any score (on a 10-point scale) below a 9.0 was greeted with a chant from the audience of "Sleep no more!"

The Ensemble Round required the groups to take Shakespeare's words and do a mash-up. In this round the creativity of the student actors emerged in full, as they used Shakespeare's language to create new scenes and new narratives. The stories the teams told ranged from classic to contemporary, with many of the groups employing Shakespeare's words to reflect current events. Niles North (Skokie, IL), the eventual winners of the competition, created a scene called "The Generation of Love," addressing the problem of bullying by taking encounters from Shakespeare and presenting them as non-examples of love through mock-abusive performance choices. The ensemble created a quasi-Greek chorus effect by commenting on the various encounters, and they resolved their scene through reversal, portraying authentic, loving exchanges.

Several other teams used Shakespeare's language to create political messages. Lindblom (Chicago) and Elk Grove both created "presidential" debates with Shakespeare's language, one featuring Beatrice vs. Iago, and the other using Shakespeare's lines as asides to mimic antics displayed in the 2016 presidential debates. Of special note was Kenwood Academy's "Dating Game" format, titled "Who Dost Thou Love?" In the scene, Hamlet, Iago, Macbeth and Ganymede (Rosalind) competed for a date with Katherine from *The Taming of the Shrew*. The scene included Wall to divide the contestants, and ended with Katherine choosing Ganymede over the hesitant Hamlet, conniving Iago, and angry Macbeth. Every scene was greeted with loud applause, and during the second round, the celebrity judges commented on the scenes, offering praise and encouragement to the actors. At the end of the competition, all student actors were invited onto the stage to take a group mannequin photo.

Reflecting on this event, I think about the motivations of the organizers, the generosity of the volunteers, and the coordination between teachers to make the event happen. But most of all, I think about the students involved and what they have at stake, what they have to gain, what they have to offer. These students from vastly different schools engaged in the same process of working to understand and interpret Shakespeare, using Shakespeare to, in essence, tell their own stories—to create new narratives. In many local schools, under the influence of the Common Core State Standards, the reading and composing of narratives has decreased significantly in favor of informational reading and argumentative writing. The Battle of the Bard occasions the development of collaborative, inventive, and powerful storytelling, shared in a mutually supportive environment between teenagers who, as Spadaro stated, "might otherwise never encounter each other."

The resulting meta-narrative created by the event has a richer significance than any of the individual stories, powerful as they were. In that theater space on that night, we didn't need to imagine teenagers from a Christian school cheering for teenagers from a Muslim school and vice versa. We saw it and heard it. We didn't need to imagine students from the suburban schools cheering for and supporting students from urban schools and vice versa, or students of multiple ethnicities, cultural backgrounds, faiths, and economic situations mingling in a spirit of camaraderie, professionalism, respect, and fun. We lived it. Stepping on stage during the intermission that night, Chicago Shakespeare Theater's Artistic Director, Barbara Gaines, commented on what she had seen thus far and mused, "Don't you wish the world could be this way?" Indeed.

Shakespeare of the Future
Rebecca L. Fall

Among the most energizing and exciting events over the course of this year's Shakespeare 400 festival has been the Battle of the Bard, a dynamic "Shakespeare slam" competition for high school students, produced in collaboration between Chicago Shakespeare Theater and Chicago Youth Shakespeare. The program brings together more than 300 students and teacher-coaches from 40 high schools across Chicagoland. Participating schools range from public schools and charters to private preps and religious academies; the students and teachers themselves represent a wide range of backgrounds, identities and communities. What all of these different individuals and groups have in common, however, is Shakespeare. Teams of four to eight students meet and work for months to prepare two scenes: a more or less straightforward Shakespeare scene and a creative "ensemble" scene that remixes and mashes up lines from any of Shakespeare's works into a new whole. To keep judge and audience attention on the performers themselves, no costumes or props are allowed; the only set pieces permitted on stage are eight plain chairs, which teams may use however they wish. Before each performance, every team lays claim to the stage by introducing their school and declaring, "We *own* this space!" It is an energizing and inspiring way to begin a performance.

This review will focus primarily on BOTB's November 14 "Final Bout," in which nine teams competed on the main stage at the Chicago Shakespeare Theater, but the BOTB program reaches far beyond one single event on Navy Pier. Prior to the competition period, teams convene for massive workshops to learn about Shakespearean language and performance techniques from expert scholars and theater practitioners. Using the skills that these workshops help them develop, the teams return to their home institutions to arrange, rehearse, and refine their two scenes. From then, they perform in one of three "preliminary bouts," held at host schools across the region. The top nine teams go on to compete in the Final Bout in front of a panel of celebrity judges on the main stage of CST; in addition, one stand-out but non-advancing team is invited to perform as an opening act.

The atmosphere at every round is overwhelmingly positive and supportive. As BOTB's organizers, emcees, and team-members often insist, "The points are not the point!" Judges do score every scene and teams are in competition with each other, but the shared objective among every BOTB participant is to empower students, teachers and performers. The rock-concert-like atmosphere of the Final Bout is especially optimistic and positive. The program's resident DJ "Iamb" Patrick Budde keeps the energy up with his dynamic music selections. Between rounds, BOTB's two emcees, Donovan Diaz and Sarah Ruggles, encourage spectators and team-members alike to dance, shout, and "own this space!" even from their seats. Every participant from the preliminary rounds is invited to attend the Final Bout at the CST main stage, and the positive energy is palpable. It is truly an extraordinary experience.

On the surface, of course, Battle of the Bard is a celebration of Shakespeare. "Bill," as he is known to participants, is the factor unifying these diverse young students; they have traveled from across a vast metropolitan region to battle over "the Bard." More precisely, though, BOTB is a celebration of young people, of multicultural community, and of creativity.

During the first "scene round" of competition, teams perform a cohesive scene from one play. At the Final Bout, these ranged from an utterly terrifying rendition of the eye-gouging scene from *King Lear*(Oak Park and River Forest High School), to the miraculous reunion scene at the end of *The Winter's Tale* (Christian Liberty Academy), to two of the funniest performances of *Midsummer*'s play-within-a-play that this lifelong Shakespeare student has ever witnessed (Prosser Career Academy in Chicago and Niles North High School in Skokie).

The second "ensemble round" allows for more flexibility and creativity: using language from any of Shakespeare's plays or poems, teams invent their own scene. Some of these are more meditative explorations of a particular theme. Niles North, for instance, delivered a scene at the Final Bout entitled "The Generation of Love," which mashed together lines and exchanges from several plays and sonnets that represent a variety of models of love. Where, the scene asked, does love originate, and how do we know it when we see it? As the scene's chorus urged, no matter how the experience manifests for us, we would do well to "make love known" (*Macbeth* 2.3). Mundelein High School, by contrast, offered a meta-dramatic examination of acting. Shakespeare himself appeared on stage as a character, primarily speaking lines from the scene in *Hamlet* when the eponymous prince gives performance directions to an acting troupe. As other performers bungled some of his most famous lines ("To be, or not to be, that is the question"; "wherefore art thou Romeo?"; "Now is the winter of our discontent"; and so forth), Mundelein's Shakespeare-as-director offered advice on delivery and language, advocating for a natural and authentic acting style. The Islamic Foundation School's all-female team, who were invited to kick-start the evening as honorary performers, presented a powerful meditation on female identity. Opening with Miranda's request in *The Tempest* that Prospero "tell me what I am," the scene assembled, line by line, all of Shakespeare's contradictory third-person definitions of women: "she is a strumpet," "she is a piece of virtue," "she is fierce," "she is wise," "she is rich in beauty," "she is spherical, like a globe; I could find out / whole countries in her." By the end, though, the syntactic formulation had shifted, and the performers went on to define themselves in the first person: "I am a woman."

Other ensemble-round performances were more narratively driven, remixing Shakespeare's lines to create a new story rather than a meditation on a theme. Two teams took on present-day politics, focusing in particular on October's contentious Presidential debates. Lindblom Math and Science Academy's aptly titled "Debate Tragedy" gave us a money-obsessed and deceitful but ironically named "honest Iago" debating an uncompromising, sharp-tongued "fair Beatrice." After knocking over his chair in anger, the debate's moderator denounced both candidates, wishing "a plague on both [their] houses!" Elk Grove High School's Shakespearean debate, meanwhile, drew on the Bard's vast trove of gender-based insults to give shape to the speech of the scene's male candidate, who repeatedly bent down to his imaginary microphone to interrupt the female candidate with a sharp and low-voiced "Nay."

Senn Arts Magnet High School's ensemble scene took a different tack but still placed Shakespeare's language firmly in a present-day context. In their "Rap Battle of the Bard," Senn's team imagined the Montagues and Capulets as rival hip hop crews. Their scene went on to offer a highlight reel of Shakespeare's greatest insults and demonstrated just how thoroughly new generations might make the Bard's four-hundred-year-old language their own, transforming his Renaissance London dialect to an African-American Vernacular-derived hip hop idiom.

Meanwhile, Kenwood Academy High School's witty ensemble scene "Who Dost Thou Love?" was modeled after a dating show: four distinct suitors—a deceptive Iago, an angry Macbeth, a weepy Hamlet, and a sensitive Ganymede—competed for the affections of one picky woman

(Katherine from *The Taming of the Shrew*). Kate picked Ganymede, who shocked the other male suitors by revealing herself to be a woman in disguise (Rosalind from *As You Like It*). The scene was uproariously funny—the violently angry male chauvinist Macbeth character being a particular standout—and cleverly used Shakespearean comedy's gender-bending formula to offer a poignant critique of the representation of sexual norms in modern popular culture.

As a teacher and scholar of Shakespeare, the primary question I found myself asking throughout Battle of the Bard's Final Bout was, "What does this program say about the value of Shakespeare today?" Every team offered a radically different (and totally fresh) perspective on his work and legacy. Even teams that presented similar content—like Prosser and Niles North, who both happened to perform the same scene from *A Midsummer Night's Dream*, or Lindblom and Elk Grove, who both drew on the recent Presidential debates—distinguished their work by advancing completely unique approaches to the same material. In the process, they did not merely articulate what is valuable about Shakespeare, but *generated* that value themselves. They used Shakespeare to examine their own multilingual and multicultural worlds—to work through very modern concerns in ways that made Shakespeare's historically distant and rhetorically difficult language seem completely familiar and immediately relevant. During the course of the program, these Battlers of the Bard came not only to "own" the space of the stage, but also the larger cultural *idea* of "Shakespeare" himself. The result was astounding. This is what Shakespeare should be. This is what Shakespeare will be. And this, the students definitively demonstrated, is what Shakespeare *is*.

THE NEWBERRY
CREATING SHAKESPEARE

Giacomo Comiati

Creating Shakespeare: An Interview with Newberry Library's Exhibit Curator
Andrew S. Keener

Recently, I sat down to talk with Jill Gage, Bibliographer for British Literature and History at the Newberry Library. She has also recently succeeded Paul Gehl as Custodian of the John M. Wing Foundation on the History of Printing. Dr. Gage and I discussed "Creating Shakespeare," an exhibition she is currently curating and which will be free and open to the public at the Newberry beginning on September 23.

Andrew S. Keener: To begin, could you tell me a little bit about your background in the world of librarianship? What brought you to the Newberry?

Jill Gage: I've never worked anywhere other than the Newberry Library. I started here as an intern while I was in library school, doing my MA in Library Science and my MA in English simultaneously, and when I finished, the Newberry created a job for me. In 2010, I went back to school to get my PhD at the University of London, specializing in eighteenth-century English literature. Now, I do all of the antiquarian acquisitions for the fields of British literature and history, and I'm the subject specialist as well, which is how I ended up being the curator of the Newberry's Shakespeare exhibition.

AK: I think this leads us into the exhibit. We're here in the midst of the 400th anniversary of Shakespeare's death, and there are hundreds of events going on all over the city for Shakespeare 400 Chicago. Could you tell us a bit about what you've been doing?

JG: We started working on the exhibit in 2012. I'm not by training a Shakespearean scholar, but I do know the Newberry's collections, and this was an opportunity to think about what we have and what we might offer.

I started out by typing the word "Shakespeare" into our catalog, and it grew from there. We've decided to call the exhibit *Creating Shakespeare* because the story of Shakespeare's survival has actually very little to do with Shakespeare himself, or at least that's one way of thinking about it. We have the First Folio, without which he might have slipped into obscurity; but then, starting in the late seventeenth century, many others have shaped Shakespeare and created Shakespeare in ways that are new for each successive generation. That's the really interesting story for me.

The hard thing about the exhibition is that there are endless ways of thinking about Shakespeare. Honestly, the Newberry's strongest collection of Shakespeare materials is seventeenth-century materials, and I'd love to do an exhibit of just those items, but one of my jobs as a curator and librarian is to think broadly. I've tried to invite people who look at the exhibition to think, "I didn't know anything like that existed," or, "I didn't know the Newberry had that." This way, visitors who aren't as interested in the quartos or the First Folio might be struck by nineteenth-century sheet music, newspapers, or a radio play.

AK: Can you tell us a few things about what sort of items will be in the exhibition? What can we look forward to? I'm aware that some of the items on display will be coming from places beyond the Newberry as well.

JG: Yes. We are borrowing from the British Library, the Folger Shakespeare Library, the Houghton Library at Harvard, Art Institute of Chicago and Chicago Shakespeare Theater, as well as four private collectors.

The British Library is sending four manuscripts and the 1603 first quarto of *Hamlet*, which is one of only two known copies. This book has been called a "bad quarto" because it's so different from the later editions; it's much shorter than the second quarto, many of the speeches are rearranged, and it has unique stage directions. There's been a lot of ink spilled about what this "bad quarto" is, and whether it is actually "bad"—it could be an adaptation from the stage, or a memorial reconstruction by actors who were in the play. I think it's really a perfect object to include, since it gives us a window into all the people who created Shakespeare and how Shakespeare has been mediated and created by other people from the beginning.

We're also borrowing the John Manningham diary from the British Library. Manningham was a seventeenth-century law student who kept very gossipy notebooks, and he recorded seeing a production of *Twelfth Night* at the Middle Temple. It reminds him of *The Comedy of Errors*, and his favorite scene is when Malvolio reads Maria's letter. From the Folger Shakespeare Library, we're borrowing a lot of theatrical materials, including David Garrick's promptbook for *Hamlet* and an Edmund Booth costume from the nineteenth century.

AK: Those seem like fantastic items. To take a step back: how, to your mind, will *Creating Shakespeare* fit into the broader landscape of events and performances around the city celebrating 400 years of Shakespeare?

JG: Shakespeare 400 Chicago is a wonderful, groundbreaking effort that Chicago Shakespeare Theater has coordinated with so many other cultural institutions, and the Newberry's role is to help provide the historical background. We have a Chicago-specific section in the exhibit, beginning in the 1860s. And, in fact, that section includes the one thing I cannot tell you about, which is going to be the most blockbuster thing of all.

But *Creating Shakespeare* is a process that is ongoing; it's still happening, and it's going to be happening in the future. Our programming around the exhibit really fits in with celebrating the way our collections have been used by scholars and artists within the local community. We do have three scholars, James Shapiro, Peter Holland, and Coppélia Kahn, who will give traditional talks. They'll all be great, but we really wanted to celebrate performance in Chicago, too. We don't want to be seen as the ivory tower part of it; I think the programming is actually an integral part of the exhibition.

AK: Here's a final question that sums up some of what we've been talking about. Simply put, what does Shakespeare mean to you, as a curator, researcher, and librarian?

JG: There's something about Shakespeare that ties us all together, which I find quite poignant. Not that much that we share stretches from

1616 to 2016. Four hundred years of people have read or seen Shakespeare and somehow been inspired, whether that means cutting out all the sad parts, or making illustrations of Falstaff. I think that idea of inspiration, of creativity, is fascinating.

Culture and Capital: *Creating Shakespeare* at the Newberry Library
Anna Ullmann

The Newberry's *Creating Shakespeare* exhibit offers visitors the rare opportunity to view the books, artifacts, posters, and drawings that visually constitute the man and the canon that we know as William Shakespeare. Arranged chronologically so that the visitor takes a virtual walk through time, surrounded by the material objects that signify first the man and his career in his own time, then his presence in the subsequent centuries, and finally in our own cultural present, the exhibit purports to explain how he is both "of an age *and* for all time," whatever Jonson's famous poetic rendering might claim.

The first gallery sets out to demonstrate Shakespeare's situation within a broader theater industry, "of an age" in that he was one among many playwrights with whom he acted, collaborated, and competed. While no manuscript versions of Shakespeare's promptbooks or plays are known to exist, the opening gallery features such items as a play manuscript by Ben Jonson and the diary of John Manningham, which gives a first-hand account of a performance of *Twelfth Night* as well as a (much-debated) account of Shakespeare's sexual exploits. This first gallery imagines and presents the early modern London of which Shakespeare was but a part, emphasizing the world that created the man.

After this initial gallery, the visitor continues into a room entirely devoted to the history of Shakespeare's *Hamlet* in print, performance, and illustration. First-edition quartos, playbills, comic books, and sculptures all pay tribute to the historical constitution of what is probably Shakespeare's best-known play. The Cranach Press illustrated *Hamlet*, in particular, is a true privilege to view. The collection is impressive in its size and scope, to be sure. And yet, it is somewhat jarring in its devotion to one piece of work in an exhibit that seeks to situate Shakespeare in historical and cultural context rather than as a brilliant and solitary author who exists in a kind of timeless continuum. For example, an 1830 playbill included in the *Hamlet* collection also advertises performances of *Macbeth* and *Julius Caesar* later in the same week, which the exhibit passes over in its description of the artifact. Similarly, a small display on Sir John Falstaff tells the visitor that he has the second most lines of any Shakespeare character and appears in three plays, and that his likeness has been used throughout history for both artistic and political purposes, and yet he is afforded a single half-wall while *Hamlet* has an entire room. Ira Aldridge, who made a career for himself as a black man on the London stage in the early nineteenth century, most famously in *Othello*, which the exhibit informs the visitor was "one of the most performed plays since the Restoration," is paradoxically given a single wall panel, while David Garrick's *Romeo and Juliet*, "performed more than any other play during the eighteenth century," is similarly given a single panel.

The issue raised by a gallery entirely devoted to *Hamlet* is that *Hamlet* is the play which theatergoers and Newberry visitors alike can almost universally name when they think of Shakespeare. *Hamlet*, that work of psychological genius, is nearly synonymous with the notion of Shakespeare as solitary and eternal artist which the exhibit claims to eschew in its opening statement. It strikes one as a bit disingenuous to establish Shakespeare as "of an age," a collaborator in a rich and thriving theater industry, in the first gallery, and then immediately reinforce the commonly held notion that he was exceptional in this second gallery. It is true that *Hamlet* has had a long and prosperous life on stage and page, but so have many, many more of Shakespeare's works, as the Newberry itself concedes in other places throughout the exhibit. The dichotomy between intentional author and social collaborator has been a polemical one in academia for at least the last century or so, and it is therefore a bit disconcerting how the exhibit straddles the fence on this issue.

However, across the lobby, the exhibit returns the visitor to the spirit of Shakespeare's work as continually reconstituted and re-appropriated, even as it was in his own time. The final gallery brings the visitor into the late nineteenth and twentieth century, emphasizing the all-important performance and visual aspects of Shakespeare's art. The gallery is bursting with color, featuring theater posters, advertisements, and even the actual costume worn by Edwin Booth in his portrayal of Iago, fitted on a mannequin. There are editions of mid-twentieth century comic book versions of plays, aimed at a young male audience, musical scores for operas and adaptations of various works, paintings, a beautifully gilded illustrated edition of *A Midsummer Night's Dream*, and even Chicago Shakespeare Theater's own recipe for stage blood. The emphasis is all on visualizing Shakespeare and the life of his works in the modern theater, and it succeeds in demonstrating the scale and value of the spectacle.

But does this modernized Shakespeare come at a cost? What is lost when we begin to commercialize the Bard? If the nineteenth- and twentieth-century attempts to re-appropriate Shakespeare seem to have one common goal, it is to make money using his image and his creations. Some of the artifacts the visitor encounters do so explicitly; a Budweiser advertisement from 1908 features Shakespeare's portrait, and another ad tells us that the 1949 Ford is "a midsummer night's dream!" But there is also the more implicit sense that the avant garde stagings, the illustrated books, and the operas and musical versions of his plays have the true purpose of boosting ticket sales and actors' careers, rather than any real commitment to artistic expression. It is a fine line, but what is most apparent is the burgeoning of the "Shakespeare industrial complex," the notion that our modern culture both constitutes and capitalizes on Shakespeare and his works even as it holds him up as an artistic genius.

But is there anything inherently wrong with this? As long as we acknowledge that we are appropriating Shakespeare for both artistic and commercial reasons, rather than hiding behind abstract or academic pretensions, perhaps this kind of cultural capitalization of the Bard is truer to his memory than anything else. It is, after all, how Shakespeare approached his own work. The Newberry's exhibit thus takes the visitor full-circle, back to the emerging theater industry of sixteenth-century London. The creating Shakespeare, that is, the man who created the plays, in his coupling of artistic and economic goals, was not so different from the industry that is perpetually creating him. In this sense, the exhibit captures both the material remnants and the profit-driven, artistically inspired essence of the man and his works, four hundred years later.

SPYMONKEY
THE COMPLETE DEATHS

adapted + directed by Tim Crouch
a Spymonkey co-production with Brighton Festival
+ Royal & Derngate Northampton
presented by Chicago Shakespeare Theater

Ludovic des Cognets

Blood, Clowns, and Metadrama
Andrea Stevens

The United Kingdom-based physical comedy troupe Spymonkey's members include Toby Park, Petra Massey, Aitor Basauri and Stephan Kreiss, all of whom play fictionalized, exaggerated versions of their own "real" identities in *The Complete Deaths*, which ran recently at the theater Upstairs at Chicago Shakespeare. The premise of the show is as follows: an ensemble troupe is performing an evening of avant-garde, serious, "anti-capitalist" Shakespeare in which all the onstage deaths in the canon are to be presented, each death commemorated on a neon sign counting down to "76." This is "art" and, as the ostensible leader of the troupe, Toby, proclaims—real art is meant to be challenging: "the first death is of the audience's complacency." There are in fact only seventy-four onstage deaths in Shakespeare's plays; if the first "death" is of the audience's horizon of expectation, the final death is of the "black ill-favored fly" from *Titus Andronicus*. This fly, in turn, poses something of a recurring gag throughout in that a fly-camera is also stuck at the end of a recording stick that occasionally travels up actors' noses and into their mouths, the resulting visions projected onto a screen at the back of the stage.

Part of the ongoing conceit of the piece is our glimpse into the complex group dynamics of the company as the performers occasionally rebel (and eventually briefly revolt) against Toby's artistic vision: leading lady Petra's insistence on playing Ophelia, even if that death technically happens offstage; German clown Stephan's penchant for pulling focus with his physical comedy; Spanish clown Aitor's ambition to become a "serious" Shakespearean actor, in part encouraged by his occasional solo communions with Shakespeare, represented as a giant face projected on a screen who coaches Aitor from the great beyond on how best to act ("point your fingers a lot"). The show was written by Tim Crouch, whom Chicago audiences might recall from his one-man show *I, Malvolio* (indeed, many of Toby's direct addresses to the audience seemed to echo, if only tonally, moments from *I, Malvolio*).

Unfolding at a rapid pace, then, are a series of dazzling set-pieces — some pure slapstick, others incorporating recorded and live music and dance, still others performed via puppets and/or screen projections, all involving innovative costuming — brilliantly realized by these four seasoned performers with extensive training in physical theater, including especially clowning. The show moves from the lesser-known deaths toward the more notable ones — Romeo, Juliet, Hamlet — which conclude the show. It should also be clear that prop blood flows in abundance, especially within a blood-wrestling scene between a dueling Aitor and Stephan that precedes the intermission.

Notable stand outs for me included the musical song and dance number performed in chef hats and aprons for *Titus Andronicus*, this tableau also including a kazoo for Lavinia's tongue and a prop meat grinder into which bodies are fed, sausage links emerging from the other side. The death of Richard III was set to blaring club music, the performers wearing gas masks and black latex bondage gear right out of a Berlin sex club. In a shift into puppetry, the company manipulated unnerving marionette stick-figures for the death of the poet Cinna at the hands of an angry mob in *Julius Caesar* (this death scene was also projected live onto a video screen). Time and time again innovative costuming helped contribute to the overall success of each scene, perhaps most memorably in the death of Cleopatra: upon intoning her "I am fire and air" speech Cleopatra whips off her dress to reveal asps dangling from each nipple of her prop breasts—and then whips up her skirt to reveal even more adders dangling from between her legs (the show was advertised for mature audiences). To be sure, the designer Lucy Bradridge deserves all praise for her efforts.

I found myself most taken, however, with the death scenes that incorporated some note of seriousness. For example, the slaughter of the Macduffs was initially performed within a riveting modern dance sequence that was both theatrically vibrant and poignant in spite of the contrast between the precision of the movements and the silly Scottish "drag" of the dancers: bare chests, yellow kilts, and Petra done up in a red beard and red chest hair.

As his colleagues push back harder and harder against his "serious" vision (Aitor deciding that bubbles are of the utmost importance), Toby eventually quits in despair—his cue to perform the death of Enobarbus, the only character in Shakespeare who dies of a broken heart and another stand-out moment for me. In Toby's absence artistic hell breaks temporarily breaks loose—Aitor and Stephan run amok in elaborately absurd clown costumes, bubbles are blown, Petra rolls in as Ophelia within a giant plastic sphere—but the cast reconcile, reaffirm Toby's vision, and the play concludes with last act of *Hamlet*—followed by, of course, the final (and protracted) death throes of the fly, as seen on the video screen.

The show as a whole ought to convince American audiences who might associate clowning with all things Bozo of the rigor and seriousness of professional "clown" training: each member of the company was an extraordinary physical performer, dancer, acrobat, and musician. If within the fiction of *The Complete Deaths* Petra was hell-bent on playing Ophelia, my wish would be for this company to devise a similarly acrobatic, physically challenging, irreverent and Grand-Guignolesque production of Middleton's *The Revenger's Tragedy*, the black camp tone of that play matching the aesthetics evident throughout this production.

The Bard Slays: (Everyone Dies in the End)
Lydia Craig

When watching a Shakespeare tragedy, I always look forward to seeing the death scene(s) "done right." What this phrase means for this theatergoer is that I prize seeing the characters themselves, as "real" people, hope against hope that this death will not in fact occur, that fate can be averted and a happy ending achieved for all. A successful performance makes me believe that just this once, Richard III may possibly find that elusive horse and rally the troops, or Romeo will prolong his rambling speech for a few more stanzas, just until Juliet rouses herself (as no doubt he easily could). Occasionally I hope along with these characters that they will talk their way out of it, as pale Desdemona begs merciless Othello, "I hope you will not kill me" (5.2. 37), or believe in a miracle as haggard King Lear desperately vacillates between despair and hope, crouching over Cordelia's body: "She's dead as earth. Lend me a looking-glass; / If that her breath will mist or stain the stone, / Why, then she lives" (5.3.260-263). At other times, this suspense builds my wicked satisfaction at a villain getting his just deserts, as when Macduff delivers the gloriously chilling line, "Macduff was from his mother's womb / untimely ripped" (5.11.15-16), to trembling, whey-faced Macbeth, at once bereft of magical protection by that most unforeseen of medical events—a Scottish cesarean section in the Middle Ages. I want to see the sneer wiped right off Macbeth's face, replaced with a knowledge of the grisly death in store for him. Within a death scene, Shakespeare often builds words upon each other to heighten suspense and to stave off the inevitable, speeches temporarily interposed between a character and their impending death. When the words stop on a Shakespearean stage, life ends.

A recent performance of Spymonkey's *The Complete Deaths* at Chicago Shakespeare Theater interjected comedy into the usual unalleviated pathos of such scenes, causing me to marvel at how some deaths can be both touching and uproariously amusing depending on atmosphere and tone. For an informative look at the entire performance and an important request for the same treatment of Thomas Middleton's *The Revenger's Tragedy*, which I heartily second, see my colleague Andrea Stevens's recent review for City Desk. Adapted and directed by Tim Crouch and co-produced with Brighton Festival and Royal & Derngate Northampton, this dark comedy was enacted by the four members of the

British comedy troupe Spymonkey, Aitor Basauri, Petra Massey, Toby Park and Stephan Kreiss, who work together as artistic directors and/or performers to craft and perform each show. A remarkable amount of physical activity went into each of the seventy-six deaths, which were counted down on one neon sign to the right of the stage, while another above the stage helpfully listed the person and play (i.e. Queen Gertrude, *Hamlet*). Particularly, I was impressed by Petra Massey's girlish leaps and bounds to get up on Juliet's tombstone, energetic asp-dance as a writhing, sensuous Cleopatra flanked by serpentine back-up dancers, and gravity-defying antics inside the giant plastic bubble during the rebellion against Toby's vision for *The Complete Deaths*. During the bloodiest death scene that "went through" a variety of deaths at one sitting and utilized an Asian-themed chopsticks-and-sponges "sword-fight," Aitor and Stephen went from sedate "touching" to all-out bucket-dumping, wrestling, strangling, and attempted murder in a pool of fake stage blood, the former furious at having his own successful hits ignored and Stephen's accepted by the omnipotent neon sign, whose approving buzzer signaled the end of a character's life. Playing out thespian animosity through the medium of successive stage deaths was a great choice, channeling vicious urgency into the most humdrum of minor character interactions.

The two deaths I laughed and cringed at the most, however, were acted out through objects, not people, using flies at the end of sticks and puppetry. One depicted Cinna the Poet's violent death in (conscious) mistake for Cinna the Conspirator in *Julius Caesar*. Wandering out of doors in answer to a fateful impulse, "I have no will to wander forth of doors, / Yet something leads me forth" (3.3.2-4), the poet encounters a rowdy mob of plebeians looking for trouble. The company acted out the menacing lead-up to the murder with small marionette stick-figures on a table who surrounded the poet-figure menacingly, while a projector portrayed the marionettes' maneuvers on the big screen overhead. Herding him into the midst of a circle, they shrieked, "Tear him for his bad verses, tear him for his bad verses!" The figure, crying, "I am Cinna the poet, I am Cinna the poet! I am not Cinna the conspirator!" was then torn apart by a baying crowd and set ablaze, burning while the company stood calmly around, satiated (3.3.28-36). Seeing such calculated, yet uncontrollable violence consuming Cinna's proxy effectively stimulated the viewer to imagine how horrific the actual encounter must have been, and reflect on how useless words are in some Shakespearean deaths to counter or even forestall violence and hate.

One of the most famous deaths in the Shakespeare canon, due to its unusual method of execution, is the drowning of George, Duke of Clarence by First and Second Murderer in a cask of Malmsey wine at the behest of Clarence's wicked brother, Richard, Duke of Gloucester, the future Richard III. To portray this death, three members of the cast solemnly recited lines from the scene as ominous music played in the stillness, holding fly sticks, which they moved to vibrate the flies in time to the words:

> **FIRST MURDERER** Take him on the costard with the hilts of thy sword, and then throw him into the malmsey butt in the next room.
> **SECOND MURDERER** O excellent device! — and make a sop of him.
> **FIRST MURDERER** Strike!
> **SECOND MURDERER** No, we'll reason with him.

> **(1.4.144-151)**

All eyes were trained on the overhead screen, where the mason jar full of water sitting on the table acted as the offending Malmsey butt. Fly Clarence awoke and eloquently pleaded for his life:

> **CLARENCE** How darkly and how deadly dost thou speak.
> Your eyes do menace me. Why look you pale?
> Who sent you hither? Wherefore do you come?
> **SECOND MURDERER** To, to, to—
> **CLARENCE** To murder me.
> **BOTH MURDERERS** Ay, ay.

> **(1.4.159-164)**

Despite pleading at some length (which was curtailed somewhat as the lead-up to the murder stretches to 190 lines in the original play), no argument fly Clarence can make will preserve him from his liquid doom. The two Murderer flies forcibly hold struggling, frantically buzzing Clarence down in the depths of the mason jar for an impossibly long time until he relaxes, floats to the top, and remains in place. *Cue buzzer!* No human-acted performance of Clarence's death has ever moved me to such helpless laughter and strange emotion: seeing his murder in fly-form reveals the utter helplessness of the duke as a character, ganged up on and completely surprised at the sudden reversal of everything he believed in and thought he knew about his world, the kingdom, and his beloved brother, Gloucester. He dies knowing the awful truth of his brother's betrayal, but such knowledge does not save him.

Seeing these deaths all at once is a rare opportunity to catch a glimpse of what Shakespeare means to say about the precariousness of life and suddenness of death by the way he pictures, speaks, and writes last words and actions before snuffing out the candle that can never be relit. Through its surface buffoonery and slapstick, especially in its appreciation for allowing contemplative stage time to certain deaths such as Clarence's and Cinna's, *The Complete Deaths* illustrates Shakespeare's philosophy of theatrical death at large: a good death is memorable and eloquent, a bad death is quick and obscure, because a good theater death needs to live on in audience memory. What weds the maudlin and absurd in this particular show, at least for me, is its full-hearted embracing of chaos as an existential concept contributing to tragedy and comedy alike insofar as such chaos recalls the uncertainty, inevitability, and apparent unfairness of death. In fearing, responding to, and experiencing their grotesque demises, Shakespearean characters mirror us, having no idea when, where, and by what method they will die. While laughing at the ridiculousness of some characters' dramatic exits into the afterlife, we as the audience acknowledge our own fragility, apprehension, and find comfort in (still) being part of the dark comedy.

CHICAGO SHAKESPEARE THEATER
SHAKESPEARE TONIGHT!

written + directed by Bob Mason
music direction + arrangements by Beckie Menzie

Cabaret, Consciousness, and the Pursuit of Excellence
Timothy J. Duggan

I love to watch people who are at the top of their profession doing what they do. Great artists, athletes, teachers, and performers who know the spirit and the craft of their disciplines can transform an idea or a text into joyful excellence. Witnessing these transformations inevitably leads me to reflect on the value and necessity of conspicuous competence in society across disciplines and professions. Such was my experience watching the cabaret performance *Shakespeare Tonight!* at Chicago Shakespeare Theater on December 5.

The show, written and directed by Bob Mason, with musical direction and arrangements by Beckie Menzie, included amusing riffs on the American Songbook, such as the opening song, Mason's parody of Stephen Sondheim's "Comedy Tonight!" from *A Funny Thing Happened on the Way to the Forum*. Much like the original, Mason's adaptation promised something for everyone, inviting us to step away from reality and into a special space: "Hamilton tomorrow, Shakespeare tonight!"

The program included an eclectic mix of musical works inspired by Shakespeare, recontextualized from sources as varied as *Gilligan's Island* and *Hallelujah, Baby!* Light numbers sprinkled throughout the program balanced forays into deeper emotions, such as Eric Lane Barnes's musical adaptation of "Sonnet 138" and Kurt Weill's setting of an Ogden Nash poem, "Speak Low." Short scene cuttings from Shakespeare performed by members of the ensemble or lines read from prompt books provided effective transitions between tunes and reminded the audience intermittently that Shakespeare, in one way or another, engendered these songs, the stories from which they came, and the very theater in which they were being sung. The beauty of history and memory allows us to take revered works from the past, such as Shakespeare, and reimagine those works in nearly infinite combinations of settings and presentational modes. As time goes by, even those derivative works become part of our collective cultural capital and can be recombined in novel ways to entertain, provoke, or enlighten, as happened in this show.

The stage setting was simple and elegant, with Menzie's grand piano stationed upstage right (house left) on the thrust and cellist Elizabeth J. Anderson's chair and music stand farther upstage left. Menzie spent the entire show seated at her piano, smiling, providing vocals on several numbers, and expertly supporting the ensemble, which included Chicago Shakespeare veterans Heidi Kettenring and Sean Allan Krill, James Earl Jones II, Jennie Sophia, and Jordan Brown. With musical staging by Tammy Mader, the performers were free to make use of the entire space. Broadway veteran Karen Mason entered partway through the first half of the show to sing Frank Loesser's amusing "Hamlet" and then returned with a beautiful performance of "Speak Low" and "Hit Me with a Hot Note" (Ellington/George) from *Play On!* She also led the ensemble in the finale, a medley from *West Side Story*. A distinct highlight of the program was Donica Lynn's appearance to sing a haunting version of a Cliff Jones piece, "The Last Blues," from *Rockabye Hamlet*.

The ensemble performed in many different combinations, with solos, duets, and collective pieces. Sean Allan Krill's rendering of "Sonnet 138" and James Earl Jones II's take on the difficult "Fear No More" (Sondheim/Shakespeare) from *The Frogs* stood out, as did Jordan Brown and Jennie Sophia's delightful balcony scene cutting from *Romeo and Juliet* leading into "Tonight" during the *West Side Story* sequence. Perhaps the biggest surprise was Christina Perri's "Jar of Hearts," a duet sung by Menzie and Kettenring, stitched into the Shakespeare theme using Ophelia's soliloquy from *Hamlet*, "Oh what a noble mind is here o'erthrown." The song's chorus stood as a fitting counter-text:

> Who do you think you are,
> Running round leaving scars,
> Collecting your jar of hearts,
> And tearing love apart?
> You're gonna catch a cold,
> From the ice inside your soul,
> So don't come back for me.
> Who do you think you are?

The cabaret framework allowed the audience to relax and focus on the songs and the performers. Applause between each piece compelled us to surface collectively and breathe, unlike the typical two- to three-hour investment of attention to language and story required by a full-length dramatic performance. Even so, during the recitation of lines from Shakespeare and the singing of familiar songs, ripples of their original contexts would take shape in the air and carry us to places like Verona and Denmark, the deep resonances found in our own learning and experience. Setting the performance in the Jentes Family Courtyard Theater provided a shared etiquette demanding silence and minimizing the distractions that one might typically find in a cabaret club or bar. The effect was mildly intoxicating.

As Robert Jourdain explains in his book, *Music, the Brain, and Ecstasy*, "When music transports us to the threshold of ecstasy, we behave almost like drug addicts as we listen..." Add rich lyrics to the music (or vice versa), and both sides of the brain fire deep showers of neural activity, leading to a heightened state of consciousness. Further fueling the audience's reverence that night was our awareness of the sheer ability of those bringing these works to us, from Shakespeare as the primogenitor, to the composers and lyricists like Sondheim, Bernstein, Porter, Ellington, et al., to the designers of the show and the performers on stage in real time, sharing their gifts. Many in the audience knew these performers and perhaps attended as much to see them as to hear what songs they would do. Fairly late in the show, sandwiched between an ensemble medley from *Kiss Me, Kate* and the *West Side Story* finale, Kettenring and Krill performed "Thank You for Dying First" from *The People vs Friar Laurence, The Man Who Killed Romeo & Juliet*. The selection showcased perfectly the combination of their comedic skills and their musical chops. It was at that point that my own thoughts turned to the value of raw talent, honed by dedication to craft and the opportunity (and willingness) to share.

I have spent the greater part of my thirty-three year career in youth development, as a teacher, as a camp director, as a musician, and for the past sixteen years, as a teacher educator. Sometimes it is nice to just attend a show and enjoy the work of the performers without thinking about how they came to be where they are in their careers. But on this night, I was accompanied by my ten-year-old daughter, whose own career ambitions vacillate between becoming a singer, an author, a pediatrician, or a scientist. Trying to imagine the experience through her eyes, I couldn't help but contemplate the life journeys of these creative artists, some still early in their careers, others midway through, and a couple of them able to look back on decades of professional work. What in their childhoods led them on this path, but more importantly, what fueled their drive for excellence? After the show, in the lobby, an older gentleman saw my daughter and asked, "Did you enjoy it?" to which she enthusiastically replied, "Yes!" He then added, "Someday, you'll be up there." My thought was, it doesn't matter to me what path you travel, just be good at what you do.

Art can provide inspiration and sustenance in a time when the consequences of inexperience and lack of dedication can prove dire. Excellence reminds us of what we are capable of if we hold on to truth. It reminds us that vision, discipline, and creative cooperation can yield up wonderful fruits. A short ninety minutes in the theater that night allowed us to forget the troubling circumstances we currently face, but we cannot take for granted that the world operates consistently as a crucible for excellence. We must dedicate ourselves to pursuing it, recognizing it in others, and appreciating it when we see it.

CHEEK BY JOWL
THE WINTER'S TALE

by William Shakespeare
directed by Declan Donnellan
designed by Nick Ormerod
presented by Chicago Shakespeare Theater

Johan Persson

A Mid-winter *Winter's Tale*
Wendy Doniger

I saw the Cheek by Jowl production of *The Winter's Tale* on December 20, the longest night of the year, and it haunted me well into the dark hours of the early morning. It's a play I've seen often before, including memorable productions at Chicago Shakespeare in 2002-2003 and 1994-1995. But Declan Donnellan's stunning, sometimes even shocking, direction made me see things in it I never saw before—which often happens in a really good production of a familiar Shakespeare play.[19]

---

19 Woody Allen (in "The Kugelmass Episode," in *Side Effects* [New York, 1975]) once satirized the way that we experience the same classic differently at different times, in a short story about a Jewish businessman from New York who got into Gustave Flaubert's novel *Madame Bovary* and had an affair with Emma Bovary at the plaza hotel in New York, so that anyone who read the book at that time read about the businessman and The Plaza Hotel. a Stanford professor, encountering this new character and new episode, explained to

The central plot is simple enough:

Jealous King Leontes accuses his innocent (and pregnant) wife Hermione of cuckolding him with his childhood friend Polixenes; he has her imprisoned, where she bears the child and dies. Leontes sends the newborn girl off to be killed by exposure. When their young son Mamillius sickens and dies, grieving for his mother, Leontes realizes his error and is overcome by self-loathing.

But, in fact, the newborn girl does not die; she is found by a shepherd, who raises her as his own daughter. Fifteen years later she meets and falls in love with Polixenes' son, Florizel. When the young couple appears in Leontes' court, it transpires that Hermione, too, did not die after all, but merely went into hiding. She emerges now, and they all live happily ever after.

Ah, but do they really? The term "winter's tale" signifies the coziness of sitting around a fire but also the coziness of a familiar and implausible fairytale. *The Winter's Tale* makes fun of its own implausibility, as when the long lost daughter—whose lostness is so basic to her that she is named Perdita—has been found, and people in Leontes' court keep saying things like, "This news, which is called true, is so like an old tale, that the verity of it is in strong suspicion" (5.2.28-30). And when Hermione, long thought to be dead, is found to be alive, they say, "That she is living, / Were it but told you, should be hooted at / Like an old tale: but it appears she lives" (5.3.115—227).

When Hermione asks her son Mamillius to tell them a story, he remarks, "A sad tale's best for winter" (2.1.25), and this is, all told, a sad tale, despite the unbelievable happy end. An inspired touch in this production illuminated the sadness for me, a haunting moment at the end when, as all the couples are assembled (Hermione and Leontes, Perdita and Florizel, and others in subplots I haven't space to tell you about), and they all hug together in one big collage of bodies, and freeze in a stop-frame, the happy ending seems glued in place. But then the dead boy, Mamillius (or rather, presumably, his ghost), wanders soundlessly on stage and walks to the petrified group of happy enders and sadly walks away, reminding us that even a happy ending has a tragic edge in a late Shakespearean romance—the dead child, who does *not* come back to life as Hermione and Perdita seem to do, not to

---

his class, "well, I guess the mark of a classic is that you can reread it a thousand times and always find something new."

mention the tragedy of the fifteen years of lonely misery for both Hermione and Leontes.

A more pervasive innovation in this production offers the answer to a question about this play that has haunted me for years: Why is Leontes so unreasonably jealous? Unlike Othello, Leontes has no Iago to blame; he does it all by himself. But under Declan Donnellan's powerful direction, the actor Orlando James, a brilliant Leontes, is constantly in motion. His frenetic agitation reveals a man about to explode, a man overpowered by his own physicality. His boyish roughhousing with Polixenes, and with Mamillius, and eventually, most inappropriately, with his extremely pregnant wife finally explodes into mad rage, as he throws her down and kicks her pregnant belly, bringing on the premature birth of Perdita. His violence is also obscene. His overheated sexual imagination is brilliantly illuminated, in this production, during his anguished soliloquy about his sexual jealousy. As Hermione and Polixenes freeze like statues, Leontes moves them into the positions of a copulating couple, making his imagined fears come vividly alive for him, and for us. "Your actions are my dreams" (3.2.82), he says to Hermione.

Polixenes, too, is well played by Edward Sayer with that same excess of energy, both violent and sexual. These qualities come out when he attacks his son Florizel for falling in love with the low-born (as they think) shepherd girl Perdita. Shakespeare gives Polixenes sharp words — he threatens to have Perdita's face scratched with briars to destroy her beauty, and to devise a "cruel death" for her if ever she might open "these rural latches" to Florizel's entrance. But Donnellan has Polixenes accompany this sadistic sentiment with an equally sadistic action, brutally groping her between her legs. At this moment I realized, for the first time, why Leontes and Polixenes were indeed such boyhood pals — they are two of a kind, which is why it is Polixenes who stirs Leontes' jealousy. This double dose of pent-up violence and sexuality is what this play has in place of a Iago. The jealousy is all the more appalling because it comes from within Leontes, whom we come to view not as a particularly twisted individual but as a member of a male world that nourishes sexuality and violence in boys from their very childhood. And the pent-up negative energy of the two men is enhanced by the extraordinary choreography of this production where, unlike most stage presentations in which everyone stands still whenever the main characters are speaking, here everyone seems to be in perpetual motion, like electrons around the nucleus of an atom, like matter itself, expressing in the ensemble the inner restlessness of the two central male characters. Moments like that change one's understanding of a great play forever after.

TIME: "I turn my glass and give my scene such growing"
Stephanie Kucsera

In Cheek by Jowl's production of *The Winter's Tale*, directed by Declan Donnellan, the operation of time is given thematic pride of place. In fact, Time herself (Grace Andrews) frames the action of the story. From the opening of the house and the commencement of the play, to the transition to the pastoral world of Bohemia, to the play's closing moments in Paulina's "gallery," Time guides this *Tale*'s major turnings. The production's choice to highlight Time's involvement in human events beyond what is explicitly provided in Shakespeare's text makes perfect sense when *The Winter's Tale* is considered in its generic context, as part of the body of Shakespeare's late romances, or tragicomedies. Many of the genre's defining features—namely the flouting of the classical unities—may be seen as directly related to its fascination with time and to its overlapping interests in movement, transformation, and the sudden, unexpected revelations brought about by time's passage. Indeed, the sheer pleasure of a romance like *The Winter's Tale* is due, in large part, to the interconnected work of these very elements, in their ability to generate the wonder excited by what Sir William Davenant referred to as "the plot's swift change and counterturn."

While some elements of Donnellan's production (such as the aforementioned pervasive presence of Time, the modality of the sparse set pieces, and the fluid use of projections) cleverly uphold romance's interest in change of all sorts, the work of these same elements is often undercut in a production that also features choices far more static. While Mamillius (Tom Cawte) indeed declares that "a sad tale's best for winter," the set design by Nick Ormerod is unchangingly cold (2.1.25). The house opens to a dark, nearly bare stage, an almost void-like space that resists any ascription of time or place. The lights (designed by Judith Greenwood) then come up at the commencement of Act I where we are introduced to Leontes' (Orlando James) Sicilian court, but the light is harsh, largely cool, and somehow just as alienating as the darkness. The members of the court, moreover, are attired by Ormerod in black, white, and shades of grey, and in styles as resistant to any particular periodization as the set. Such stark choices might have been more effective for the disturbed Sicilian kingdom if they had been met with a marked transition into the Bohemian pastoral world. Bohemia, though, is just as harsh as Sicilia. In this production, Bohemia is dark and rain-drenched from the requisite shipwreck that lands baby Perdita (Eleanor McLoughlin) on the coast all the way through the sheep shearing festival sixteen years later. The drab (gray palette) costumes of the first half of the play are matched by the similarly drab (brown palette) overcoats, wellies, and stocking caps featured at the festival. As the cold downpour continues in the dark outside the festival space, the only real visual hint at the regeneration traditionally signaled by the move to the pastoral world is found in Perdita's flowers (which now seem strangely incongruous).

But it is also the alterations to play text itself that deprive the last two Acts of much of their warmth and downplay their investment in the power of restorative change. One of the most obvious examples is the short, comedic altercation between Mopsa (Joy Richardson) and Dorcas (Natalie Radmall-Quirke) at the festival that, here, is exploded into an overly long, Jerry Springer-esque showdown complete with catfight between scantily-clad, sequined combatants and audience participation. While this is certainly a fresh, modernized rendition of this moment, the trashy daytime talk show interpretation undercuts the earnestness of the country festival that functions in the text as another one of the romance's celebrations of renewal and which, ultimately, points us forward to the play's maybe-miraculous revivification of the Sicilian queen (also Natalie Radmall-Quirke). Other examples include the brutal groping of Perdita by the disguised Polixenes (Edward Sayer), the downplaying of Leontes' penitence prior to the courtiers' trip into Paulina's "gallery," and the trimming of the play's final social resolutions to exclude the pairing of the faithful servant Camillo (Abubakar Salim) with the widowed Paulina (also Joy Richardson). The final moments of the play feature little Mamillius's ghost walking the stage, sensed by a freshly anguished Leontes.

At least for this viewer, the sum of these edgy choices lends the impression that perhaps nothing much has really changed in Sicilia (or anywhere or anytime else). Certainly, they only add to the residual ambiguity that Shakespeare himself invites us to grapple with at the story's end: the drama is indebted to fairy tale and myth, but what should be a happy ending is tinged with sorrow. The young Mamillius remains dead. Leontes' family is not quite whole. The fairy tale is ruined. But romance isn't just a fairy tale—is also the literary heir to the Gospel narratives and to the late medieval miracle and mystery plays still familiar to Shakespeare and his original audiences. For these stories, as in *The Winter's Tale,* time, mistakes, death and sorrow are painfully real. But they are not allowed to have the final word. It is the warm and hopeful counterturn, the *growing* through such pain, that this *Winter's Tale* seems to lack.

CULINARY COMPLETE WORKS
38 PLAYS. 38 CHEFS.

curated + developed by Alpana Singh + Rick Boynton

In Shakespeare's Kitchen
Clark Hulse

As a theatrical chef, Shakespeare can serve you up some pretty wild dishes. His menu might begin and end with *Richard III*, starting with a vegetarian first course with ingredients of Richard's "green and salad days," and ending with "good strawberries" from the Bishop of Ely's garden. The featured dish in the middle of course will come from *Titus Andronicus*, where Titus prepares a pasty made from Queen Tamora's two evil sons. Tending bar will be the two Sirs, John Falstaff and Toby Belch.

Such menus lend themselves to the dramatic. When Queen Tamora asks what has become of her sons, Titus—routinely costumed these days in a tall chef's hat—reveals the dish and declares: "Why, there they are, both baked in this pie!"

The anthropologists long ago taught us that food is central to culture. In addition to just keeping us alive, it expresses our environment, forms and reaffirms our social groups, and shapes the rhythm of our day. When I described the subject of this post to an anthropologist friend (as we were leaving a first-rate restaurant where the winter menu included corn chowder with green chile and marrow and pork chops with smoked pork belly, polenta and mushrooms, etc.), she simply said, "a meal is poetry and performance."

It seems natural, then, that the yearlong cultural holiday of Shakespeare 400 Chicago should include at least thirty-eight meals, one for each of his plays. The idea began in a conversation about a Shakespearean meal between Chicago Shakespeare Creative Producer Rick Boynton and Alpana Singh, the celebrated sommelier and restaurateur. Alpana immediately thought, "this can't just be about turkey drumsticks at the Renaissance fair. It's not about what Shakespeare ate, or his characters might have eaten. Everyone who has gone through an English-language education has read Shakespeare. I still remember reading him in third-period English. Shakespeare is something we share now, today. Let's gather great chefs, and let each one interpret Shakespeare in his or her own way."

And so the chefs were recruited, each distinguished by the quality of their cooking and their unique approaches, but reaching across a range of neighborhoods and price points to reflect the culinary diversity of the city. Art Jackson at the Pleasant House Bakery immediately snared *Titus Andronicus* and prepared a Roman-style braised pork pie with blood pudding, fennel, olives and spices. Tigist Reda of Demera prepared a royal Ethiopian feast for *Henry VIII*, including spiced beef tartare and chicken Doro Wat stewed with Berbere sauce. John Manion, an English major in college, reportedly exclaimed, "Only if I get *Othello!*" Dan Pancake, another English major, was heard to proclaim, "Shakespeare's my dude!"

But what does it mean when a chef interprets Shakespeare? What stirs in the mind that stirs the sauce? Alpana Singh remarked that all chefs have access to the same ingredients and the same sauces, just as writers have access to the same words. All the magic, the singular mixture, the sublime taste, come after that shared beginning. The chef is as fully an interpreter as the director, or actor, or literary critic, and the restaurant is as fully a collaborative, creative space as the theater.

Some approaches were thematic. Tony Mantuano of Café Spiaggia went full Veronese to celebrate *Romeo and Juliet*. J. Joho at Everest went to ancient Rome to create dishes in honor of *Julius Caesar*. Michael Kornick of mk the Restaurant collaborated with an interdisciplinary artist to create an evening-long event around *The Merchant of Venice*, where guests would "borrow" gold and silver ducats to buy Venetian culinary creations, Italian wines and Amaro cocktails while listening to Vivaldi, Monteverdi, Gabrieli.

Others focused on the combination of ingredients and the preparation to find their line of interpretation. Ryan McCaskey sought out contrasting flavors to express the clashing moods of *The Winter's Tale* at his Acadia restaurant, only to bring them together in harmony at the end. Tanya Baker at The Boarding House carefully basted a young chicken until it was tender, in honor of Kate in *The Taming of the Shrew*, and served it with creamy polenta, pickled asparagus and a sour cherry sauce. Reflecting on the British wilderness setting of *Cymbeline*, Iliana Regan served a continuously varying selection of foraged vegetable crudités to diners at her restaurant Elizabeth.

Carrie Nahabedian at Naha chose *Measure for Measure* at the encouragement of her brother-in-law, who teaches Shakespeare. The title seemed wondrously culinary. The menu she designed expressed the play's contrasts of passion and rationality, and of temptation and purity: Hudson Valley Foie Gras with Tarte Tatin of Rhubarb, Young Chicken with Root Vegetables, Floating Island with Summer Fruits. Response among diners at first was slow, so the staff developed a theatrical printed menu and Carrie promoted it on social media, and it took off. What had been planned as a feature for two weeks ran for four months. "The Tarte Tatin was huge," she said, "and I was making it every night." Nahabedian made changes of ingredients and preparations as diners responded, staff made suggestions, and purveyors brought new foodstuffs with the shifting season. "Once apricots were gone," she concluded, "we had to stop."

The *Culinary Complete Works* ran from late February to mid-December, 2016, often in multiple locations at any one time, predominantly in the central city, but also in neighborhoods from Berwyn to Uptown to Beverly. Overhead, Chicago nights were filled with Michelin stars. And then, yes, it had to stop. Each meal was, as my friend put it, poetry and performance. But feasts like these are difficult to memorialize, even more difficult than either verse or theater. You can print a poem, or tape a performance. You can even print a menu, videotape a preparation, or put a photo of a dish on your Facebook page. But the singularity of food-as-culture is that we have as yet no way to reproduce the sensation of that first taste as it touches the tongue.

Three Takes: Two Gentlemen
Lydia Craig

Recently, Berwyn's Autre Monde Café & Spirits played host to 16th Street Theater's performances of three sketches inspired by William Shakespeare's *The Two Gentlemen of Verona* as part of Shakespeare 400 Chicago's *Culinary Complete Works* series. Providing delectable fare for both the mind and body, this event held on November 16 provided a new way of transporting the body through taste into a different time period and culture while exploring how controversial Shakespearean themes and conventional devices can be updated and revised to provoke self-reflection in a twenty-first-century context. Sending their dinner guests on a gastronomical excursion from Verona to Milan, Chefs Dan Pancake and Beth Partridge of Autre Monde served up a delicious gourmet meal following champagne and hors d'oeuvres, concluding with dessert and coffee. Welcoming guests to the Berwyn community to "see what we do," Sommelier John Aranza provided regional wine pairings to complement each course, explaining that his choices were inspired by the culture and history of northern Verona. Between each serving, dinner guests were transformed into members of a theater audience as actors performed scenes composed by playwrights Rob Koon, Arlene Malinowski and Juan Villa, inspired by the work, but not written in the original language of Shakespeare.

Following applause, the first course was immediately served, consisting of Poached Lake Trout, Pesto Prezzemolo, a delicious dish which had a sour, herbal sauce lavished on the meat accompanied by warm, well-cooked purple cauliflower. This was paired with Ca' Di Rajo's Le Moss from Trentino, made with unfiltered Glera grapes, which was described to me by the sommelier as "fresh and harmonious, with an exotic muskiness." Taste-wise, this sparkling white wine possessed a tart, earthy tang, with a bouquet like an apple orchard in harvest. Experienced simultaneously, such a counterintuitive taste and smell agreeably confused the palate.

After the first course, two actors played the roles of Shelly and David in "Coffeehouse" by Robert Koon in a scene based loosely on Proteus's deceitful love for Valentine's fiancée in *Two Gentlemen*. Likely written and performed between 1590 and 1593, this play is an early comedy, possibly representing Shakespeare's initial, or at least first successful, foray as a playwright. In a hilarious subplot that delighted Queen

Elizabeth, Sir Proteus's bumbling Lance, prone to spouting malapropisms and acting out tearful family partings with old shoes, carries on a fraught, but devoted relationship with his misbehaving dog, Crab. Despite hinting at Shakespeare's budding comedic genius, this comedy contains near tragedy, its main plot depicting how a devoted friendship between two men, Proteus and Valentine, flounders in jealousy and betrayal due to mutual passion for the same woman, the fair Silvia. After pretending to promote his friend's suit, Proteus lays siege to Silvia's heart and, proving unsuccessful in his endeavor, threatens her with rape:

> **PROTEUS** Nay, if the gentle spirit of moving words
> Can in no way change you to a milder form
> I'll woo you like a soldier, at arm's end,
> And love you 'gainst the nature of love: force ye.
> **SILVIA** O heaven!
> **PROTEUS** (*assailing her*) I'll force thee yield to my desire.

(5.4. 55-59)

After rescuing Sylvia from Proteus's onslaught, Valentine appears to offer his fiancée to him for the sake of preserving their comradeship in a scene that has long puzzled Shakespearean critics and embarrassed directors keen for an alternative. All is resolved, however, with Valentine and Silvia reunited and repentant Proteus returning to his longsuffering love Julia, who has followed him disguised in male attire.

Though "Coffeehouse" eloquently speaks to the conflict between succumbing to the temptations of mimetic desire and conforming to standard morality in the name of friendship, the piece largely sidesteps the original play's issues with rape, sexual consent, and the commodification of women. Of course, such delicacy may be due to the undeniable fact that such repellent scenes might put diners off their food, exemplified by the shocking lack of Thomas Middleton and John Webster-themed dinner theater. Meeting for drinks tête à tête, DAVID ponders aloud to SHELLY, his best friend JOHN'S girlfriend and his not-so-secret crush, "...Sometimes I wonder what it would be like not to be a good friend. Sometimes I wonder what it would be like to be an asshole...Not making a choice, it's just easier. Doesn't mean you're not an asshole, you're just an internal asshole." After being reassured by an anxious SHELLY that he is "...not an asshole. Not even an internal one," David gives the following response, a mightily ambiguous one, considering the original character Proteus's justification of rape as a mechanism for physically overcoming female disinterest and rejection:

> Oh, I could be. All it takes is justification. And you can justify anything. I could justify all sorts of things. It's easy. You just say something's really important to have, say, love, and then all you have to do is say, hey, if love's the most important thing, you have to go after what you love. And anything that stands in your way, well, it's not as important as love, so it's got to go. You can justify anything.

Clearly, ignoring female autonomy is not at issue here in Koon's scene so much as the question of potential heterosexual betrayal, contingent on violating masculine trust. Being an "asshole" does not equate to threatening rape, nor does "love" serve as a substitute for sexual assault. But David's use of phrases such as "You have to go after what you love" and belief that "You can justify anything" if it stands in the way of love, indicates the moral fragility of David's character and recalls Proteus's willingness to overcome Sylvia if he cannot win her verbal acceptance of his suit. However, differences do exist between Shakespeare's Sylvia and SHELLY, who, while also reminding DAVID of his prior romantic interest JULIE (Julia) seems physically responsive to DAVID, holding his hand and lingering when she should leave. These changes effectively downplay the Sylvia character's disinterest, call her own motivations into question in meeting up *sans* boyfriend in the first place, and suggest that the themes of faithfulness and betrayal, not the threat of sexual violence, occupy the focus of Koon's contemporary scene.

The second course was Tortallacci Bergamese, made with brown butter, sage, and parmigiano, paired with a refreshingly crisp and sharp Freccioarossa "Sillery" Pinot Nero Bianco, from Lombardia (2015). The main dish, my favorite of the evening, had a sweet nut garnish with a savory veal pasty, amoretti, pinenuts and raisins. Judging from the taste I thought hazelnut or almond liquor might have been mixed into the sauce. Apparently, if a Pinot Noir is denied skin contact with the grape it has a clear juice; thus, the wine was a *white* Pinot Noir, which blew my uncultured mind.

Next, diners viewed "Tinderella" by Arlene Malinowski based on Act 1, Scene 2 of *Two Gentlemen*, which provoked many laughs with its indication of the discrepancy in using social media that often exists between contemporary generations, unique dating app take on Julia's interest in her suitor, Proteus, and timely questions it raised about whether using different forms of communication to romantically connect in the digital age shifts the power dynamic between genders at all. Shakespeare's scene depicts Julia and her maid Lucetta debating the merits of her various suitors until the latter angers her mistress. After dropping a love letter from Proteus, Julia is further teased by her maid until she angrily tears it to pieces, crying: "Go, get you gone and let the papers lie. / You would be fing'ring them to anger me." Lucetta responds in an aside: "She makes it strange, but she would be best pleased / To be so angered with another letter" (101-104). After Lucetta's exit, Julia frantically recovers the scattered letter, searching for both lovers' names and lamenting her rash act: "I'll kiss each several paper for amends / ... And here is writ 'Love-wounded Proteus.' / Poor wounded name, my bosom as a bed / Shall lodge thee till thy wound be thoroughly healed" (109-116). By directly addressing the letter, Julia's speech emphasizes the powerful, but ephemeral nature of the written word. Paper seems to be contrasted with the fickle yet elastic state of love, which can be lost and found as a letter can be torn and reassembled.

It is doubtful whether electronic communication can serve as an exact substitute for this metaphor (partial data recovery, encountering the same Tinder profile again, unblocking someone on Facebook), but there are parallels. In Malinowski's scene, a young girl, JULIA, describes her attempts to find love on Tinder to her family's old maid, LUCHETTA. She explains, "Tinder is, like this app on your phone. It, ummm helps you- you know like, find guys that are a match." LUCHETTA responds, unexpectedly, "Oh, like Grinder and Scruff." Giggling in mock horror, JULIA demands, "Luchetta, how do you EVEN know about that?" Another intergenerational moment involves Luchetta's ignorance of the "secret" meaning of certain emojis to great comedic effect.

> **LUCHETTA** Oh look, you got something back. He says. "Hey girl. Thanks for hitting me up" and then he sent a picture of an eggplant?
> **JULIA** Ewww. Forget it. He's gross.
> **LUCHETTA** What's wrong with that? So he likes vegetables.

After encountering a dud or two, JULIA swipes right on "Proteus. An Italian foreign exchange student from Verona," who she says "looks a little like that guy from *Game of Thrones*, right? OK, He likes Fetty Wap.

Me too! He reads Vonnegut and Hemingway." LUCHETTA observes drily, "That's a little too predictable if you ask me. Trying too hard." Though this scene relied heavily on audience knowledge of the Tinder app's twists and turns, there was one reference to the original play's underlying gender issues, contemplating female powerlessness when it comes to romantic initiative and the fulfilment of desire.

Still somewhat mystified by Tinder as JULIA messages PROTEUS, LUCHETTA asks, "Now, we wait for him to message back?" After being answered in the affirmative, LUCHETTA reflects,

> You know, women waste too much time waiting for men. We've done it for centuries. Waiting for them to notice us. Waiting for them to propose. Now you, waiting for them to swipe right. I don't know why smart, independent women do that to ourselves.

According to LUCHETTA, like the tragic Julia pursuing fickle Proteus, modern women still "wait" for men to respond to them on dating apps, desperately hoping that they will be interested in pursuing a romantic relationship (and, it must be admitted, vice-versa). However, this scene generally maintained a lighthearted, amusing tone stressing the comfortable intimacy and trust between the two women as opposed to their tense back-and-forth in *Two Gentlemen*.

At this stage, the third course arrived, the delectable Bollito Misto, a northern Italian beef and chicken (or veal) stew, Corn Polenta, which is a cornmeal and cheese side dish rather like Southern grits, and Grilled Radicchio, radishes prepared in olive oil and sea salt, all paired with Malvira Nebbiolo, in Roero, from Piedmonte (2009). This red wine's bark was worse than its bite: though it smelled acidic, the actual taste was like currents and berries with a fine aftertaste.

In the final sketch, "Camaraderie" by Juan Francisco Villa, two old friends, Rad and Jaff, discuss the tricky issue of communal identity, uneven loyalties, and the failure to "make it" in the big outside world. Of the three scenes, this last seemed most divorced from the themes of *Two Gentlemen,* appearing to combine Valentine's abandonment of Proteus and Proteus's sexual betrayal of his friend into Rad's person and to excise specific references to romantic and sexual rivalries. Refusing Proteus's attempts to dissuade him from his journey in Act 1, scene 1, Valentine bids farewell to his friend: "Cease to persuade, my loving

Proteus. / Home-keeping youth have ever homely wits." Were Proteus
not in love with a local girl, he claims,

> I rather would entreat thy company
> To see the wonders of the world abroad,
> Than, living dully sluggardized at home,
> Wear out thy youth with shapeless idleness.

(1.1.1-8)

When they do meet again Proteus deceitfully and unsuccessfully
woos Sylvia and the pair are momentarily estranged until Valentine
makes peace with Proteus, urging the superior claims of their masculine
brotherhood over the female influence that has interfered throughout the
play to separate them.

Similarly, in "Camaraderie," Rad's return to the neighborhood he
lived in throughout childhood with his friend Jaff recalls their old
history, such as covering for each other's fancied sexual transgressions.
Time has passed, however, and the dynamic has shifted between the two
during Rad's prolonged absence. Perceiving Rad to be looking down on
him while refusing to face his own failures, Jaff exclaims,

> DON'T PLAY ME RAD! Do. Not. Play me like I'm some
> hipster who buys elotes for twice the price cuz it's "local." I
> did alla' that shit for you so that you can get the fuck outta
> here and do something with your life.

He demands of his friend why he moved back, only for Rad to admit
his fear of failing again, a move Jaff interprets as cowardly, seeking after
unprofitable stasis. He conducts an interrogation to help Rad discover
the truth about himself and change his attitude before it is too late to
escape being a failure at home, like Jaff believes himself to be.

> **JAFF** Coming back here is succeeding to you?
> **RAD** No.
> **JAFF** So then it's failing.
> **RAD** No.
> **JAFF** So you're not succeeding or failing by moving back
> home?
> **RAD** Kind of.

In a final magnanimous gesture, Jaff urges Rad to forget about his own betrayals as a friend and instead focus on making his dreams come true, since he has a chance to succeed. This scene seemed extremely relevant for millennials finding their career path, or those familiar with leaving home to "make it" in the big world.

The evening concluded with dessert, or "Dolci," as the menu stylishly termed it: Pumpkin Ricotta Torta, garnished with a Semolina Cookie. This was paired with a moscato, Tenuta Gambalonga, "Jelmo" Fior d'Arancio, from Veneto (2015) and gloriously strong coffee. Though it was beautifully presented, the pumpkin dessert was the only indifferent culinary moment to me in an otherwise delicious meal, since it preserved the original sourness of pumpkin without sugar and I have a sweet tooth when it comes to dessert. The moscato, on the other hand, was dry and refreshing, spritzy, with a hint of orange peel.

Feeling physically like the most contented of boa constrictors, I returned home pondering the difficulties inherent in translating a play like *Two Gentlemen* to modern times. As demonstrated by the modern scenes inspired by the play, male friendship endures today with its code of duty and loyalty, as it did in Shakespeare's day and age, male rivalry over females also persists, and so does a culture of entitlement and rape. Perhaps in future productions this play should be staged in full as it reads, not avoided or softened, demonstrating the dangers of acting wrongly towards people of both sexes either for personal benefit or selfish revenge.

SCHOLARS

Joseph Alulis is a professor of politics and government at North Park University, Chicago. He earned his PhD in political science from the University of Chicago with a dissertation on Alexis de Tocqueville. He has published a number of articles on Shakespeare as a political thinker, most recently, "The Very Heart of Loss" (2012) on *Antony and Cleopatra*, and is co-editor of a collection of critical essays entitled *Shakespeare's Political Pageant* (1996). He is also an instructor in University of Chicago's Graham School, Continuing Liberal and Professional Studies.

Alexandra Bennett is a Chicago-based actor, dramaturg, and an associate professor of English at Northern Illinois University, where she specializes in Shakespeare, early modern drama, modern British and American drama, and women's and gender studies. She holds her PhD in English literature from Brandeis University, an MA in English literature from Western University (Canada) and a BA in English and history from Queen's University (Canada).

David Bevington is the Phyllis Fay Horton Distinguished Service Professor Emeritus in the Humanities at University of Chicago, where he has taught English language, literature and comparative literature since 1967. He earned his BA, MA and PhD degrees from Harvard University. Dr. Bevington is one of the world's eminent Shakespeare scholars. His numerous publications and editions include: *Murder Most Foul: "Hamlet" Through the Ages, Shakespeare and Biography, This Wide and Universal Theater: Shakespeare in Performance Then and Now, Action Is Eloquence: Shakespeare's Language of Gesture, The Bantam Shakespeare, The Complete Works of Shakespeare,* and the *Norton Anthology of Renaissance Drama.*

Katie Blankenau is a doctoral student in English literature at Northwestern University. She specializes in early modern drama and theater history, with a particular interest in hospitality and privacy on the early modern stage. She received her MA from Southern Methodist University, her BA in English and a BS in journalism from the University of Kansas.

Regina Buccola is a professor and the chair of the Department of Literature and Languages at Roosevelt University in Chicago, where she also serves as core faculty in Women's and Gender Studies. She has published several books on early modern British drama and culture, most recently as editor of *A Midsummer Night's Dream: A Critical Guide* and co-editor, with Peter Kanelos, of *Chicago Shakespeare Theater: Suiting the Action to the Word*. Recent journal publications have appeared in *Medieval and Renaissance Drama in England* and *Borrowers and Lenders: The Journal of Shakespeare and Appropriation*. She serves as the scholar-in-residence at Chicago Shakespeare Theater, and is one of the Midwest American reviewers for the online journal, *Reviewing Shakespeare*.

Casey Caldwell is a doctoral candidate in English at Northwestern University, where he specializes in the ontology and sexuality of money in early modern drama and intellectual texts. He holds his MFA in Shakespeare and performance, with a concentration on directing, from Mary Baldwin College, an MA in philosophy from University of Auckland, and a BA in philosophy from University of Texas at Austin.

Lydia Craig is a doctoral candidate at Loyola University Chicago, where she specializes in Victorian studies, with an additional focus on early modern drama. She holds an MA in English literature from Loyola University Chicago and a BA in English and history from the University of Georgia.

Gina Di Salvo is an assistant professor of theatre history and dramaturgy at the University of Tennessee. She is also a professional dramaturg and an Artistic Associate of Sideshow Theatre Company in Chicago.

Wendy Doniger [O'Flaherty] is the Mircea Eliade Distinguished Service Professor of the History of Religions at the University of Chicago. She earned her BA at Radcliffe College, her PhD from Harvard University, and a DPhil from Oxford University. She is the author of over forty books, most recently *The Woman Who Pretended to Be Who She Was* (2005), *The Hindus: An Alternative History* (2009), *On Hinduism* (2013) and *Hinduism* in the Norton Anthology of World Religions (2015).

Timothy J. Duggan is an associate professor of Education at Northeastern Illinois University in Chicago, where he teaches English education and English courses, including Shakespeare, and coordinates a partnership between the University and Amundsen High School. He earned his EdD in curriculum and instruction from the University of South Dakota, his MA in English literature from the University of Nebraska and his BA in English literature from University of California at Santa Barbara. He is the author of three books, including *Advanced Placement Classroom: Hamlet* and *Advanced Placement Classroom: Julius Caesar* from Prufrock Press.

Rebecca L. Fall is a visiting assistant professor in the Department of English at Northwestern University, where she teaches courses on Renaissance literature and media history. She is currently writing a book on nonsense writing, clownish language and silly jokes in sixteenth- and seventeenth-century English literature. Her research has been supported by several nationally competitive fellowships, including the Mellon/ACLS and Mellon-CES Dissertation Completion Fellowships. Rebecca holds a PhD and an MA in English from Northwestern University, and a BA in English from the University of Virginia.

Verna Foster is a professor of English at Loyola University Chicago, where she specializes in modern drama, dramatic theory and Shakespeare. She holds her PhD, MPhil and BA in English from University of London. Her publications include a book on tragicomedy, as well as numerous articles.

Richard Gilbert is a doctoral student in the English department at Loyola University Chicago. His research focuses on representations of violence in the theater, as well as adaptations and versionality. He holds an MA in humanities from University of Chicago, and a BA in theater from Brandeis University.

Cherrie Gottsleben is a doctoral student of early modern British literature at Northern Illinois University, where she is also undertaking undergraduate studies in French. Her areas of interest include Shakespearean politics of identity, John Milton, and the religio-political pamphlet wars of seventeenth-century Britain. Her interests in theory focus on the thought of Michel de Certeau, René Girard, Michel Foucault and Tzvetan Todorov. She holds an MA in English from Northeastern Illinois University.

Hilary J. Gross is a graduate student and instructor at the University of Illinois at Urbana-Champaign, where she is pursuing her Master's and PhD in the English department with a focus on early modern theatre and Shakespeare through the inter-disciplinary lenses of affect, adaptation, and performance. She was the inaugural British Literature Fellow at UIUC, and previously graduated cum laude from Wellesley College with her BA in English literature as a member of the Phi Beta Kappa Eta Chapter of Massachusetts.

Kyle Haden is an assistant professor of theatre at Carnegie Mellon University in Pittsburgh, as well as a professional actor and director, and the artistic director of the Ashland New Plays Festival in Ashland, Oregon. He holds his MFA from Columbia University in New York and his BA from Wake Forest University.

 **Clark Hulse** is a professor emeritus of English and art history at the University of Illinois at Chicago and chair of the Board of Directors of the Chicago Humanities Festival. He is author of numerous books and articles about Shakespeare, Renaissance literature and visual culture. Hulse is a Guggenheim and NEH Fellow and curator of the award-winning exhibition *Elizabeth I: Ruler and Legend* at the Newberry Library.

 **Andrew S. Keener** is a doctoral candidate in English at Northwestern University, where he researches drama, literary translation and the publication and use of bilingual dictionaries and grammar books in Renaissance England. He also has interests in rare book exhibit curation and computational approaches to language and literature. He holds an MA in English from North Carolina State University and a BA in English from Boston College.

 **Aaron Krall** is a lecturer in the department of English at the University of Illinois at Chicago, where he teaches drama and first-year writing, and writes about theater and the city. He holds his PhD in English from the University of Wisconsin-Milwaukee, an MS in theatre history from Illinois State University and his BA in English from University of St. Francis.

Stephanie Kucsera is a doctoral candidate in English at Loyola University Chicago, where she specializes in early modern drama with a focus in inter-religious encounter and constructions of English nationhood. She holds an MA in English from Loyola University Chicago, an inter-disciplinary MA from the University of Chicago, and her BA in theatre and English literature from the University of Indianapolis.

Ira S. Murfin is currently completing his doctorate in the Interdisciplinary PhD in Theatre & Drama at Northwestern University. His research focuses on the relationship between language, performance, and media across arts disciplines in the post-1960s American avant-garde. He holds an MFA in writing from the School of the Art Institute of Chicago and a BFA in playwriting from New York University.

Lori Humphrey Newcomb is an associate professor in the department of English at the University of Illinois at Urbana-Champaign. Her research puts Shakespeare's plays in dialogue with other printed books of the era. She earned her MA and PhD in English at Duke University and her BA in British Studies at Yale University.

Martha C. Nussbaum is the Ernst Freund Distinguished Service Professor of Law and Ethics at University of Chicago, appointed in the philosophy department and the law school. She writes on ethical and political philosophy, the history of Greek and Roman philosophy, feminism, gay rights and the nature of the emotions. She is the 2016 winner of the Kyoto Prize in Philosophy and the 2017 Jefferson Lecturer in the Humanities. She received her MA and PhD from Harvard, her BA from New York University and fifty-six honorary doctorates from universities in various countries.

Raashi Rastogi recently completed her doctoral work in English at Northwestern University. She studies and teaches Shakespeare and the literature of the English Renaissance with an emphasis on classical reception, gender and sexualities studies, and history of the book and media theory. She also holds an MA in English literature from Northwestern University and a BA in English literature and International Relations from the University of Virginia.

Cynthia Rutz is an instructor and past chair of University of Chicago's Basic Program of Liberal Education, a great books discussion program for adults. She also teaches at and is director of faculty development for Valparaiso University. She earned her PhD from the University of Chicago, with her dissertation on Shakespeare's *King Lear* and its folktale analogues. She received her BA in mathematics and philosophy from St. John's College, Santa Fe, New Mexico.

Lise Schlosser is a doctoral candidate at Northern Illinois University completing her dissertation on narrative and crisis in the early seventeenth century in England. Her research interests include Shakespeare and early modern drama, performance studies, gender studies and metaphor. She holds her MA in English literature and her BA in anthropology from Northern Illinois University.

Andrea Stevens is an associate professor of English, theatre and medieval studies at the University of Illinois at Urbana-Champaign, where she specializes in the drama of Shakespeare and his contemporaries. She holds a PhD in English literature from the University of Virginia, an MA in literature from Dalhousie University in Halifax, Nova Scotia, and a BA (Honors) in English from Huron University College in London, Ontario.

Elizabeth Elaine Tavares is an assistant professor of Medieval and Renaissance Literature in the English department at Pacific University. Specializing in Shakespeare and Tudor drama, her research foci include playing companies, theater history and performance. Her publications have appeared in *Shakespeare Bulletin* and *Shakespeare Studies* among others. She currently serves as scholar-in-residence with the Original Practice Shakespeare Festival in Portland, Oregon. She holds advanced degrees in English Literature and History from DePaul University and the University of Illinois at Urbana-Champaign.

 **Alfred Thomas** is a professor of English at the University of Illinois at Chicago, where he teaches courses on medieval and Renaissance literature. He has published eight books, including *A Blessed Shore: England and Bohemia from Chaucer to Shakespeare* (2007), *Prague Palimpsest: Writing, Memory and the City* (2010), *Shakespeare, Dissent, and the Cold War* (2014), and *Reading Women in Late Medieval Europe: Anne of Bohemia and Chaucer's Female Audience* (2015). His new book project is tentatively titled *Maimed Rights: Shakespeare, Religion, and the Middle Ages*.

 **Anna Ullmann** is a doctoral candidate at Loyola University Chicago specializing in Shakespeare and non-Shakespearean early modern drama, early modern historiography, and Marxist literary theory. She received an MA in English literature from Loyola University Chicago and her BA in English and sociology from Kalamazoo College.

APPENDIX

Shakespeare 400 Chicago
Programs by Month

JANUARY

Measure for Measure (Cheek by Jowl + Pushkin Theatre, Moscow) Chicago Shakespeare
  Theater
*Shakespeare and the Citizen Soldier (Pritzker Military Museum & Library + Chicago
  Shakespeare Theater) Pritzker Military Museum & Library
*City Desk 400 Online + On the Go
Prospero's Storm (The Theatre School at DePaul) DePaul's Merle Reskin Theatre
*Shakespeare on Air (Network Chicago WTTW Channel 11 + WFMT 98.7 FM) On TV + On the
  Radio

FEBRUARY

King Lear (Belarus Free Theatre) Chicago Shakespeare Theater
Romeo and Juliet (Chicago Symphony Orchestra + Chicago Shakespeare Theater) Symphony
  Center
A Midsummer Night's Dream (Chicago Symphony Orchestra + Chicago Shakespeare
  Theater) Symphony Center
*Culinary Complete Works: 38 Plays. 38 Chefs. Restaurants across Chicago
Shakespeare a cappella (Chicago *a cappella* + Chicago Shakespeare Theater) across
  Chicagoland
Sancho: An Act of Remembrance (Pemberley Productions + Oxford Playhouse)
  Chicago Shakespeare Theater
Othello (Hamburg Ballet) Harris Theater for Music and Dance
(In) Complete Works: Table Top Shakespeare (Tim Etchells + Forced Entertainment) Museum of
  Contemporary Art
The Bell Invited Me: Shakespeare at the Carillon (Joey Brink) Rockefeller Memorial Chapel
Music in the Time of Shakespeare (The Decani) Rockefeller Memorial Chapel

MARCH

Othello (Chicago Shakespeare Theater) Chicago Shakespeare Theater
Gounod's Romeo and Juliet (Lyric Opera of Chicago) Lyric Opera of Chicago
Twelfth Night (Filter Theatre, in association with the Royal Shakespeare Company)
  Chicago Shakespeare Theater
Short Shakespeare! Twelfth Night (Chicago Shakespeare Theater) Chicago Shakespeare
  Theater
"King Lear Screenings" (Richard Strier) Reva and David Logan Center for the Arts
What Are We Worth? (Professor Michael Sandel with Illinois Humanities + Chicago
  Shakespeare Theater) Chicago Shakespeare Theater

APRIL

Shakespeare Screenings The Gene Siskel Film Center
The Tallis Scholars Fourth Presbyterian Church of Chicago
Berlioz's Romeo and Juliet (Chicago Symphony Orchestra) Symphony Center
Othello: The Remix (The Q Brothers) Chicago Shakespeare Theater
Tchaikovsky's The Tempest, Op. 18 + Romeo and Juliet, Mahler's Symphony No. 4 in G major
   (Chicago Symphony Orchestra) Symphony Center
Falstaff (Chicago Symphony Orchestra) Symphony Center
Catch My Soul (Alice Kaplan Institute for the Humanities + Mary and Leigh Block Museum
   of Art) Mary and Leigh Block Museum of Art
"Play the Knave: An Interactive Shakespeare Video Game" (Gina Bloom + the ModLab,
   University of California, Davis) Northwestern University

MAY

Richard III (The Gift Theatre Company, in association with Steppenwolf Theatre Company
   + The Rehabilitation Institute of Chicago) Steppenwolf's Merle Reskin Garage
CSO Chamber at the AIC: A World of Characters (Chicago Symphony Orchestra + Art Institute
   of Chicago) Art Institute of Chicago
*Check Out Shakespeare (Chicago Public Library) Library branches across the city
A Midsummer Night's Dream (The Civic Orchestra of Chicago + Chicago Shakespeare
   Theater) Symphony Center
Twelfth Night (Artists Breaking Limits + Expectations) Chicago Shakespeare Theater
*Improvised Shakespeare (The Improvised Shakespeare Company) The iO Theater

JUNE

Tug of War: Foreign Fire (Edward III + Henry V + Henry VI, Part 1) (Chicago Shakespeare
   Theater) Chicago Shakespeare Theater
I, Malvolio (Tim Crouch) Chicago Shakespeare Theater
"To Make High Majesty Look Like Itself" (Joseph Alulis) Claudia Cassidy Theater at
   Chicago Cultural Center
Silent Shakespeare (Chicago Humanities Festival + Chicago Shakespeare Theater) Music Box
   Theatre
A Distant Mirror (Yo-Yo Ma with musicians from Chicago Symphony Orchestra)
   Symphony Center
The People vs Friar Laurence, The Man Who Killed Romeo & Juliet (Steppenwolf Theatre
   Company + Second City Theatricals) Steppenwolf Theatre Company
Supernatural Shakespeare Art Institute of Chicago

JULY

Celebrity One-Man Hamlet (David Carl) Chicago Shakespeare Theater
"Shakespeare at War" (University of Chicago's Basic Program of Liberal Arts Education for Adults) Gleacher Center
Chicago Shakespeare in the Parks: Twelfth Night (Chicago Shakespeare Theater) Neighborhood parks across Chicago
Grant Park Chorus (Grant Park Music Festival) Columbus Park Refectory + South Shore Cultural Center
Workshop for Girls (The Viola Project) Library branches across the city

AUGUST

West Side Story (Millennium Park Film Series) Millennium Park, Pritzker Pavilion
Puck: The Beer (North Coast Brewing Co.) Shops, bars + restaurants across the US
The Merchant of Venice (Shakespeare's Globe) Chicago Shakespeare Theater
Macbeth (Theater Zuidpool) Thalia Hall
"Shakespeare's *The Merchant of Venice* as Christian Comedy" (University of Chicago's Basic Program of Liberal Arts Education for Adults) Gleacher Center

SEPTEMBER

Tug of War: Civil Strife (Henry VI Parts 2 and 3 + Richard III) (Chicago Shakespeare Theater) Chicago Shakespeare Theater
"Man as Woman as Man" (University of Chicago's Basic Program of Liberal Arts Education for Adults + Graham School) Gleacher Center
Songs of Lear (Song of the Goat Theatre) Chicago Shakespeare Theater
Enamorarse de un incendio (Foro Shakespeare) Chicago Shakespeare Theater
Bon Appétit Presents Chicago Gourmet, *Grand Cru* (Chicago Shakespeare Theater) Millennium Park
"Shakespeare's Henriad" (University of Chicago's Basic Program of Liberal Arts Education for Adults) Gleacher Center
Shakespeare in the Criminal Justice System: A Panel Discussion Chicago Shakespeare Theater
"Legality and Morality: The Quest for Certainty" (University of Chicago's Basic Program of Liberal Arts Education for Adults) Gleacher Center
Piya Behrupiya (Twelfth Night) (Company Theatre Mumbai) Chicago Shakespeare Theater
The Revenge of Prince Zi Dan (Hamlet) (Shanghai Jingju Theatre) Harris Theater for Music and Dance
"Equivocation in 1606" (James Shapiro) The Newberry + Chicago Shakespeare Theater

OCTOBER

undreamed shores (one step at a time like this) Navy Pier
"Shakespeare on Screens in the 21st Century" (Peter Holland) The Newberry
  + Chicago Shakespeare Theater
Romeo & Juliet (Joffrey Ballet) Auditorium Theatre
"Interpreting Shakespeare through Alderman Boydell's Print Collection" (David
  Bevington) Smart Museum of Art University of Chicago
"Exploring Cultural Identity: Shakespeare on Stage" (Aaron Todd Douglas) Reva and
  David Logan Center for the Arts
"Eros & Power, Hidden & Confused: Shakespeare's *As You Like It* and *Twelfth Night*"
  (University of Chicago's Basic Program of Liberal Arts Education for Adults) Gleacher
  Center
Bloody, Bold + Resolute (The Dilettantes) CH Distillery
"Speed-reading Shakespeare" (Michael Witmore) Reva and David Logan Center for the
  Arts

NOVEMBER

Creating Shakespeare The Newberry
Macbeth (Georges Bigot + Theatre Y) Chopin Theatre
"Shakespeare's War of the Roses: The Original Game of Thrones" (University of Chicago's
  Basic Program of Liberal Arts Education for Adults) Gleacher Center
The Fairy Queen (Chicago Opera Theater) The Studebaker Theater
"Victorian American Shakespeare" (Richard Mallette) Glessner House Museum
Battle of the Bard: High School Shakespeare Slam (Chicago Shakespeare Theater + Chicago
  Youth Shakespeare) Across Chicagoland

DECEMBER

The Complete Deaths (Spymonkey) Chicago Shakespeare Theater
"The Complete Shakespeare The Tragedies" (University of Chicago's Basic Program of
  Liberal Arts Education for Adults) Gleacher Center
"Shakespeare the Master of Ambiguity" (University of Chicago's Basic Program of Liberal
  Arts Education for Adults) Gleacher Center
Shakespeare Tonight! (Chicago Shakespeare Theater) Chicago Shakespeare Theater
"The Man, the Myth, the Works: The Challenge of Celebrating Shakespeare" (Coppélia
  Kahn) The Newberry + Chicago Shakespeare Theater
The Winter's Tale (Cheek by Jowl) Chicago Shakespeare Theater

* indicates a yearlong program

Made in the USA
Lexington, KY
10 March 2017